# Learning Blockchain in Java
# A step-by-step approach with P2P demonstration

Hong Zhou

Copyright © 2019 Hong Zhou

All rights reserved.

ISBN: 978-1-69466-067-1

# DEDICATION

In memory of my parents who live in my heart forever.

# CONTENTS

ACKNOWLEDGMENTS .................................................................................................. i

1 BLOCKCHAIN: A NEW TECHNOLOGY PARADIGM.................................................. 1

2 MINING BLOCKS AND SECURE HASH ALGORITHM .............................................. 5

3 TRANSACTION AND CRYPTOGRAPHY.................................................................. 13

4 TRANSACTION, WALLET AND MINER .................................................................. 31

5 BLOCK AND BLOCKCHAIN ..................................................................................... 46

6 BLOCKCHAIN IMPROVED ....................................................................................... 59

7 NETWORK AND NETWORK MESSAGING ............................................................. 82

8 DISTRIBUTED BLOCKCHAIN SYSTEM ................................................................ 107

9 PEER-TO-PEER BLOCKCHAIN SYSTEM .............................................................. 166

10 UNIDIRECTIONAL P2P BLOCKCHAIN SYSTEM ................................................ 211

11 SECURE CODING ................................................................................................. 217

INDEX .......................................................................................................................... 223

# ACKNOWLEDGMENTS

First, I must credit my son, Michael Zhou, with both inspiration and editing help. Michael is currently a freshman majoring in computer science and engineering at the University of Connecticut. One day he approached me asking what blockchain is, and it was his question that motivated me to eventually write this book. Foremost, I must thank Daisy Li, a freshman at Emory University studying biology and integrated visual arts with pre-med aspirations. She completed comprehensive revision of the first edition of this book. My thanks also go to my colleague and friend Joe Cheah who revised part of the first edition for me. And last but not least I would like to thank my wife, Yufang Wang, for all her support.

# 1 BLOCKCHAIN: A NEW TECHNOLOGY PARADIGM

Ever since the bitcoin white paper of 2008 by Satoshi Nakamoto (identity still unknown), blockchain technology has gradually pervaded the public eye. Intended to serve as an alternative or replacement for traditional financial institutions because of their expensive transaction cost and vulnerability to double spending, bitcoin presents the world with a transparent electronic cash system in which chains of transaction blocks are distributed among users and secured by cryptographic technology. Distributed systems are not a new concept in computer science – it has been studied and applied since the last century. A number of powerful Internet tools today are built upon distributed systems, appearing to users as one "central" system. One example that comes to mind is the ubiquitous Google search engine – a distributed system that provides an efficient web-surfing service. But if such technology is already so commonplace, what is new about blockchain?

There are in fact several new and promising concepts to blockchain that set it apart from the traditional distributed systems. A search engine like Google, which runs on a distributed system, depends on a network of distributed computers belonging to Google, each of which can provide responses to search inquiries without obtaining consensus from other computers. In blockchain, however, for a decision to become final, the majority of the participants need to reach a consensus while they are not the private property of the blockchain. In this sense, blockchain is more distributed.

Using a chain to warrant trust is not a novel concept either. For example, Java employs a certificate chain to verify the trustworthiness of certificates. At the beginning of this chain is the root of trust. Take, for example, the financial world, where institutions form a chain of trust with the root trust in the central bank. Now let's suppose the central bank certifies bank A, which then in turn certifies bank B. If we trust the central bank, we can also trust bank A, bank B, and whichever banks A and B certify and so on and so forth. Such a trust system seems to work well, but it can fail if an important link is broken, or even worse, if the central bank becomes not trustworthy. Blockchain solves this problem by several means. First, it has no root trust – the trust of the system is distributed among the participants so that no single source grounds the validity of the entire operation. Secondly, the blocks are transparent, and a block is always built with information from the immediately previous block. Therefore, if changes are made to one block, then there is a domino effect all the way down the chain, which requires that all subsequent blocks must also undergo modification accordingly, a task proven impossible by another key concept of blockchain – proof-of-work. Thirdly, blockchain is built upon cryptography, which provides a mechanism to guarantee that finding a solution to a difficult puzzle is time consuming while validating a solution is easy and straightforward. The proof-of-work requires that in order for a participant to claim the validity of his/her block, the participant must conduct a labor-intensive work to find a solution to a computationally expensive puzzle. The solution to this puzzle becomes part of the block and can be easily validated by other participants. Once a block is added to the blockchain, it cannot be removed or modified, and new blocks are quickly added afterwards. Any attempts to modify a block must involve redoing the convoluted procedure of puzzle-solving. Plainly speaking, the only way to modify a specific block in a blockchain is to change that block and all blocks afterwards. For example, blocks A, B, C, …, Z form a blockchain. After modifying block P, all blocks after P (Q, R, …, Z) must be modified accordingly as well. If, for instance, block Q is not modified, Q will fail validation, as would all blocks following Q. Therefore, modifying an existing block becomes computationally impossible unless the attacker is armed with computation power superior to all other participants combined.

Blockchain started from bitcoin. However, its applications are not limited to digital cryptocurrency alone. An underemphasized but significant feature of blockchain is the fact that it is composed entirely of recognizable computer science technology. Bitcoin was written in C++, adopted peer-to-peer network architecture, and coupled public and private key technology together with other cryptography algorithms. It is through the creative combination of these existing technologies that bitcoin presented the world the innovative genius of blockchain technology. And bitcoin is likely only the beginning – inventors will continue to explore the potential applications of blockchain (Ethereum blockchain being one example). In the near future, it is expected that we will see the same technology expanding beyond uses in financial transactions and onto new frontiers.

In recent decades, the Internet has grown into a technological giant that has a hand in everything from propagating our social lives to increasing productivity in the workplace. It owes its popularity to its accessibility, curating a world where anyone can log on and participate in just about anything. In a similar vein, the stock market is hailed as one of the greatest inventions in human history partly because it allows "everyone" to participate, a sharp contrast from the self-contained giants of the financial world that operate within elite circles. Bitcoin is simply the newest invention in a long line of accessible platforms and it is revolutionizing the traditional financial system by allowing individuals all over the world to engage in a distributed financial system. This is the value of bitcoin. Beyond bitcoin, blockchain technology has the potential to include everyone in a world that no longer plays by the rules of centralized governance but instead decentralizes control so that anyone who chooses to can play a role. The development of blockchain are still in early growth, however, the potential is undeniable.

In its current form, blockchain is unaltered but transparent. But if there was a way to make it both unalterable and also private, the result could be a hypothetical "unhackable" computing paradigm. The internet is a heterogeneous place where trust is highly demanded but always in low supply. Blockchain has the capacity to build peer-to-peer trust. If harnessed properly, blockchain's trust-building capacity could become a great business opportunity.

There is no definite answer as to why bitcoin was developed in C++. It could just be that Satoshi Nakamoto is skilled at C++ (he is for sure), or it could be the fact that C++ is object-oriented but still gives programmers control over memory usage. The latter likely has some influence since memory usage is a heavily-weighted issue directly addressed by the bitcoin white paper. In 2013, the blockchain protocol Ethereum was proposed and eventually Ethereum Virtual Machine (EVM) has been implemented in several different programming languages including C++, Python, Solidity and Java. Building upon C++, Java has been ranked the most commonly used programming language for several years including 2017 and 2018 by TIOBE index. This indicates that there are a large number of Java applications and Java programmers. So, this book is intended for Java programmers who are interested in blockchain technology. Though EVM has been implemented in Java, this book does not discuss how to write Ethereum applications in Java. Instead, this book explains blockchain concepts and some technical issues using Java programs. No third-party packages are required to follow along with the tutorials – everything explained in this book can be accomplished with OpenJDK, and the sample codes are written entirely in Java. The book is divided into multiple chapters with succeeding chapters building upon the concepts reviewed in previous chapters. However, each chapter covers inherently different material and so they can also be taken independently.

The fundamental requirements of a blockchain include security (cryptography), distributed (decentralized) network, and concurrency. The open JDK is capable of meeting all three requirements, though open JDK does not have Java Message Service (JMS). Rest assured that this book will show you how to implement a simple message communication system. Please bear in mind that this book will, for the most part, be following bitcoin's ideas. Each chapter will begin with an explanation of blockchain concepts before moving on to discuss relevant Java programs that implement those concepts. You will accumulate knowledge via hands-on experience in code-writing and learn several versions of blockchain "systems". In the last chapter, we will discuss the importance of secure coding. The book ends with case studies of several malicious attacks that had occurred in the cryptocurrency world.

Before we conclude this chapter, let us examine the life cycle of a typical block in a blockchain. The cycle begins with transactions, and ends with the block being chained to the blockchain. For a specific block, there might have many similar copies, but only one wins the opportunity to be added to the blockchain while the others are discarded. The life cycle is illustrated in **Figure 1**.

In a blockchain system, there are different types of nodes. The simplest nodes are wallets which only utilize the blockchain system for trade. They are not interested in block mining. In contrast, another type of nodes are mining nodes (usually called miners) which are mostly interested in mining blocks to sustain the validation and growth of the blockchain. There are several other types of nodes as well. One, for example, acts like regional centers, providing services to wallets and some miners. What types of nodes a blockchain system possesses depends on the preferences of the blockchain platform designers and developers. Only two types of nodes are covered in this book: wallet and mining nodes, and the mining nodes in this book are also interested in trade and have a full copy of the blockchain. We will have more discussion about this later. The basic life cycle of a block provides an overview of this book: transaction, block, nodes including wallet and miner, block and block mining, blockchain genesis and update, and message communication among nodes.

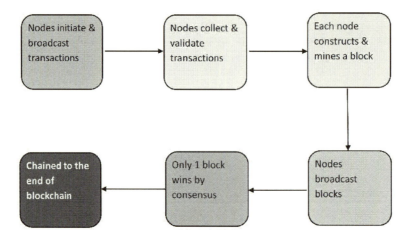

Figure 1  The life cycle of a block.

## 2 MINING BLOCKS AND SECURE HASH ALGORITHM

A quick note before we begin: we will be writing programs in each chapter, so it is important to organize them chapter by chapter. All sample programs in this book were written using Eclipse IDE, a free and fully functional IDE tool. You are strongly encouraged to write and organize your programs with Eclipse as you follow along. It is also strongly advised that you organize all your programs from each chapter into a folder (directory) to remain neat and keep track of everything you have accomplished.

Mining might perhaps be the most interesting topic to readers. So what is mining? What is proof-of-work? To answer these questions, we need to begin by studying the basics of cryptography and the Java security package.

The first concept in this chapter is hashing. You may have used class java.util.Hashtable and/or class java.util.HashMap before. Both classes allow you to store objects and quickly find any objects based on a key. For example:

```
Hashtable<String, String> table = new Hashtable<String, String>();
table.put("mykey", "Once upon a time");
```

What happens here is that, the string "mykey" is transformed into an index based on a hash function such that the value "Once upon a time" can be quickly retrieved using the index. A hash function here, is to transform "mykey" into a unique indexed value. The very first requirement of a hash function is to consistently generate the same hash value for the same input string and a different hash value for a different input string (understand that a hash is a value, so the terms "hash" and "hash value" are interchangeable). Therefore, you can be assured that the input string "mykey" can always successfully retrieve the target "Once upon a time".

Secure hash algorithms (SHA), provide one-way hashing algorithms where it is impossible to identify the original string from the hash value of it. Such an algorithm can accept an input of arbitrary length and output a hash of fixed-length. SHA-1 outputs a 160-bit hash while SHA-256, the most popular

SHA-2 algorithm, outputs a 256-bit hash. An output of 256-bit means that the algorithm can generate 2^256 ($2^{256}$) different hash values based on different inputs. This amount of variation is enough to meet all of the theoretical needs of hashing. The most critical requirement for a secure hash algorithm is to avoid a "collision", a case when two different inputs are given the same hash output. Collisions cause the hashing process unsafe. For SHA-256, the chance to have a collision is practically zero.

As hashing is used frequently in blockchain, it is a good idea to write a static method that generates a secure hash based on any string input. Thus, let's write the following UtilityMethods class and its first several static methods like so:

```java
import java.security.MessageDigest;
import java.util.Base64;
public class UtilityMethods{
    public static byte[] messageDigestSHA256_toBytes(String message){
        try{
            MessageDigest md = MessageDigest.getInstance("SHA-256");
            md.update(message.getBytes());
            return md.digest();
        }catch(java.security.NoSuchAlgorithmException e){
            throw new RuntimeException(e);
        }
    }

    public static String messageDigestSHA256_toString(String message){
        return Base64.getEncoder().encodeToString(
                        messageDigestSHA256_toBytes(message));
    }

    public static long getTimeStamp(){
        return java.util.Calendar.getInstance().getTimeInMillis();
    }
}
```

Here is what you need to understand about this class:

- As a major part of the Java Cryptography Architecture (JCA), the java.security package contains quite a few classes we are going to learn. The MessageDigest class is one of them. It takes in a byte array and returns a hash value also in the form of byte array. Code line 6 obtains an object of MessageDigest that applies SHA-256 algorithm. Currently JDK automatically supports MD2, MD5, SHA-1, SHA-256, SHA-384, SHA-512 algorithms. For our purpose, we will be using SHA-256. Remember that you can check the names of the supported algorithms for each JCA class through Java API documentation (JDK1.8) at https://docs.oracle.com/javase/8/docs/technotes/guides/security/StandardNames.html.
- To hash an input, the input must be loaded into the MessageDigest object first by the method update() which takes a byte array argument (code line 7). After that, the digest() method (code line 8) can be called to return the hash value which is in the form of a byte array as well. Please note that once the digest() method is called, the input previously loaded in the MessageDigest object is automatically cleared.
- Since JDK1.8, Java provides the Base64 class which can convert any byte array into a readable

string and turn a readable string back into the original byte array. As demonstrated in the code above, the second method (code lines 13-15) converts a hash value in byte array into a readable string.

- What is RuntimeException in code line 10? The instantiation of a MessageDigest instance in code line 6 requires catching a potential NoSuchAlgorithmException. Assuming there is no such RuntimeException in the method `messageDigestSHA256_toBytes()`. What we can do is either letting the method to throw this NoSuchAlgorithmException or writing a try-catch clause inside the method to handle this exception and return null in the catch clause. Either way is not ideal. When this method throws the exception, all statements calling this method must be placed in another try-catch clause. When this method has the potential to return null, the codes become unsafe. In fact, we are certain that SHA-256 algorithm is supported in MessageDigest class. Thus, catching this NoSuchAlgorithmException and throwing a RuntimeException is a perfect solution. No null will ever be returned, and RuntimeException does not require the method header to throw any exception, i.e. codes calling this method does not need to explicitly handle this RuntimeException. That said, please do not abuse and overuse RuntimeException, use it only when it is guaranteed that the occurrence of the original exception is impossible.

Once the above class is finished, you can write a test program to try it out. Following is an example:

```java
public class TestHashing{
    public static void main(String[] args){
        String mesg = "If you are a drop of tears in my eyes";
        String hash = UtilityMethods.messageDigestSHA256_toString(mesg);
        System.out.println(hash);
    }
}
```

Please note that if you copy and paste the above codes into your Eclipse or other programming editor you may be using, the double quotation marks are not always recognized and can cause errors. Double quotation marks in Word documents have special formatting and are not pure text. They cannot be properly compiled by Java. Additionally, please modify the message a tiny bit in the above program and then execute it again. You will observe that a minor change will result in a totally different hash.

Once we understand how a secure hash can be obtained, it is time to learn what mining means in blockchain. Data items in blockchain are contained within blocks, and each block contains a number of transactions. Mining a block means generating a hash ID for the block based on the transactions' hash IDs and the previous block's hash ID such that the newly generated hash ID meets the given difficulty level requirement. Generating a secure hash value based on transactions and other data items in the block is simple and takes little time. However, making the hash value meet a given requirement can be a time consuming task. That is why generating a valid hash ID is called "proof-of-work".

In bitcoin, a satisfactory hash ID must have a certain number of leading zeros bits (called leading zeros from now on). The number of leading zeros required is called the difficulty level. Higher the difficulty level, the more leading zeros required. Since we are using SHA-256, our hash ID has a fixed length of 256 bits. Evidently, we can neither ask for 256 leading zeros in the hash ID, nor we should ask for too many leading zeros. The MessageDigest object only generates one unique hash value for a given input string, and very likely this hash value does not have enough leading zeros. Therefore, we must make small changes to the input string until a valid hash value is found. This is where the keyword nonce comes to the stage. The integer nonce is incorporated into the input string and is constantly changed to obtain a different hash until the hash meets the requirement. In essence, mining is the process of finding the right nonce.

To demonstrate the mining of a block, we first need to add two more methods to the UtilityMethods class.

```
1    public static boolean hashMeetsDifficultyLevel(String hash, int difficultyLevel){
2        char[] c = hash.toCharArray();
3        for(int i=0; i<difficultyLevel; i++){
4            if(c[i] != '0'){
5                return false;
6            }
7        }
8        return true;
9    }

10   public static String toBinaryString(byte[] hash){
11       StringBuilder sb = new StringBuilder();
12       for(int i=0; i<hash.length; i++){
             // Transform a byte into an unsigned integer.
13           int x = ((int)hash[i])+128;
14           String s = Integer.toBinaryString(x);
15           while(s.length() < 8){
16               s = "0"+s;
17           }
18           sb.append(s);
19       }
20       return sb.toString();
21   }
```

The first method hashMeetsDifficultyLevel() examines if a hash string has at least a certain number of leading zeros. What it does is to convert the string into a char array and then count the leading zeros. If the digit "1" shows up before enough leading zeros are found, the hash fails the requirement.

The second method converts a hash in bytes form into a bit string. As Java uses Two's complement system to store numbers, in this method a byte is converted into an unsigned integer first (line 13) and then translated into a bit string (line 14). However, it is not necessary to use unsigned integers, so line 13 can be changed to: int x = ((int)hash[i]).

Method toBinaryString() makes use of class Integer's static method toBinaryString() so that we do not need to write our own method to generate the bit string for a given byte. To use the Integer.toBinaryString() method, we need to cast each byte into an integer first, as delineated in line 13. However, the Integer.toBinaryString() method truncates leading zero bits for every byte. So, we need to make sure that each byte has eight bits in its bit string, which is achieved with the while loop (lines 15-17).

Having written the two aforementioned methods, we are almost ready to mine a block. The next step is to write the Block class that include the mining process. The Block class is supposed to contain a number of transactions and since we do not have the Transaction class, we will just replace String for Transaction in our current Block class. Please reference the Block class below (we will update it later).

```java
import java.util.ArrayList;
import java.util.Calendar;
public class Block implements java.io.Serializable{
    private static final long serialVersionUID = 1L;
    private int difficultyLevel = 20;
    private ArrayList<String> transactions = new ArrayList<String>();
    private long timestamp;
    private String previousBlockHashID;
    private int nonce = 0;
    private String hashID;

    public Block(String previousBlockHashID, int difficultyLevel){
        this.previousBlockHashID = previousBlockHashID;
        this.timestamp = UtilityMethods.getTimeStamp();
        this.difficultyLevel = difficultyLevel;
    }

    protected String computeHashID()
    {
        StringBuilder sb = new StringBuilder();
        sb.append(this.previousBlockHashID + Long.toHexString(this.timestamp));
        for(String t : transactions){
            sb.append(t);
        }
        sb.append(Integer.toHexString(this.difficultyLevel) + nonce);
        byte[] b = UtilityMethods.messageDigestSHA256_toBytes(sb.toString());
        return UtilityMethods.toBinaryString(b);
    }

    public void addTransaction(String s){
        this.transactions.add(s);
    }

    public String getHashID(){
        return this.hashID;
    }

    public int getNonce(){
        return this.nonce;
    }

    public long getTimeStamp(){
        return this.timestamp;
    }

    public String getPreviousBlockHashID(){
        return this.previousBlockHashID;
    }

    protected boolean mineTheBlock()
    {
        this.hashID = this.computeHashID();
```

```
45              while(!UtilityMethods.hashMeetsDifficultyLevel(this.hashID,
                                                  this.difficultyLevel)){
46                  this.nonce++;
47                  this.hashID = this.computeHashID();
48              }
49              return true;
50          }

51          public int getDifficultyLevel(){
52              return this.difficultyLevel;
53          }
54      }
```

Let's take a closer look at this class. There are a few concepts that require some clarification.

- Why does the Block class need to implement java.io.Serializable? Well, if objects of a class need to be transported across network or written into a file as bytes for later retrieval, then this class must implement java.io.Serializable interface. When a class implements Serializable interface, we do not need to write any extra codes as it is just a gesture to inform Java Virtual Machine (JVM) that objects of this class should be serialized into bytes when needed. A class is serializable when all of its instance variables are also serializable. All Java primitive data types are serializable, and many more classes are, too. To make sure if a Java class is serializable, please check Java API. The opposite of the serialization process is deserialization, which means to convert an array of bytes into an object. Looking ahead, we will need to transport blocks across networks in versions of blockchain that this book will cover later. In preparation for that, we will implement the Serializable interface now. Though it is not mandatory, it is strongly suggested that any user-defined classes implementing Serializable have code line 4. What is line 4 for? Taking our Block class as an example, this variable *serialVersionUID* is important only when our package is used across multiple locations and there is a risk that different locations may have a different version of Block class. Say, for example, that a Block object is serialized at location A, JVM associates it with the serialVersionUID. When the object is deserialized at another JVM, say, location B, the JVM of location B needs to load Block class as a template for this object to be reconstructed. The class loader checks if Block class at location B and the Block object from location A have the same serialVersionUID value. If they have different UID values, the program will throw an exception that is easy to catch and fix. This mechanism ensures that the classes in use are consistent and compatible.
- Timestamp is another important concept in blockchain. All transactions and blocks are time stamped such that blocks too old or too far in the future are not accepted. This is why there is an instance variable named timestamp in line 7.
- In cryptography, a nonce is an arbitrary number (line 9). This is a number that will keep increasing until a required hash is found. If the input for the MessageDigest object does not change, the generated hash won't ever change. However, even a small change in the input results in a totally different hash.
- You may notice that there are no setter methods in this class except for adding transaction(s). This is because we do not want a block object to be unnecessarily changed. In fact, once a block is signed, the method to add transaction will be disabled, too. We will see to that later. In addition, for every instance variable there is a getter method except for the transactions.

- Code lines 16-26 include the method computeHashID(). The hash ID should be built upon the values of all the instance variables including nonce and the transactions. Thus, this method generates a string based on all instance variables before calling one static method in the UtilityMethods class to compute a hash value. The order of those instance variables in the string generation process does not matter, so you can rearrange the structure of this method the way you prefer. However, once you are certain how a string is generated based on all instance variables, please keep it constant.
- Code lines 42-50 present the mineTheBlock() method in which a loop is used to repeat the hash generation process until a valid hash meeting the required difficulty level is produced. In average, more leading zeros required, more repetitions spent. This process can be very time consuming. Note that in line 46, the integer variable "nonce" is continuously increased by one until a valid hash (proof-of-work) is found. The nonce plays such a critical role that the mining can be understood as a process of "mining the right integer". We will revisit this method in the last chapter when we discuss secure coding.

Now that you have the Block class written, it is time to write a class to experience the mining process.

```java
public class TestBlockMining {
    public static void main(String[] args) {
        Block b = new Block("0", 20);
        for(int t=0; t<10; t++){
            b.addTransaction("Transaction"+t);
        }
        System.out.println("Start mining the block");
        b.mineTheBlock();
        System.out.println("block is successfully mined, hash ID is:");
        System.out.println(b.getHashID());
    }
}
```

Setting the difficulty level to be 20 in this testing class will probably take a few seconds for your mining process to complete. However, should you increase the difficulty level to 30, you will notice that the CPU time will be dramatically increased. Figure 2 shows the CPU time consumption for different difficulty levels (15-28) on a Windows 7 Professional computer with Intel Xeon 2.7 GHz CPU and 128 GB RAM. Process was repeated 30 rounds. Mining times were averaged and then logged (base 2).

Try experience the mining time yourself and note the changes in mining time. If you plan to draw a graph akin to Figure 2, you need to repeat the process multiple times. Drawing a graph based on only one round may not produce an accurate result.

You can download this chapter's programs at https://github.com/hhohho/Learning-Blockchain-in-Java-Edition-2. The programs presented in the book belong to a Java default package, while programs deposited at GitHub are in the package mdsky.applications.blockchain. The following steps demonstrate how to execute this chapter's program without using an IDE on a computer:
1) Assume that you have downloaded this chapter's programs from github into a directory (folder) named blockchain. The downloaded file should be: Learning-Blockchain-in-Java-Chapter2-src.rar.

2) Unzip the compressed file inside the blockchain folder. There should be a subfolder named "src" inside.
3) Please open a terminal window and navigate into the blockchain/src folder.
4) Continue navigate into blockchain/src/mdsky/applications/blockchain. You will see a few Java programs (source codes).
5) Execute the command: "javac *.java" without the quotation marks.
6) The above command compiles all the java source codes into .class files.
7) Navigate back to the blockchain/src folder. The reason to do so is because the downloaded Java programs are in the mdsky.applications.blockchain package. To execute them, you need to navigate into the folder where "mdsky" subfolder is located.
8) Execute the command: "java mdsky.applications.blockchain.TestHashing" without the quotation marks.
9) If step 8 does not work, it is very likely that the CLASSPATH of your computer is not set correctly: you then need to include the "." (the dot represents the current folder/directory) into your CLASSPATH.

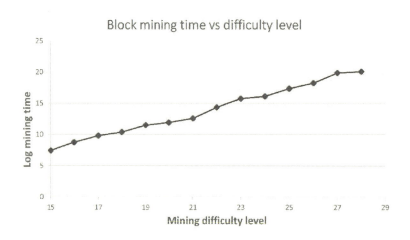

**Figure 2. The difficult level can significantly affect the mining time.**

# 3 TRANSACTION AND CRYPTOGRAPHY

Before we begin the programming in this chapter, please copy the programs from chapter 2 into a folder (directory) dedicated for chapter 3. Again, we suggest using Eclipse to write and organize your programs, but it is not the only editor that would suffice. If you are using Eclipse, please start a new Java project named "chapter3" and import all the programs from chapter 2 into the source directory of Java project chapter3.

Transaction is probably the central tenet in digital cryptocurrency. Bitcoin, the initial blockchain system, was developed to ensure that transactions are transparent, secure and irreversible in a distributed environment. Transaction is so important that bitcoin had Script specifically developed to safeguard transactions. Before we dive deeper into blockchain transactions, let's review a couple real world business transaction scenarios.

In the first scenario, suppose you go to a market to purchase a product that costs $59.12 and you can only pay with cash. To purchase the product, you would first need to have enough cash in your pocket – this we will delineate as "unspent" money. It is possible that you have just the right amount so you can pay without getting leftover change, but usually this is not the case. Let's assume you only have a few $50 bills. You hand over two $50 bills to the seller, and the seller acknowledges your payment. In addition to giving you your purchase, the seller also hands you $40.88 as the change. Blockchain transactions follow a similar logic, where available cash is known as unspent transaction output (let's call them UTXO by following bitcoin tradition). Only UTXOs can be used as transferable fund, and these UTXOs are considered input in transactions. Payments are considered outputs. To transfer enough fund, enough UTXOs are collected to pay the receiver. At the same time, the change is collected as another UTXO. Once the transaction is completed, the original inputs have been spent and can no longer be spent again, but the change in the form of UTXO is available for further spending. From the buyer's point of view, the change is part of the output in the transaction and is marked as payment from and to yourself. From the seller's perspective, he receives your UTXO(s) and these UTXO(s) become spendable funds to him. This concept is further explained in Figure 3.

In the second scenario, the transaction goes through a third party, in this case a bank. Suppose two people A and C are making a deal and the transaction is made through banks B1 and B2, where B1 is A's bank and B2 is C's bank. A trusts bank B1, while C trusts bank B2, and both banks trust each other. Assuming that A is paying C a sum of $1000 dollars. A initiates the transaction with B1 and B1 verifies that A has enough fund to conduct this transaction. B1 contacts B2, acknowledging that A's account is now $1000 dollar less, while B2 acknowledges that C's account has now acquired $1000 dollars. The transaction would appear on two different bank statements, A's stating that its account is now short $1000 and C's stating that its account gained $1000. Similarly, in a blockchain system, how much fund a user has is determined by "statements". When a user pays, the statement shows that he pays out from his pocket; and when a user receives, the statement shows that he carries into his pocket. In this sense, the blockchain system is akin to the bank in the scenario above – the middleman conducting the transaction. However, a blockchain "statement" is different from a bank statement. Bank statements are private (e.g. A's statements are only accessible to A), while in a typical blockchain (public blockchain), all statements are public and accessible to anyone with internet access. Moreover, the amount of funds a user has is computed from all the transactions posted in all public statements. Of course the computation only includes transactions the user is involved, either as the payer or the payee.

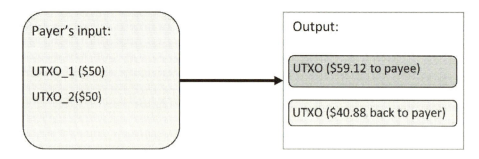

**Figure 3    Scenario 1: a blockchain transaction is similar to a real market transaction.**

But you may be thinking: if blockchain simply acts like any another bank, why would we choose to use it in lieu of the systems already in place? And you're right, for simple wallet-users who only care about trading, blockchain does act like another bank or trade agency. When it comes to mining nodes, however, blockchain is much more than a bank or trade agency.

We trust banks for their historical credits and certificates. How does blockchain procure our trust? How can we trust a transaction when there is no physical bank? To beget confidence, blockchain takes the following precautions.
- Examine if the user has enough UTXO to cover the transaction cost (including transaction fee if there is any).
- Verify that the transaction is initiated by the right payer, i.e. only the genuine payer can make a transaction under his "name".
- Publish the transaction such that it is transparent, final and unchangeable.

In chapter 5 we will discuss how to examine a user's balance. In this chapter, let's figure out how to verify if a transaction is genuinely initiated by the payer. We then need to learn more about cryptography in Java, specifically the public and private key technology and its applications.

Encryption techniques have been around for thousands of years. In the digital world, encryption has become more sophisticated and challenging as the digital world is facing various malicious and smart hackers. To encrypt a digital message, we use a key (e.g. a password), to turn the message into a byte array via a specific algorithm or process, and then later we can use another key, which might be the same as or different from the original key, to decrypt the byte array into the original message. If the key to decrypt is the same as the key to encrypt, it is called symmetric encryption, and the key in symmetric encryption is usually called a secret key. This is the traditional encryption approach. Its advantage lies in the fact that it can encrypt/decrypt an arbitrary length of data. Its disadvantage, however, lies in the fact that if you want to allow another user to decrypt your data, you must give the user your own key first – inconvenient when trying to share secure data. A workaround is achieved through the use of the public and private key algorithm, an asymmetric encryption in which the key to decrypt and the key to encrypt are different.

We won't be delving into the mathematics behind the public and private key technology. What you do need to know is that it is ingenious innovation that has brought the world of cryptography significant breakthroughs. Public keys and private keys are paired entities, in other words, a public key has exactly one private key to match. Using a public and private key pair, a user can publish the public key for communal usage, keep the private key, and not worry about information leakage. The original challenge with symmetric keys, of course, was sending the secret key out safely. And additionally, there was never a guarantee that the users who obtained the secret key would use it securely and responsibly. The public and private key technology offers an inventive solution to these problems. Suppose user A wants to send user B a secret key. B would first create a public/private key pair and send A the public key without any protection. A encrypts the secret key using B's public key and sends the encrypted data to B. This encrypted data can be decrypted by B only as he is the only person having the corresponding private key. You might be confused at this point. Well, please just remember, public key and private key are a key pair. Anything encrypted by the private key can only be decrypted by the public key, and vice versa, i.e. anything encrypted by the public key can only be decrypted by the private key. You cannot use the same key to encrypt and decrypt. Therefore, as long the private key is safe, it does not matter who has access to the public key. Figure 4 visually illustrates the application of the public and private key technology.

As innovative as this technology is, public and private key technology has its limitations, too. Public and private key pairs are not suitable for encrypting and decrypting large amounts of data. For example, if we use RSA algorithm to generate public and private key pairs with key size of 2048 bits (256 bytes), then the public and private keys can only encrypt and decrypt a block of data no larger than 256 bytes. Considering that some encryption algorithms use padding to fill up in a certain number of bytes, the space available for encryption can be even smaller. As a result, public and private key technology is primarily used for secret key transportation and signature verification only. Of course, if the data size is small, we can use public key and private key technology to encrypt and decrypt. This does not mean you cannot apply this technology to encrypt data of large size. Certainly, you can. You can divide your data into a number of small blocks, encrypt each block individually by applying a public key and transport each block separately. On the receiver's side, decrypt each block individually using the private key and then reassemble the blocks. However, this incurs much more work and is not practical.

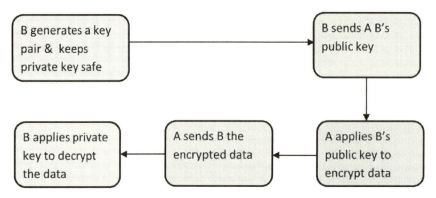

Figure 4    Applying public key to encrypt and private key to decrypt.

By this point you should have a pretty good idea of why the secure transportation of secret keys is so important. But just in case you are not convinced, here is another example of the technique in action. Assume two entities, a client and a server, are starting up a secure network connection for data transportation. The client sends his public key to the server. The server randomly generates a secret key, utilizes the client's public key to encrypt the secret key and gives it to the client. The client uses his own private key to decrypt the secret key. After this conversation, a secure connection has been established so that all messages between the server and the client are encrypted using the secret key. The beauty is, next time when the client logs in again, the secure connection is rebuilt with a different secret key, making the connection difficult to hack. This is one reason why after you have finished your transaction online, you should log out. If you stay logged in for too long, it gives malicious hackers enough time to figure out the secret key.

Nearly everyone is familiar with the concept of signature verification – the act of signing paper documents by hand to confirm the authenticity of the documents. A digital signature works in a similar way by verifying the authenticity of data. Assume user A is sending user B a data package. To ensure that the data package is not tampered during transportation, A generates a hash value based on the data and includes it inside the data package. When the data package arrives, B regenerates a hash value based on the data in the package and compares it with the hash value generated by A. If there is any difference, then the data package must have been altered. Unfortunately a hacker who knows what he's doing can easily outsmart that method. The hacker simply changes the data and regenerates the hash value based on the modified data so the hash seems unaltered. A better method of detecting data alteration is using public and private key technology. User A would apply a private key to the hash value and generate a signature in a byte array. This signature would be sent together with the data to user B. Now, even if the hacker were to regenerate the hash value based on the modified data, his hash value would not be properly encrypted without the private key. When B receives the package, B can use A's public key and signature to verify if the data has been modified. Any modification to either the data or the signature will result in a failed verification. Figure 5 explains this visually.

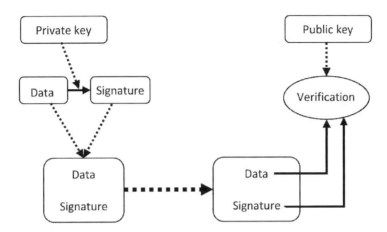

**Figure 5** The signature is generated by applying the private key to the data. The verification can be successful only if the public key is the right key, the data is the original, and the signature has never been altered.

Now that we have a better understanding of certain cryptography techniques, it is time to learn how to make use of JCA which includes classes MessageDigest, Cipher, SecureRandom, KeyGenerator, KeyPairGenerator, Signature, etc. But first, let's learn how to use a Cipher instance to encrypt and decrypt a digital message.

```
1   import java.security.SecureRandom;
2   import javax.crypto.Cipher;
3   import javax.crypto.KeyGenerator;
4   import javax.crypto.SecretKey;
5   public class TestCipher_1 {
6       public static void main(String[] args) throws Exception{
7           Cipher cipher = Cipher.getInstance("AES");
8           KeyGenerator keyGen = KeyGenerator.getInstance("AES");
9           SecureRandom sr = SecureRandom.getInstance("SHA1PRNG");
10          keyGen.init(sr);
11          SecretKey key = keyGen.generateKey();
12          cipher.init(Cipher.ENCRYPT_MODE, key);
13          String message = "If you were a drop of tear in my eyes";
14          byte[] cipherText = cipher.doFinal(message.getBytes());
15          Cipher cipher2 = Cipher.getInstance("AES");
16          cipher2.init(Cipher.DECRYPT_MODE, key);
17          byte[] decoded = cipher2.doFinal(cipherText);
18          String msg = new String(decoded);
19          System.out.println(msg);
20      }
21  }
```

Code line 7 instantiates a Cipher instance which is capable of encrypting and decrypting data based on a proper algorithm. Currently JDK Cipher class supports AES, DES, DESede, and RSA algorithms. Except for RSA, AES, DES and DESede are all symmetric-key algorithms and AES is believed to be more powerful and secure than DES.

Code line 8 obtains a KeyGenerator object using the AES algorithm.

Code line 9 obtains a SecureRandom instance. A SecureRandom generator is required by the KeyGenerator since all secret keys are randomly created. JDK only supports SHA1PRNG algorithm for secure random number generation.

Code line 10 shows that a key generator must be initialized with a SecureRandom object before it can generate a random key.

Code line 11 creates an instance of SecretKey by the KeyGenerator instance.

Code line 12 sets the Cipher instance's mode for encryption using the secret key.

Code line 14 calls the doFinal() method to encrypt the given byte array and returns another byte array containing the encrypted data. It is important to notice that the input byte array and the output byte array are not necessarily the same size, though they happen to be in the given example above.

Code lines 15-17 construct another Cipher instance with the same encryption algorithm (this is important). The mode of the instance is set to be decryption, and then the encrypted data is decrypted. Note that you do not need to construct another Cipher instance. The same Cipher instance can be used by switching its mode from ENCRYPT_MODE to DECRYPT_MODE for decryption. Because in blockchain applications the instance decrypting data is usually not the one encrypting data, the program constructs a second Cipher instance for decryption.

The following code example shows how to generate a pair of public and private keys to encrypt and decrypt data.

```
1    import java.security.KeyPair;
2    import java.security.KeyPairGenerator;
3    import javax.crypto.Cipher;
4    public class TestCipher_2 {
5        public static void main(String[] args) throws Exception{
6            String msg = "If you were a drop of tear in my eyes, I will never cry";
7            KeyPairGenerator kpg = KeyPairGenerator.getInstance("RSA");
8            kpg.initialize(4096);
9            KeyPair pair = kpg.generateKeyPair();
10           Cipher cipher = Cipher.getInstance("RSA");
11           cipher.init(Cipher.ENCRYPT_MODE, pair.getPublic());
12           byte[] bb = cipher.doFinal(msg.getBytes());
13           cipher.init(Cipher.DECRYPT_MODE, pair.getPrivate());
14           byte[] b2 = cipher.doFinal(bb);
15           System.out.println(new String(b2));
```

```
16      }
17  }
```

Code line 7 creates a KeyPairGenerator object using RSA algorithm. Class KeyPairGenerator supports four different algorithms. They are DiffieHellman, DSA, RSA, and EC. They are all for generating public and private key pairs.

Code line 8 initializes the key size. For RSA and DSA, the key size can be 128, 256 and 512 bytes using the inherent algorithms provided by Java JDK. However, Java specifies that every custom implementation must support DSA 1024 bits, RSA 1024 and 2048 bits. This means that a third party package may or may not support RSA 4096 bits. In this tutorial we are using RSA 4096 bits (512 bytes). In later chapters, we will switch over to RSA 2048 bits. Note that while longer bits can make hacking more difficult, the drawback is poorer efficiency. RSA 2048 is used the most currently.

Code line 9 generates a pair of public key and private key.

Code line 10 creates a Cipher instance that encrypts and decrypts using the RSA algorithm. It is worth noting that Cipher class does not support DSA algorithm. That leaves RSA the only choice here if we are going to apply public key and private key technology with Java Cipher class.

Code lines 11-12 apply the public key to initiate the Cipher instance into encryption mode, and then encrypts the message.

Code line 13-14 apply the private key to switch the Cipher instance to decryption mode and then decrypt the encrypted data. Please notice here that we are making use of the same Cipher instance for both encryption and decryption.

It is worth mentioning again that you can encrypt the data by private key and then decrypt the data by the paired public key if you are using a Cipher instance.

The message size in the above example is very small. If you make the message size twenty times larger and then try the above program, you will get an Exception "javax.crypto.IllegalBlockSizeException: Data must not be longer than 501 bytes". As the above program sets 4096 bits (512 bytes) as the key size, the encrypted data size must be no more than 512 bytes. If the encrypted data is much smaller, extra bytes are added to make it 512 bytes. RSA algorithm also automatically applies padding, which takes up 11 bytes. So, the input must be 512-11 = 501 bytes or less. Similarly, a key size of 2048 bits means that the largest data size possible is 245 bytes. Clearly, public and private key technology is lousy at encrypting large blocks of data.

Hope you are not bored so far. There is one more program for you to experience what is digital signature before we resume our learning of transactions.

```
1   import java.security.KeyPair;
2   import java.security.KeyPairGenerator;
3   import java.security.Signature;
4   public class TestSignature {
```

```
5       public static void main(String[] args) throws Exception{
6           String msg = "If you never come, how do I age alone?";
7           KeyPairGenerator kpg = KeyPairGenerator.getInstance("RSA");
8           kpg.initialize(2048);
9           KeyPair pair = kpg.generateKeyPair();
10          Signature sig = Signature.getInstance("SHA256withRSA");
11          sig.initSign(pair.getPrivate());
12          sig.update(msg.getBytes());
13          byte[] digitalSignature = sig.sign();
14          System.out.println(new String(digitalSignature));
15          Signature sig2 = Signature.getInstance("SHA256withRSA");
16          sig2.initVerify(pair.getPublic());
17          sig2.update(msg.getBytes());
18          boolean verified = sig2.verify(digitalSignature);
19          System.out.println("verified=" + verified);
20      }
21  }
```

Code line 10 instantiates a Signature object that applies RSA SHA-256 algorithm. SHA-1 algorithm is not secure enough now, and therefore it is necessary to use SHA-2 algorithms which include SHA-256, SHA-384, and SHA-512.

Code line 11 initializes the Signature object to be ready to sign a byte array with a private key. Unlike the Cipher class, the Signature class can generate a signature only with a private key, and can verify a signature only by a public key.

Code line 12 loads the data to sign into the Signature object.

Code line 13 signs the data and returns a byte array as the signature.

Code line 14 displays the signature with unreadable characters.

Code line 15 instantiates another Signature object with the same algorithm.

Code lines 16-18 initialize the second Signature object to be ready for verification with the public key, load the data and verify it with the signature. If the data and signature are intact, the verification returns true; otherwise false. Try it for yourself: modify the data or signature to inspect if the verification process still returns true.

That concludes our study into public and private key technology. Now, we will return to our blockchain programming in Java, and this chapter will show you how to write the UTXO and Transaction classes. Since we will be using public and private keys to generate signatures, it is a good idea to update our UtilityMethods class by adding a few more static methods to take care signature and key generation. In addition, let's add one static field named "uniqueNumber" in this UtilityMethods class because we need to generate a unique number for both UTXO and Transaction instances later.

Please add the following import statements at the top of your UtilityMethods class (above the class header).

```java
import java.security.PublicKey;
import java.security.PrivateKey;
import java.security.KeyPair;
import java.security.KeyPairGenerator;
import java.security.Key;
import java.security.Signature;
```

Then please add the following codes into your UtilityMethods class body.

```java
private static long uniqueNumber = 0;

public static long getUniqueNumber(){
    return UtilityMethods.uniqueNumber++;
}

public static KeyPair generateKeyPair()
{
    try{
        KeyPairGenerator kpg = KeyPairGenerator.getInstance("RSA");
        kpg.initialize(2048);
        KeyPair pair = kpg.generateKeyPair();
        return pair;
    }catch(java.security.NoSuchAlgorithmException e){
        throw new RuntimeException(e);
    }
}

public static byte[] generateSignature(PrivateKey privateKey, String message){
    try{
        Signature sig = Signature.getInstance("SHA256withRSA");
        sig.initSign(privateKey);
        sig.update(message.getBytes());
        return sig.sign();
    }catch(Exception e){
        throw new RuntimeException(e);
    }
}

public static boolean verifySignature(PublicKey publicKey, byte[] signature,
                                            String message){
    try{
        Signature sig2 = Signature.getInstance("SHA256withRSA");
        sig2.initVerify(publicKey);
        sig2.update(message.getBytes());
        return sig2.verify(signature);
    }catch(Exception e){
        e.printStackTrace();
        return false;
    }
}

public static String getKeyString(Key key){
    return Base64.getEncoder().encodeToString(key.getEncoded());
}
```

Why do we need the method getKeyString? This is because when we compute the hash ID for UTXO or Transaction, we need to include the sender's public key and the receiver's public key as strings. Class PublicKey extends class Key which has a method "byte[ ] getEncoded()" that returns a byte array containing the key value. This byte array represents the key. The getKeyString method then transforms this byte array into a comprehensible and readable string. Thus, this method takes in a Key object and returns a readable String uniquely for the Key object. Through this book, you will experience how we add more and more utility methods into the class UtilityMethods to make our programming handy.

A UTXO represents a spendable fund. It should include the following data.
1) Where it comes from. This has two avenues of data. First, a UTXO is generated inside a transaction. So, we need to know inside which transaction this UTXO is. Second, it is a good idea to record who sends the fund (technically this is optional, but we are going to do it here). In blockchain, a user is referred as an address, which is just a public key. Therefore, either it is a sender or receiver, a user is represented by a public key.
2) The owner of the UTXO. The receiver (in the form of a public key) is the owner of the UTXO.
3) How much fund available inside the UTXO.
4) A timestamp.
5) A unique ID identifying this UTXO. This is another hash based on the above data items: the transaction the UTXO is from, the sender, the receiver, the amount of fund, and a timestamp. However, to make the ID absolutely unique, the above information is still not enough. We need a unique sequential number that is different for each UTXO to make the ID absolutely unique.

The program for our UTXO class is displayed as the following.

```
1    import java.security.PublicKey;
2    public class UTXO implements java.io.Serializable {
3        private static final long serialVersionUID = 1L;
4        private String hashID;
5        private String parentTransactionID;
6        private PublicKey receiver;
7        private PublicKey sender;
8        private long timestamp;
9        private double fundTransferred;
10       private long sequentialNumber = 0;
11       public UTXO(String parentTransactionID, PublicKey sender,
                         PublicKey receiver, double fundToTransfer){
12           this.sequentialNumber = UtilityMethods.getUniqueNumber();
13           this.parentTransactionID = parentTransactionID;
14           this.receiver = receiver;
15           this.sender = sender;
16           this.fundTransferred = fundToTransfer;
17           this.timestamp = UtilityMethods.getTimeStamp();
18           this.hashID = computeHashID();
19       }

20       protected String computeHashID(){
21           String message = this.parentTransactionID
                         + UtilityMethods.getKeyString(this.sender)
                         + UtilityMethods.getKeyString(receiver)
                         + Double.toHexString(this.fundTransferred)
                         + Long.toHexString(this.timestamp)
```

```
                        +Long.toHexString(this.sequentialNumber);
22              return UtilityMethods.messageDigestSHA256_toString(message);
23          }

24          public String getHashID(){
25              return this.hashID;
26          }

27          public String getParentTransactionID(){
28              return this.parentTransactionID;
29          }

30          public PublicKey getReceiver(){
31              return this.receiver;
32          }

33          public PublicKey getSender(){
34              return this.sender;
35          }

36          public long getTimeStamp(){
37              return this.timestamp;
38          }

39          public long getSequentialNumber(){
40              return this.sequentialNumber;
41          }

42          public double getFundTransferred(){
43              return this.fundTransferred;
44          }

45          public boolean equals(UTXO uxo){
46              return this.getHashID().equals(uxo.getHashID());
47          }

48          public boolean isMiningReward(){
49              return false;
50          }
51      }
```

Code line 2 specifies that UTXO needs to be serialized and deserialized.

Code line 3 specifies a serialVersionUID for the UTXO class. If you recall, serialization and serialVersionUID were explained in chapter 2. Let's do a quick review to jog our memories. When a UTXO object at location A is serialized into bytes and transported to another location B, the JVM at location B determines that the incoming bytes are for an instance of class UTXO. The JVM's class loader uploads the class structure of the UTXO class to reconstruct the UTXO object based on the incoming bytes. It is possible that location A and location B are using different, incompatible versions of UTXO classes, and if this is the case, unexpected errors can occur. Therefore, it is a good programming convention to specify a serialVersionUID and update it whenever the class is modified in an effort to avoid unexpected errors.

The parentTransactionID in code line 5 is the unique hash value of the transaction in which this UTXO is created as an element. We can always track back to the transaction owning this UTXO via this hash value.

Code lines 20-23 illustrate that all instance fields are incorporated into the hash ID computation.

Code lines 48-50 require some explanation. In blockchain, a miner is rewarded an incentive for mining a block successfully. The reward is in the form of a UTXO. To track where the fund is from, it would be a good idea to tell the difference between a general UTXO and a UTXO of reward.

The codes for class Transaction are illustrated in the following.

```
1      import java.security.PrivateKey;
2      import java.security.PublicKey;
3      import java.util.ArrayList;
4      public class Transaction implements java.io.Serializable {
5          private static final long serialVersionUID = 1L;
6          public static final double TRANSACTION_FEE = 1.0;
7          private String hashID;
8          private PublicKey sender;
9          private PublicKey[] receivers;
10         private double[] fundToTransfer;
11         private long timestamp;
12         private ArrayList<UTXO> inputs = null;
13         private ArrayList<UTXO> outputs = new ArrayList<UTXO>(4);
14         private byte[] signature = null;
15         private boolean signed = false;
16         private long mySequentialNumber;

17         public Transaction(PublicKey sender, PublicKey receiver,
                       double fundToTransfer, ArrayList<UTXO> inputs)
18         {
19             PublicKey[] pks = new PublicKey[1];
20             pks[0] = receiver;
21             double[] funds = new double[1];
22             funds[0] = fundToTransfer;
23             this.setUp(sender, pks, funds, inputs);
24         }

25         public Transaction(PublicKey sender, PublicKey[] receivers,
                       double[] fundToTransfer, ArrayList<UTXO> inputs)
26         {
27             this.setUp(sender, receivers, fundToTransfer, inputs);
28         }

29         private void setUp(PublicKey sender, PublicKey[] receivers,
                       double[] fundToTransfer, ArrayList<UTXO> inputs) {
30             this.mySequentialNumber = UtilityMethods.getUniqueNumber();
31             this.sender = sender;
32             this.receivers = new PublicKey[1];
33             this.receivers = receivers;
34             this.fundToTransfer = fundToTransfer;
35             this.inputs = inputs;
36             this.timestamp = java.util.Calendar.getInstance().getTimeInMillis();
37             computeHashID();
38         }
```

```java
39      public void signTheTransaction(PrivateKey privateKey){
40          if(this.signature == null && !signed){
41              this.signature = UtilityMethods.generateSignature(privateKey,
                                            getMessageData());
42              signed = true;
43          }
44      }

45      public boolean verifySignature(){
46          String message = getMessageData();
47          return UtilityMethods.verifySignature(this.sender, this.signature, message);
48      }

49      private String getMessageData(){
50          StringBuilder sb = new StringBuilder();
51          sb.append(UtilityMethods.getKeyString(sender)
                    +Long.toHexString(this.timestamp)
                    +Long.toString(this.mySequentialNumber));
52          for(int i=0; i<this.receivers.length; i++){
53              sb.append(UtilityMethods.getKeyString(this.receivers[i])
                        + Double.toHexString(this.fundToTransfer[i]));
54          }
55          for(int i=0; i<this.getNumberOfInputUTXOs(); i++){
56              UTXO ut = this.getInputUTXO(i);
57              sb.append(ut.getHashID());
58          }
59          return sb.toString();
60      }

61      protected void computeHashID(){
62          String message = getMessageData();
63          this.hashID = UtilityMethods.messageDigestSHA256_toString(message);
64      }

65      public String getHashID(){
66          return this.hashID;
67      }

68      public PublicKey getSender(){
69          return this.sender;
70      }

71      public long getTimeStamp(){
72          return this.timestamp;
73      }

74      public long getSequentialNumber(){
75          return this.mySequentialNumber;
76      }

77      public double getTotalFundToTransfer(){
78          double f = 0;
79          for(int i=0; i<this.fundToTransfer.length;i++){
80              f += this.fundToTransfer[i];
81          }
82          return f;
83      }
```

```
84          protected void addOutputUTXO(UTXO ut){
85              if(!signed){
86                  outputs.add(ut);
87              }
88          }

89          public int getNumberOfOutputUTXOs(){
90              return this.outputs.size();
91          }

92          public UTXO getOuputUTXO(int i) {
93              return this.outputs.get(i);
94          }

95          public int getNumberOfInputUTXOs(){
96              if(this.inputs == null){
97                  return 0;
98              }
99              return this.inputs.size();
100         }

101         public UTXO getInputUTXO(int i){
102             return this.inputs.get(i);
103         }

104         public boolean equals(Transaction T){
105             return this.getHashID().equals(T.getHashID());
106         }
107 }
```

The Transaction class requires some in-depth explanation.

Code line 6 specifies a constant TRANSACTION_FEE. In bitcoin, transaction fee is dynamically allocated by the transaction sender, in which case the transaction fee can be more or less. To simplify things in our blockchain system and make it easier as to manually verify balances later on, we are making the transaction fee constant.

Code lines 8-10 specify the sender (there should be only one sender), the recipients (called receivers in the program. There can be one or more recipients), and the funds intended to be transferred to recipients. Both the sender and recipients are represented by their public keys. Please observe that we need to guarantee that the number of recipients matches the number of funds.

Code lines 12-13 indicate that both the input and output can have multiple UTXOs.

The two instance fields in code lines 14-15 are closely related. The signature is initially null. Once it is generated successfully, i.e. not null, the instance variable *signed* is set to be true. In the Transaction class, only the method signTheTransaction() in lines 39-44 can change the values of variable *signature* and variable *signed*. Moreover, once *signature* is not null or *signed* becomes true, the signature cannot be regenerated. This is a secure coding practice to ensure that a transaction cannot be signed more than once.

The Transaction class provides two constructors: one accepts one receiver, the second one accepts an array of receivers (code lines 17-28).

Code lines 39-48 include two methods. Though the method signTheTransaction() takes a PrivateKey as the input argument, it only uses it and never stores it. This is another secure coding practice – any private key should never be stored outside the key owner. The method verifySignature() calls a method in the UtilityMethods class to complete the signature verification. Plesae note that both the method signTheTransaction() and the method verifySignature() make use of the getMessageData() method (lines 49-60). This is important because the data prepared for signature generation and verification must be the same. How the data are prepared in the getMessageData() method is not critical, as long as all the necessary data items are included.

Code lines 61-64 presents the computeHashID() method which also makes use of the method getMessageData(). Please note that the output UTXOs are not included in the hash computation because a Transaction object must be instantiated before any output UTXOs are created, and output UTXOs need to reference the hash value of the Transaction object to which they belong.

Code lines 77-83 are for method getTotalFundToTransfer(). The Transaction class does not provide any access to the instance variable "double[ ] fundToTransfer" for two reasons. One reason is that the content of the double array can be obtained from the output UTXOs. A more important reason is for secure coding practice. We cannot have a method that returns an array of doubles because arrays are accessed by reference. If we provide a method "double[ ] getFundsToTransfer()" which returns the original array *fundToTransfer*, then when the returned array is modified outside the Transaction object, the content of the Transaction object is altered. Such a scenario should never be allowed to happen. Of course we can provide a deep copy of the instance field *fundToTransfer* so that it cannot be modified outside the transaction, but for the purpose of this book, that is unnecessary.

The method to add one UTXO into the transaction as an output is presented in code lines 84-88. Please note the safeguard mechanism there – once the transaction has been signed, no more UTXO can be added.

Code lines 89-103 provide methods to access the UTXOs in the input array list and the output array list. Please note that access to UTXOs is limited to one UTXO at a time. There is no method to return an array list of UTXO for access. This is again for secure coding.

We also need to write a test class that initiates a transaction. The following class TestTransaction is right for such a purpose. Note that comments are added inside the class to help explain the logics and details.

```
1     import java.security.KeyPair;
2     import java.security.PublicKey;
3     import java.util.ArrayList;
4     public class TestTransaction {
5         public static void main(String[] args) {
              // Generate the sender.
6             KeyPair sender = UtilityMethods.generateKeyPair();
              // Let us have two recipients.
7             PublicKey[] receivers = new PublicKey[2];
```

```
8              double[] fundsToTransfer = new double[receivers.length];
9              for(int i=0; i<receivers.length; i++){
10                 receivers[i] = UtilityMethods.generateKeyPair().getPublic();
11                 fundsToTransfer[i] = (i + 1) * 100;
12             }
               // As we do not have a Wallet class to make the transaction,
               // we need to manually create the input UTXOs and output UTXO.
13             UTXO uin = new UTXO("0", sender.getPublic(), sender.getPublic(), 1000);
14             ArrayList<UTXO> input = new ArrayList<UTXO>();
15             input.add(uin);
16             Transaction T = new Transaction(sender.getPublic(),
                                               receivers, fundsToTransfer, input);
               // Make sure that the sender has enough fund.
17             double available = 0.0;
18             for(int i=0; i<input.size(); i++){
19                 available += input.get(i).getFundTransferred();
20             }
               // Compute the total cost and add the transaction fee.
21             double totalCost = T.getTotalFundToTransfer()
                                               + Transaction.TRANSACTION_FEE;
               // If fund is not enough, abort.
22             if(available < totalCost){
23                 System.out.println("fund available=" + available
                                       + ", not enough for total cost of " + totalCost);
24                 return;
25             }
               // Generate the output UTXOs.
26             for(int i=0; i<receivers.length; i++){
27                 UTXO ut = new UTXO(T.getHashID(),
                                      sender.getPublic(), receivers[i], fundsToTransfer[i]);
28                 T.addOutputUTXO(ut);
29             }
               // Generate the change as an UTXO to the sender.
30             UTXO change = new UTXO(T.getHashID(),
                                      sender.getPublic(), sender.getPublic(), available-totalCost);
31             T.addOutputUTXO(change);
               // Sign the Transaction.
32             T.signTheTransaction(sender.getPrivate());
               // Display the transaction to take a look.
33             displayTransaction(T);
           }

           // A method written to display the transaction properly.
34         private static void displayTransaction(Transaction T){
35             System.out.println("Transaction{");
36             System.out.println("\tID: " + T.getHashID());
37             System.out.println("\tsender: "
                                   + UtilityMethods.getKeyString(T.getSender()));
38             System.out.println("\tfundToBeTransferred total: "
                                   + T.getTotalFundToTransfer());
39             System.out.println("\tReceivers:");
40             for(int i=0; i<T.getNumberOfOutputUTXOs() - 1; i++){
41                 UTXO ut = T.getOuputUTXO(i);
42                 System.out.println("\t\tfund=" + ut.getFundTransferred()
                                       + ",receiver=" + UtilityMethods.getKeyString(ut.getReceiver()));
43             }
44             UTXO change = T.getOuputUTXO(T.getNumberOfOutputUTXOs() - 1);
45             System.out.println("\ttransaction fee: " + Transaction.TRANSACTION_FEE);
46             System.out.println("\tchange: " + change.getFundTransferred());
```

```
47              boolean b = T.verifySignature();
48              System.out.println("\tsignature verification: " + b);
49              System.out.println("}");
50      }
51  }
```

After executing the TestTransaction program, you should see the output shown in Figure 6.

```
Transaction{
    ID: qyGVkXXwhnrAFAtmsyCKGRNm/dnkxsfYhhIS0KIHg40=
    sender: MIIBIjANBgkqhkiG9w0BAQEFAAOCAQ8AMIIBCgKCAQEAi8V0h
    fundToBeTransferred total: 300.0
    Receivers:
        fund=100.0, receiver=MIIBIjANBgkqhkiG9w0BAQEFAAOCAQ
        fund=200.0, receiver=MIIBIjANBgkqhkiG9w0BAQEFAAOCAQ
    transaction fee: 1.0
    change: 699.0
    signature verification: true
}
```

**Figure 6** The output of program TestTransaction. The information of the sender and receivers are truncated.

Hope you are enjoying the learning so far. You can download this chapter's programs at https://github.com/hhohho/Learning-Blockchain-in-Java-Edition-2. The programs presented in the book belong to a Java default package, while programs deposited at GitHub are in the package mdsky.applications.blockchain. The following steps demonstrate how to execute this chapter's program without using an IDE on a computer:

1) Assume that you have downloaded this chapter's programs from github into a directory (folder) named blockchain. The downloaded file should be: Learning-Blockchain-in-Java-Chapter3-src.rar.
2) Unzip the compressed file inside the blockchain folder. There should be a subfolder named "src" inside.
3) Please open a terminal window and navigate into the blockchain/src folder.
4) Continue navigate into blockchain/src/mdsky/applications/blockchain. You will see a few Java programs (source codes).
5) Execute the command: "javac *.java" without the quotation marks.
6) The above command compiles all the java source codes into .class files.
7) Navigate back to the blockchain/src folder. The reason to do so is because the downloaded Java programs are in the mdsky.applications.blockchain package. To execute them, you need to navigate into the folder where "mdsky" subfolder is located.
8) Execute the command: "java mdsky.applications.blockchain.TestTransaction" without the

quotation marks.
9) If step 8 does not work, it is very likely that the CLASSPATH of your computer is not set correctly: you then need to include the "." (the dot represents the current folder/directory) into your CLASSPATH.

# 4 TRANSACTION, WALLET AND MINER

Before we begin the programming in this chapter, please copy the programs from chapter 3 into a folder (directory) dedicated for chapter 4. Once again, we suggest using Eclipse to write and organize your programs, but there are other editors out there that would suffice. If you are using Eclipse, please start a new Java project named "chapter4" and import all the programs from chapter 3 into the source directory of Java project chapter4.

In blockchain, transactions are initiated by wallets. There are different understandings of what a wallet is. The most sophisticated wallets serve as a user interface that communicates with the user and manages the user's identity including all private and public keys. These wallets also track the user's balance and conduct transactions on the user's behalf, among other things. The bitcoin white paper suggests that users should utilize a different pair of public/private keys for each transaction to ensure security. If this suggestion is followed, a wallet must be capable of storing a large number of keys belonging to the same user. Less sophisticated wallets are solely holders of users' keys. By the end of this chapter, you should be able to code for a wallet capable of initiating transactions, checking balances, and storing a pair of public and private keys.

Software development is a dynamic process that requires continuous revision, and learning blockchain is no exception. We may find ourselves modifying programs or even radically redesigning software architecture. In fact, let's start chapter 4 by revising our Transaction class by adding another method called prepareOutputUTXOs().

Initiating a transaction requires preparing input UTXOs and output UTXOs. The input is usually prepared by a wallet outside the transaction, while the output can be prepared by the transaction internally – the method prepareOutputUTXOs() being one example. It is listed below.

```
1    public boolean prepareOutputUTXOs(){
2        if(this.receivers.length != this.fundToTransfer.length){
3            return false;
```

```
4      }
5      double totalCost = this.getTotalFundToTransfer() + Transaction.TRANSACTION_FEE;
6      double available = 0.0;
7      for(int i=0; i<this.inputs.size(); i++){
8          available += this.inputs.get(i).getFundTransferred();
9      }
10     if(available < totalCost){
11         return false;
12     }
13     this.outputs.clear();
14     for(int i=0; i<receivers.length; i++){
15         UTXO ut = new UTXO(this.getHashID(), this.sender,
                      receivers[i], this.fundToTransfer[i]);
16         this.outputs.add(ut);
17     }
18     UTXO change = new UTXO(this.getHashID(), this.sender,
                      this.sender, available - totalCost);
19     this.outputs.add(change);
20     return true;
21 }
```

Taking a closer look at the method above, you will notice that the method has two check points to safeguard that the initiation of a transaction is valid. First, the number of receivers must match exactly the number of fundToTransfer (lines 2-4). Next, the available funds from the input UTXOs must be enough for total cost (lines 5-12). If there is at least one condition unmet, the method aborts and returns false. Are there any other conditions this method should safeguard? Yes, there is another one, which we will leave for the last chapter when we analyze some blockchain attacking cases.

Code line 13 empties the output container. This is necessary, otherwise multiple calling of this method in preparation of a transaction can result in overpayment to the receipients.

This method automatically prepares the output UTXOs including the UTXO used as change (lines 14-19), making the programming of other classes easier. For example, in this chapter we will learn about wallets – the entities that initiate transactions. Either we can write many lines of codes to prepare the output of a transaction in the Wallet class, or we can move those codes into the Transaction class.

To properly display the content of transactions and UTXOs, relevant methods can be added to the UtilityMethods class. Shown below are three more static methods that have been supplemented:

```
public static void displayTab(PrintStream out, int level, String s){
    for(int i=0; i<level; i++){
        out.print("\t");
    }
    out.println(s);
}

public static void displayUTXO(UTXO ux, PrintStream out, int level){
    displayTab(out, level, "fund: " + ux.getFundTransferred()
               + ", receiver: " + UtilityMethods.getKeyString(ux.getReceiver()));
}

public static void displayTransaction(Transaction T, PrintStream out, int level){
    displayTab(out, level, "Transaction{");
```

```
            displayTab(out, level + 1, "ID: " + T.getHashID());
            displayTab(out, level + 1, "sender: " +
                            UtilityMethods.getKeyString(T.getSender()));
            displayTab(out, level + 1, "fundToBeTransferred total: "
                            + T.getTotalFundToTransfer());
            displayTab(out, level + 1, "Input:");
            for(int i=0; i<T.getNumberOfInputUTXOs(); i++){
                UTXO ui = T.getInputUTXO(i);
                displayUTXO(ui, out, level + 2);
            }
            displayTab(out, level + 1, "Output:");
            for(int i=0; i<T.getNumberOfOutputUTXOs() - 1; i++){
                UTXO ut = T.getOuputUTXO(i);
                displayUTXO(ut, out, level + 2);
            }
            UTXO change = T.getOuputUTXO(T.getNumberOfOutputUTXOs()-1);
            displayTab(out, level + 2,"change: " + change.getFundTransferred());
            displayTab(out, level + 1, "transaction fee: " + Transaction.TRANSACTION_FEE);
            boolean b = T.verifySignature();
            displayTab(out, level + 1, "signature verification: " + b);
            displayTab(out, level, "}");
        }
```

These three methods mainly serve cosmetic purposes, inserting tab spaces for the proper content display of Transactions and UTXOs. However, be aware that after these methods have been added to the UtilityMethods class, the program will not compile because PrintStream is not recognized as a type. You need to import java.io.PrintStream into your UtilityMethods class. Once you have added the statement "`import java.io.PrintStream;`" above the class header, the error will go away.

After putting together all the modifications, the TestTransaction class from chapter 3 should now look like this:

```
1     import java.security.KeyPair;
2     import java.security.PublicKey;
3     import java.util.ArrayList;
4     public class TestTransaction {
5         public static void main(String[] args) {
              // Generate the sender.
6             KeyPair sender = UtilityMethods.generateKeyPair();
              // Let's have two receivers.
7             PublicKey[] receivers = new PublicKey[2];
8             double[] fundsToTransfer = new double[receivers.length];
9             for(int i=0; i<receivers.length; i++){
10                receivers[i] = UtilityMethods.generateKeyPair().getPublic();
11                fundsToTransfer[i] = (i + 1) * 100;
12            }

13            UTXO uin = new UTXO("0", sender.getPublic(), sender.getPublic(), 1000);
14            ArrayList<UTXO> input = new ArrayList<UTXO>();
15            input.add(uin);
16            Transaction T = new Transaction(sender.getPublic(),
                                          receivers, fundsToTransfer, input);
17            boolean b = T.prepareOutputUTXOs();
18            if(!b){
19                System.out.println("Transaction failed");
20            }else{
```

```
21                    T.signTheTransaction(sender.getPrivate());
22                    UtilityMethods.displayTransaction(T, System.out, 1);
23              }
24         }
25    }
```

Try executing the TestTransaction class to make sure that it still works well. You should obtain the same output as shown in Figure 6.

The wallet class is one of the most complicated programs in blockchain. To make the learning process as painless as possible, we will simplify our wallet design and delegate certain functionalities to other classes whenever possible. To begin let's have our wallet store just a single pair of public and private keys.

So what information should a wallet contain? The most basic requirements are a pair of keys and a name. Wallets are represented by their public keys, but for the sake of easier identification, we will give each wallet a name. We will begin by letting our wallet class have the following instance fields:
- A pair of public and private keys
- A name

The initial version of our Wallet class can be presented as the following:

```
import java.security.KeyPair;
import java.security.PrivateKey;
import java.security.PublicKey;
public class Wallet {
    private KeyPair keyPair;
    private String walletName;

    public Wallet(String walletName){
        this.keyPair = UtilityMethods.generateKeyPair();
        this.walletName = walletName;
    }

    public String getName(){
        return this.walletName;
    }

    public PublicKey getPublicKey(){
        return this.keyPair.getPublic();
    }

    protected PrivateKey getPrivateKey(){
        return this.keyPair.getPrivate();
    }
}
```

Simple enough, right? A question to ask is if a wallet needs to store its keys locally. In reality, the keys are stored locally with password protection. Let's store keys locally, too. We then need to include two additional data items: 1) a password, and 2) a location where the keys are to be stored. The password is used only for the wallet creation and retrieval. The location for key storage should be a specific directory added as a static field in the Wallet class.

```
private static String keyLocation = "keys";
```

To use a password to protect our saved keys, we need a mechanism that will encrypt the keys using the password. You will be taught two methods of accomplishing this task, the reason being that password-based encryption in Java can be a little bit complicated.

The bitwise exclusive OR (XOR) operator has an outstanding property: if A XOR B = C, then B XOR C = A. Assuming B is the password, A is the data, and C is the encrypted data obtained by A XOR B. To obtain A from C, we just need to perform the XOR action between B and C. In Java, the exclusive OR operator is represented by "^", which can only be performed between two integers.

Let's add in two more static methods to the UtilityMethods class to make it handy to apply the XOR to encrypt and decrypt data.

```
1   public static byte[] encryptionByXOR(byte[] key, String password){
2       int more = 100;
3       byte[] p = UtilityMethods.messageDigestSHA256_toBytes(password);
4       byte[] pwds = new byte[p.length * more];
5       for(int i=0,z=0; i<more; i++){
6           for(int j=0; j<p.length; j++, z++){
7               pwds[z] = p[j];
8           }
9       }
10      byte[] result = new byte[key.length];
11      int i = 0;
12      for(i=0; i<key.length && i<pwds.length; i++){
13          result[i] =(byte)((key[i] ^ pwds[i]) & 0xFF);
14      }
15      while(i < key.length){
16          result[i] = key[i];
17          i++;
18      }
19      return result;
20  }
21  public static byte[] decryptionByXOR(byte[] key, String password){
22      return encryptionByXOR(key, password);
23  }
```

Code lines 2-9 show that we do not directly use the password to perform the XOR operation. Instead, we generate a hash value first based on the password. This provides an extra layer of security. The hash value has only 32 bytes (256 bits) based on the algorithm we have been using, which may not be long enough to XOR every bit in the byte array *key*. Instead, the hash value is amplified 100 times and stored in the variable *pwds*.

Code lines 12-14 perform the XOR operation on every byte in the byte array *key* unless *key* is longer than *pwds*. If *key*'s size is greater than *pwds*' size, lines 15-18 copy the remaining bytes in *key* into *result* without any operation on them. Line 13 needs some more explanation here. key[i] ^ pwds[i] performs an XOR operation between a byte in *key* and a byte in *pwds*, the result of which is further performed an AND (&) operation with the hexadecimal number 0xFF. 0xFF is a 4-byte integer with every bit being 1. We know that the AND operation can only result in 1 if both bits are 1, otherwise the result will be 0. This AND operation here is to guarantee that the result is preserved properly. In fact, as `key[i]` and `pwds[i]` are both of data type byte, it is not necessary to add this AND operation here. So, code line 13 can also read as the following:

```
result[i] = (byte)(key[i] ^ pwds[i]);
```

Code lines 21-23 reveal the fact that the decryptionByXOR() method calls encryptionByXOR() method to covert the encrypted data back to the original using the same password.

To evaluate our XOR encryption and decryption methods, you can write a simple program:

```java
public class TestXOR {
    public static void main(String[] args) {
        String message = "At the most beautiful place, "
            + "remember the most beautiful you.";
        String password = "blockchains";
        byte[] encry = UtilityMethods.encryptionByXOR(message.getBytes(), password);
        // Take a peek at the encrypted data.
        System.out.println(new String(encry));
        byte[] decrypted = UtilityMethods.decryptionByXOR(encry, password);
        System.out.println("after proper decryption, the message is:\n");
        System.out.println(new String(decrypted));
        System.out.println("\nwith an incorrect password, "
                + "the decrpted message looks like:");
        // Let's try an incorrect password.
        decrypted = UtilityMethods.decryptionByXOR(encry, "Block Chain");
        // Exmaine the wrongly decrypted message.
        System.out.println(new String(decrypted));
    }
}
```

The AES encryption algorithm can also be used for password-based encryption, but it is much more complicated than the XOR encryption and decryption. The central ideas are explained below:
1) Apply the password and a random large number called *salt* to prepare a KeySpec object *spec*, then create a temporary key based on *spec*.
2) Obtain a SecretKey instance compatible with the AES encryption algorithm by using the temporary key's information.
3) Create a Cipher object and initialize it with the secret key to encrypt the data. The password is incorporated into the key generation process so that only the authentic password can repeat this process to construct a correct SecretKey instance to decrypt the data.
4) Data items such as *salt* must remain constant for proper decryption and so they must also be incorporated into the encrypted data.

Before writing the encryptionByAES() method, first we need to import a few classes into the UtilityMethods class. They are listed below:

```java
import java.security.AlgorithmParameters;
import java.security.SecureRandom;
```

```
import java.security.spec.KeySpec;
import javax.crypto.Cipher;
import javax.crypto.SecretKey;
import javax.crypto.SecretKeyFactory;
import javax.crypto.spec.IvParameterSpec;
import javax.crypto.spec.PBEKeySpec;
import javax.crypto.spec.SecretKeySpec;
```

Let's analyze the UtilityMethods.encryptionByAES() method to develop some understanding.

```
1   public static byte[] encryptionByAES(byte[] key, String password){
2       try{
3           byte[] salt = new byte[8];
4           SecureRandom rand = new SecureRandom();
5           rand.nextBytes(salt);
6           SecretKeyFactory factory =
                        SecretKeyFactory.getInstance("PBKDF2WithHmacSHA1");
7           KeySpec spec = new PBEKeySpec(password.toCharArray(), salt, 1024, 128);
8           SecretKey tmp = factory.generateSecret(spec);
9           SecretKey secretKey = new SecretKeySpec(tmp.getEncoded(), "AES");
10          Cipher cipher = Cipher.getInstance("AES/CBC/PKCS5Padding");
11          cipher.init(Cipher.ENCRYPT_MODE, secretKey);
12          AlgorithmParameters params = cipher.getParameters();
13          byte[] iv = params.getParameterSpec(IvParameterSpec.class).getIV();
14          byte[] output = cipher.doFinal(key);
15          byte[] outputSizeBytes = UtilityMethods.intToBytes(output.length);
16          byte[] ivSizeBytes = UtilityMethods.intToBytes(iv.length);
17          byte[] data = new byte[Integer.BYTES * 2
                        + salt.length + iv.length + output.length];
            // The order of the data is arranged as the following:
            // int_forOutputSize + int_forIVsize + 8_byte_salt + iv_bytes + output_bytes
18          int z = 0;
19          for(int i=0; i<outputSizeBytes.length; i++, z++){
20              data[z] = outputSizeBytes[i];
21          }
22          for(int i=0; i<ivSizeBytes.length; i++, z++){
23              data[z] = ivSizeBytes[i];
24          }
25          for(int i=0; i<salt.length; i++, z++){
26              data[z] = salt[i];
27          }
28          for(int i=0; i<iv.length; i++, z++){
29              data[z] = iv[i];
30          }
31          for(int i=0; i<output.length; i++, z++){
32              data[z] = output[i];
33          }
34          return data;
35      }catch(Exception e){
36          throw new RuntimeException(e);
37      }
38  }
```

Code line 3 initializes a byte array of size 8. Plain text does not taste good, so salt is needed – or so the joke goes. *"salt"*, as we mentioned before, is the large random number that exists as an extra layer of security. If we only relied on the plain text password protection (like our XOR encryption), it would be relatively easy for a type of attack called "library attack" to breach security because there are only a finite number of character combinations. However, by using a "salt" in addition to the "plain" text password, the difficulty level for a breach to happen is dramatically increased.

Code lines 4-5 initialize an instance of SecureRandom and then utilize it to generate an 8-bytes large number. The eight bytes of this number are stored in the variable *salt*.

PBEKeySpec class implements KeySpec interface in Java Cryptography Extension (JCE). KeySpec specifies the key material used in constituting a cryptographic key. PBEKeySpec is specifically for the key material of password-based encryption and it has several constructors. The constructor used in code line 7 has four arguments: the password in char array, *salt*, 1024, and 128. The number 1024 stands for the iteration count, which specifies how many times the password is hashed for the derivation of the cryptographic key. Generally speaking, the larger the number, the more secure the cryptographic key is and so some choose to use a larger iteration count. The number 128 specifies the key size. For the AES algorithm, keys of 128-bits are the most common.

Code line 8 generates a temporary key based on the PBEKeySpec instance created in line 7.

Code line 9 constructs a cryptographic key (a secret key in this case) based on the bytes contained within the temporary key and the desired AES algorithm.

Code line 10 obtains a Cipher instance with a proper algorithm name. Please remember that you can check the supporting algorithm names for each JCE class at Java API document. For JDK8, the link is at: https://docs.oracle.com/javase/8/docs/technotes/guides/security/StandardNames.html.

Code line 11 initiates the Cipher instance into encryption mode with the proper key.

Code lines 12-13 record the Cipher instance's algorithm parameters for future decryption. The decryption must apply the same secret key, and the same algorithm parameters to construct the key in the first place. These two lines of code preserve the algorithm parameter in a byte array named *iv*.

Code line 14 encrypts the data and returns it as a byte array named *output*.

Code lines 15-33 organize all data required for successful decryption: *output*, *salt*, and *iv*. All of the data are stored as separate byte arrays but they need to be copied into a single byte array. It is necessary that we place them in a specific order and record their lengths.

In code line 15, a static method named intToBytes() of class UtilityMethods is used to convert the length of *output* (an integer) into a byte array. We need to know how many bytes the *output* has when we copy it into a single byte array.

In code line 16, the integer representing the length of *iv*, is converted into an array of bytes as well.

Code line 17 prepares a byte array named *data* that can store all the necessary information in order:

*output* length, *iv* length, *salt*, *iv*, and *output*. Later on, code lines 18-33 copy those individual byte arrays into the single storage named *data*.

Before we continue with the decryption process, please remember to add the method we just went over into the UtilityMethods class first. Please note that you will encounter two error messages stating that there is no intToBytes() method. Disregard those error messages because the mentioned method is being introduced next with a paired method bytesToInt().

```
public static byte[] intToBytes(int v){
    byte[] b = new byte[Integer.BYTES];
    for(int i=b.length-1; i>=0; i--){
        b[i] = (byte)(v & 0xFF);
        v = v >> Byte.SIZE;
    }
    return b;
}

public static int bytesToInt(byte[] b){
    int v = 0;
    for(int i=0; i<b.length; i++){
        v = v << Byte.SIZE;
        v = v | (b[i] & 0xFF);
    }
    return v;
}
```

If you do not have any experience working with bytes and bits, please do not worry about what is being presented below. We are simply explaining some of the theory behind converting an integer into an array of bytes and vice versa. The operator "<<" shifts bits to the left while the operator ">>" shifts bits to the right. As Byte.SIZE is always 8 in Java, the statement `v = v >> Byte.SIZE` shifts bits in *v* 8 bits to the right and updates *v* with the shifted result. For example, suppose integer *v* (int is always 4 bytes in Java) has the bit string shown below:

01101010 00111010 10001110 11111110

The statement `b[i] = (byte)(v & 0xFF)` in the method intToBytes() stores 11111110 inside the last spot of the byte array *b* (the least significant byte). The next statement `v = v >> Byte.SIZE` shifts to the right for 8 bits.

01101010 00111010 10001110 11111110 >> 8

After the above operation, *v* becomes:

00000000 01101010 00111010 10001110

The rightmost 8 bits are dropped while an additional 8 bits of zeros are added on the left. In the next round, the statement `b[i] = (byte)(v & 0xFF)` stores 10001110 in the second last spot of the byte array *b*. Once again 10001110 is dropped and another 8 bits of zeros are added to the left. Plainly, the method intToBytes() obtains the first byte of the integer *v* via the statement b[i] = (byte)(v & 0xFF), and subsequent bytes acquired by repeatedly shifting the bit string of *v* to right. Eventually, as this process is repeated, we end up with the four bytes of the integer *v* into an array of bytes. The method bytesToInt() works in the reverse and converts a byte array into an integer by shifting bits to the left.

The decryptionByAES() method does the reverse of the encryptionByAES() method and is represented by the following:

```java
    public static byte[] decryptionByAES(byte[] key, String password){
        try{
            // Divide the input data key[] into proper values.
            // Please remember the order of the data is:
            // int_forOutputSize + int_forIVsize + 8_byte_salt + iv_bytes + output_bytes
            int z = 0;
            byte[] lengthByte = new byte[Integer.BYTES];
            for(int i=0; i<lengthByte.length; i++, z++){
                lengthByte[i] = key[z];
            }
            int dataSize = bytesToInt(lengthByte);
            for(int i=0; i<lengthByte.length; i++, z++){
                lengthByte[i] = key[z];
            }
            int ivSize = bytesToInt(lengthByte);
            byte[] salt = new byte[8];
            for(int i=0; i<salt.length; i++, z++){
                salt[i] = key[z];
            }
            // iv bytes.
            byte[] ivBytes = new byte[ivSize];
            for(int i=0; i<ivBytes.length; i++, z++){
                ivBytes[i] = key[z];
            }
            // Real data bytes.
            byte[] dataBytes = new byte[dataSize];
            for(int i=0; i<dataBytes.length; i++, z++){
                dataBytes[i] = key[z];
            }
            // Once data are ready, reconstruct the key and cipher.
            PBEKeySpec pbeKeySpec =
                    new PBEKeySpec(password.toCharArray(), salt, 1024, 128);
            SecretKeyFactory secretKeyFactory =
                    SecretKeyFactory.getInstance("PBKDF2WithHmacSHA1");
            SecretKey tmp = secretKeyFactory.generateSecret(pbeKeySpec);
            SecretKey secretKey = new SecretKeySpec(tmp.getEncoded(), "AES");
            Cipher cipher2 = Cipher.getInstance("AES/CBC/PKCS5Padding");
            // Algorithm parameters (ivBytes) are necessary to initiate cipher.
            cipher2.init(Cipher.DECRYPT_MODE, secretKey,
                    new IvParameterSpec(ivBytes));
            byte[] data = cipher2.doFinal(dataBytes);
            return data;
        }catch(Exception e){
            throw new RuntimeException(e);
        }
    }
```

Please remember to add this decryptionByAES() method into the UtilityMethods class. You will notice that the class UtilityMethods is growing fast. If you would like to test out methods encryptionByAES() and decryptionByAES(), you can write a small program that looks something like the following:

```java
public class TestEncryptionDecryptionWithAES {
    public static void main(String[] args) {
        String message = "At the most beautiful place, "
                + "remember you the most beautiful.";
        String password = "blockchains";
        byte[] encrypted = UtilityMethods.encryptionByAES(message.getBytes(), password);
        // Take a peek at the encrypted data.
        System.out.println(new String(encrypted));
        byte[] decrypted = UtilityMethods.decryptionByAES(encrypted, password);
        // Examine the decrypted message.
        System.out.println("The encrypted message below is not readable");
        System.out.println(new String(decrypted));
        // Let's try an incorrect password.
        try{
            System.out.println("When using an incorrect password");
            decrypted = UtilityMethods.decryptionByAES(encrypted, "Block Chain");
            // Exmaine the wrongly decrypted message.
            System.out.println(new String(decrypted));
        }catch(Exception e){
            System.out.println("Runtime exception happened. Cannot work");
        }
    }
}
```

Now that we have mastered the tools for storing and retrieving keys, we can return to working on the Wallet class. We will expand it by adding methods, such as constructors, to properly create new and load existing wallets. Please note that the existing codes have been highlighted in the following code list for your convenience:

```
1    import java.io.ByteArrayInputStream;
2    import java.io.ByteArrayOutputStream;
3    import java.io.File;
4    import java.io.FileInputStream;
5    import java.io.FileNotFoundException;
6    import java.io.FileOutputStream;
7    import java.io.ObjectInputStream;
8    import java.io.ObjectOutputStream;
9    import java.io.IOException;
10   import java.security.KeyPair;
11   import java.security.PrivateKey;
12   import java.security.PublicKey;

13   public class Wallet {
14       private KeyPair keyPair;
15       private String walletName;
16       private static String keyLocation = "keys";

17       public Wallet(String walletName, String password){
18           this.keyPair = UtilityMethods.generateKeyPair();
19           this.walletName = walletName;
20           try{
21               populateExistingWallet(walletName, password);
22               System.out.println("A wallet exists with the same name "
```

```
                                    + "and password. Loaded the existing wallet");
23              }catch(Exception ee){
24                  try{
25                      this.prepareWallet(password);
26                      System.out.println("Created a new wallet based on "
                                    + "the name and password");
27                  }catch(IOException ioe){
28                      throw new RuntimeException(ioe);
29                  }
30              }
31          }

32          public Wallet(String walletName){
33              this.keyPair = UtilityMethods.generateKeyPair();
34              this.walletName = walletName;
35          }

36          public String getName(){
37              return this.walletName;
38          }

39          public PublicKey getPublicKey(){
40              return this.keyPair.getPublic();
41          }

42          protected PrivateKey getPrivateKey(){
43              return this.keyPair.getPrivate();
44          }

45          private void prepareWallet(String password)
                                    throws IOException, FileNotFoundException {
46              ByteArrayOutputStream bo = new ByteArrayOutputStream();
47              ObjectOutputStream out = new ObjectOutputStream(bo);
48              out.writeObject(this.keyPair);
49              byte[] keyBytes =
                        UtilityMethods.encryptionByXOR(bo.toByteArray(), password);
50              File F = new File(Wallet.keyLocation);
51              if(!F.exists()){
52                  F.mkdir();
53              }
54              FileOutputStream fout = new FileOutputStream(Wallet.keyLocation
                                    + "/" + this.getName().replace(' ', '_') + "_keys");
55              fout.write(keyBytes);
56              fout.close();
57              bo.close();
58          }

59          private void populateExistingWallet(String walletName, String password)
                        throws IOException, FileNotFoundException, ClassNotFoundException {
60              FileInputStream fin = new FileInputStream(Wallet.keyLocation
                                    + "/"+walletName.replace(' ', '_') + "_keys");

61              byte[] bb = new byte[4096];
62              int size = fin.read(bb);
63              fin.close();
64              byte[] data = new byte[size];
65              for(int i=0; i<data.length; i++){
66                  data[i] = bb[i];
67              }
```

```
68              byte[] keyBytes = UtilityMethods.decryptionByXOR(data, password);
69              ObjectInputStream in =
                    new ObjectInputStream(new ByteArrayInputStream(keyBytes));
70              this.keyPair = (KeyPair)(in.readObject());
71              this.walletName = walletName;
72          }
73      }
```

Code lines 17-31 present a new constructor for Wallet. This constructor requires two arguments one of which is password. Keys generated by this constructor are stored and encrypted. The program will first try to load an existing Wallet instance by searching for a matching name and password (line 21). If a match cannot be found, it usually means that no such a wallet exists, and so the program would go ahead to create a new Wallet instance (line 25).

Note that the old constructor in code lines 32-35 has been kept, but it is no longer relevant and can be deleted if you so choose (it is deleted in the chapter 9 programs).

Code lines 45-58 illustrate the structure of the method prepareWallet() which is called in line 25 in a constructor. Its function is to encrypt the public and private keys of the wallet and store them locally inside a file. Java has an ObjectOutputStream class that can serialize any classes implementing the Serializable interface into a byte array. Therefore, an instance of ObjectOutputStream (*out*) is created from an instance of ByteArrayOutputStream (*bo*) in code line 47. The goal is to have the bytes inside *out* be stored in *bo* so that the serialized bytes from a ByteArrayOutputStream instance can be easily obtained (*bo.toByteArray()* in line 49).

Code Line 48 writes the key pair into the ByteArrayOutputStream object referenced by the variable *bo*, and line 49 fetches the bytes from *bo*, encrypts them, and stores the encrypted data.

Code lines 51-53 checks if the directory for storing keys exists in the file system. If not, then creates this directory.

Code lines 54-57 write the encrypted data into a file.

An important note: code line 49 uses the UtilityMethods.encryptionByXOR() method to encrypt the data via the XOR algorithm. If you would rather use the AES algorithm simply change "XOR" to "AES" in this statement. Remember that the encryption method must match the decryption method, so you would also need to replace "XOR" with "AES" in code line 68.

Code lines 59-72 present another private method populateExistingWallet() which reads and decrypts stored key data based on the given password.

Code Line 60 creates a FileInputStream object referenced by *fin*.

Code Line 61 creates a byte array *bb* of size 4096 which is large enough for key data. After reading the encrypted bytes in line 62, line 63 closes the FileInputStream since it is no longer being used. The statement *fin.read(bb)* reads the encrypted bytes into *bb* and then returns an integer indicating how many bytes have been loaded into *bb*. From the integer, we are able to tell the size of the encrypted data.

Code Lines 64-67 copy the bytes stored in *bb* into another byte array named *data*.

Code Line 68 decrypts *data* based on the given password and stores the decrypted data as bytes in *keyBytes*. At this point, the byte array *KeyBytes* contains the serialized bytes for the KeyPair object of this wallet.

Code Line 69 makes use of ObjectInputStream to deserialize the bytes back into an object, which is then cast to a KeyPair object and assigned to the proper variable *this.keyPair* in line 70.

It is a good practice to write a testing program to examine if the above codes are working as expected. The program TestWallet_1.java, below, is an example of such a test. If you are interested, you can add a login feature for a wallet. It should be fun.

```java
public class TestWallet_1 {
    public static void main(String[] args){
        java.util.Scanner in = new java.util.Scanner(System.in);
        System.out.println("To create a wallet, please give your name:");
        String name = in.nextLine();
        System.out.println("please create a password");
        String password = in.nextLine();
        in.close();
        Wallet w = new Wallet(name, password);
        System.out.println("wallet created for " + w.getName());
        // Let's load this wallet.
        Wallet w2 = new Wallet(name, password);
        System.out.println("wallet loaded successfully, " + "wallet name=" + w2.getName());
    }
}
```

In bitcoin blockchain, there are some fully functional nodes that are much more powerful than a wallet. They keep a latest copy of the public blockchain (usually referred to as ledger), respond to queries, mine and broadcast blocks, and participate in votes. In this book, we will not be creating one of these fully functional nodes, but we will be creating a participating role that can mine blocks and keep a local copy of the public ledger. Let's call such a mining node miner.

A Miner class is an extension of the Wallet class, with the extra capability to mine and broadcast a block. At this point a Miner class can be as simple as the following:

```java
public class Miner extends Wallet {
    public Miner(String minerName, String password) {
        super(minerName, password);
    }

    // This constructor is not necessary. You can delete it.
    public Miner(String minerName){
        super(minerName);
    }
```

```
        public boolean mineBlock(Block block) {
            return (block.mineTheBlock());
        }
    }
```

Chapter 4 covered the Wallet and Miner classes, yet neither are very functional because the Block and Blockchain classes have not been set up (that's chapter 5). But by the end of the next chapter, we will have a functioning blockchain system, albeit with limited capabilities. You can download this chapter's programs at https://github.com/hhohho/Learning-Blockchain-in-Java-Edition-2. The programs presented in the book belong to a Java default package, while programs deposited at GitHub are in the package mdsky.applications.blockchain.

# 5 BLOCK AND BLOCKCHAIN

By this point you should already know the drill, but I'll reiterate for old time's sake. Please copy the programs from chapter 4 into a folder (directory) dedicated for chapter 5. Once again, we suggest using Eclipse to write and organize your programs, but feel free to use other available editors. If you are using Eclipse, please start a new Java project named "chapter5" and import all the programs from chapter 4 into the source directory of Java project chapter5. After that, it would be a good idea to remove all testing programs but only keep the six programs to start with Chapter 5: Block, Miner, Transaction, UTXO, UtilityMethods, and Wallet.

In Chapter 2, you were taught how to mine a block. At the time, the Transaction class was incomplete and so we substituted string for transaction. It is time to revise the old Block class and implement more functions, though it will not be much more complicated than the class we came up with in Chapter 2. By the end of this chapter, however, we will end up with our first functional version of blockchain. So let us begin; the revised Block class is laid out below:

```
1    import java.util.ArrayList;
2    public class Block implements java.io.Serializable{
3        private static final long serialVersionUID = 1L;
4        public final static int TRANSACTION_UPPER_LIMIT = 2;
5        private int difficultyLevel = 25;
6        private ArrayList<Transaction> transactions = new ArrayList<Transaction>();
7        private long timestamp;
8        private String previousBlockHashID;
9        private int nonce = 0;
10       private String hashID;

11       public Block(String previousBlockHashID, int difficultyLevel){
12           this.previousBlockHashID = previousBlockHashID;
13           this.timestamp = UtilityMethods.getTimeStamp();
14           this.difficultyLevel = difficultyLevel;
15       }

16       protected String computeHashID(){
```

```java
17              StringBuilder sb = new StringBuilder();
18              sb.append(this.previousBlockHashID + Long.toHexString(this.timestamp));
19              for(Transaction t : transactions){
20                  sb.append(t.getHashID());
21              }
22              sb.append(Integer.toHexString(this.difficultyLevel) + nonce);
23              byte[] b = UtilityMethods.messageDigestSHA256_toBytes(sb.toString());
24              return UtilityMethods.toBinaryString(b);
25          }

26          public boolean addTransaction(Transaction t){
27              if(this.getTotalNumberOfTransactions() >= Block.TRANSACTION_UPPER_LIMIT){
28                  return false;
29              }
30              this.transactions.add(t);
31              return true;
32          }

33          public String getHashID(){
34              return this.hashID;
35          }

36          public int getNonce(){
37              return this.nonce;
38          }

39          public long getTimeStamp(){
40              return this.timestamp;
41          }

42          public String getPreviousBlockHashID(){
43              return this.previousBlockHashID;
44          }

45          protected boolean mineTheBlock(){
46              this.hashID = this.computeHashID();
47              while(!UtilityMethods.hashMeetsDifficultyLevel(this.hashID, this.difficultyLevel)){
48                  this.nonce++;
49                  this.hashID = this.computeHashID();
50              }
51              return true;
52          }

53          public int getDifficultyLevel(){
54              return this.difficultyLevel;
55          }

56          public int getTotalNumberOfTransactions(){
57              return this.transactions.size();
58          }

59          public Transaction getTransaction(int index){
60              return this.transactions.get(index);
61          }
62      }
```

Deviating from the former Block class, code line 6 declares and initializes an ArrayList of Transactions. Each transaction's hash is added to the computation of the block's hash ID in the loop found in lines

19-21. Method addTransaction has been changed as well. In this method, a new instance field TRANSACTION_UPPER_LIMIT is used to make sure that the number of transactions in a block does not exceed the limit. For demonstration purposes, this limit is set to be 2, but know that bitcoin does not set an upper limit on the number of transactions a block can undertake. Rather, a block's transactions are somewhat limited by its size. Each bitcoin block could not exceed 1Mb (this limit was increased since 2016). In this book, we set an upper number limit to simulate this bitcoin feature.

For secure coding, a block does not allow fetching more than one transaction a time. To iterate through all transactions in a block, a loop can be used.

```
for(int i=0; i<block.getTotalNumberOfTransactions(); i++){
    Transaction t = block.getTransaction(i);
}
```

To develop the class Blockchain, the chain must be a list. Available data structures can be Java's ArrayList or LinkedList. The disadvantage of LinkedList lies in its slow linear searching for a block. The ArrayList is a perfect data structure for this purpose except that it allows elements to be inserted and deleted. To avoid accidental misuse of the data structure for our blockchain, we will build our Blockchain class on another customized class named LedgerList. The LedgerList wraps an ArrayList instance and provides necessary functions for blockchain to add a block at the end and find a block quickly with an index. It does not allow a block to be inserted or deleted. Nevertheless, the LedgerList class is not absolutely necessary.

```
1   import java.util.ArrayList;
2   public class LedgerList<T> implements java.io.Serializable {
3       private static final long serialVersionUID = 1L;
4       private ArrayList<T> list;

5       public LedgerList(){
6           list = new ArrayList<T>();
7       }

8       public int size(){
9           return this.list.size();
10      }

11      public T getLast(){
12          return this.list.get(size() - 1);
13      }

14      public T getFirst(){
15          return this.list.get(0);
16      }

17      public boolean add(T e){
18          return this.list.add(e);
19      }

20      public T findByIndex(int index){
21          return this.list.get(index);
22      }
23  }
```

This LedgerList is built upon ArrayList, but for the purpose of secure coding, it does not allow direct access to the underline ArrayList instance. The elements of LedgerList can only be accessed one at a time.

The functions we will be adding to the class Blockchain include the ability to add new blocks to the chain and being able to find the balance for a specific public key (wallet). The following implementation also includes several other methods that will become important later on:

```
1   import java.security.PublicKey;
2   import java.util.ArrayList;
3   import java.util.HashMap;

4   public class Blockchain implements java.io.Serializable {
5       private static final long serialVersionUID = 1L;
6       public static final double MINING_REWARD = 100.0;
7       private LedgerList<Block> blockchain;

8       public Blockchain(Block genesisBlock){
9           this.blockchain = new LedgerList<Block>();
10          this.blockchain.add(genesisBlock);
11      }

12      public synchronized void addBlock(Block block){
13          if(block.getPreviousBlockHashID().equals(this.getLastBlock().getHashID())){
14              this.blockchain.add(block);
15          }
16      }

17      public Block getGenesisBlock(){
18          return this.blockchain.getFirst();
19      }

20      public Block getLastBlock(){
21          return this.blockchain.getLast();
22      }

23      public int size(){
24          return this.blockchain.size();
25      }

26      public Block getBlock(int index){
27          return this.blockchain.findByIndex(index);
28      }

29      public double findRelatedUTXOs(PublicKey key, ArrayList<UTXO> all,
                                        ArrayList<UTXO> spent, ArrayList<UTXO> unspent,
                                        ArrayList<Transaction> sentTransactions) {
30          double gain = 0.0, spending = 0.0;
31          HashMap<String, UTXO> map = new HashMap<String, UTXO>();
32          int limit = this.size();
33          for(int a=0; a<limit; a++){
34              Block block = this.blockchain.findByIndex(a);
35              int size = block.getTotalNumberOfTransactions();
36              for(int i=0; i<size; i++){
37                  Transaction T = block.getTransaction(i);
38                  int N;
```

```java
39                  if(a != 0 && T.getSender().equals(key)){
40                      N = T.getNumberOfInputUTXOs();
41                      for(int x=0; x<N; x++){
42                          UTXO ut = T.getInputUTXO(x);
43                          spent.add(ut);
44                          map.put(ut.getHashID(), ut);
45                          spending += ut.getFundTransferred();
46                      }
47                      sentTransactions.add(T);
48                  }
49                  N = T.getNumberOfOutputUTXOs();
50                  for(int x=0; x<N; x++){
51                      UTXO ux = T.getOuputUTXO(x);
52                      if(ux.getReceiver().equals(key)){
53                          all.add(ux);
54                          gain += ux.getFundTransferred();
55                      }
56                  }
57              }
58          }
59          for(int i=0; i<all.size(); i++){
60              UTXO ut = all.get(i);
61              if(!map.containsKey(ut.getHashID())){
62                  unspent.add(ut);
63              }
64          }
65          return (gain - spending);
66      }

67      public double checkBalance(PublicKey key){
68          ArrayList<UTXO> all = new ArrayList<UTXO>();
69          ArrayList<UTXO> spent = new ArrayList<UTXO>();
70          ArrayList<UTXO> unspent = new ArrayList<UTXO>();
71          return findRelatedUTXOs(key, all, spent, unspent);
72      }

73      public double findRelatedUTXOs(PublicKey key, ArrayList<UTXO> all,
                        ArrayList<UTXO> spent, ArrayList<UTXO> unspent) {
74          ArrayList<Transaction> sendingTransactions = new ArrayList<Transaction>();
75          return findRelatedUTXOs(key, all, spent, unspent, sendingTransactions);
76      }

77      public ArrayList<UTXO> findUnspentUTXOs(PublicKey key){
78          ArrayList<UTXO> all = new ArrayList<UTXO>();
79          ArrayList<UTXO> spent = new ArrayList<UTXO>();
80          ArrayList<UTXO> unspent = new ArrayList<UTXO>();
81          findRelatedUTXOs(key, all, spent, unspent);
82          return unspent;
83      }

84      public double findUnspentUTXOs(PublicKey key, ArrayList<UTXO> unspent){
85          ArrayList<UTXO> all = new ArrayList<UTXO>();
86          ArrayList<UTXO> spent = new ArrayList<UTXO>();
87          return findRelatedUTXOs(key, all, spent, unspent);
88      }
89  }
```

There is only one constructor requiring a genesis block, as explained in code lines 8-11 (shown below).

```
public Blockchain(Block genesisBlock){
    this.blockchain = new LedgerList<Block>();
    this.blockchain.add(genesisBlock);
}
```

The reason why a blockchain must be constructed with a genesis block is because a genesis block is very special. In blockchain, a block must be built upon its previous block. What about the first block which does not have a previous block? This very first block is called the genesis block. Every blockchain starts from a genesis block, therefore it would be a good idea to request a genesis block in order to construct a blockchain. This is pretty much debatable, as different software developers may initiate a blockchain in a different way.

The method addBlock() (code lines 12-16, presented below) is marked "synchronized" because we must guarantee that only one calling method can append a block to the blockchain at a time. As of now, such a scenario would be impossible anyhow, but we should be proactive and prepare for when it does happen down the line. The addBlock() method examines if the block to be added is supposed to be right after the last block. Please recall that a block (except for the genesis block) stores the hash ID of its previous block. So, for this block to be added, its previous-block's hash ID must be the same as the hash ID of the last block in the chain. Later, we will revise this method so that it conducts more tests before a block can be added.

```
public synchronized void addBlock(Block block){
    if(block.getPreviousBlockHashID().equals(this.getLastBlock().getHashID())){
        this.blockchain.add(block);
    }
}
```

Methods size() and getBlock() in code lines 23-28 delineate the security protocol of only accessing one block at a time. This warrants that changing the order of the blocks is impossible.

Let's examine the code lines 29-66. Why should there be the method findRelatedUTXOs() that requires five arguments: `PublicKey key, ArrayList<UTXO> all, ArrayList<UTXO> spent, ArrayList<UTXO> unspent,` and `ArrayList<Transaction> sentTransactions`? The purpose of this method is to help with finding the balance for a given public key. We do need to know and display a wallet's balance. However, simply displaying the final balance of a wallet does not provide enough information. We need to know the amount of funds spent and unspent, as well as the origins of UTXOs involved in transactions. This method collects such required information. For miners, we also want to keep track of the amount of transaction fees and mining rewards that have been collected, but this kind of information is not provided by this method. Therefore, please be prepared that this method will have to be revised later on.

This method findRelatedUTXOs() is computationally expensive because it searches through the entire blockchain looking for UTXOs related to the public key. In reality, a complete search process is only necessary when validating a blockchain. A wallet is only concerned with its own ledger, so searching through the entire blockchain to find its balance is unnecessary. If every blockchain user must do so to find his/her balance, the blockchain system would be highly inefficient and dysfunctional. That being said, our program will conduct the chain-wide search because 1) blockchain users are typically granted the right to view the whole blockchain; and 2) our blockchain is small enough to have little to no issue with efficiency.

Code line 31, presented below, creates a HashMap object to store those UTXOs that were found by the search to be the input of transactions sent by this public key. These UTXOs count as spent funds and should not be double spent.

```
HashMap<String, UTXO> map = new HashMap<String, UTXO>();
```

The loop between lines 33 and 58 goes through every block, while the loop in lines 36-57 goes through every transaction in each block. Line 37, shown below, fetches a transaction in a block.

```
Transaction T = block.getTransaction(i);
```

The transactions we are looking at can be categorized as either transactions sent or received by the public key. If it is sent by the public key, then all of the input UTXOs in the transaction have already been spent by the public key. All the spent funds by the public key are accumulated in the variable *spending*. These input UTXOs are collected by the *spent* variable (an ArrayList instance) in code line 43, and stored in the hash map in line 44. For both types of transactions, we need to check for output UTXOs that transfer funds to the public key (code lines 49-56). An output UTXO is stored in the variable *all* if its receiver is the public key (lines 52-54). The loop between lines 59 and 64 goes through every UTXO in *all* to examine if it has been spent (if so, the UTXO must have been collected into the HashMap referenced by the variable *map*; if no, it is collected into the unspent storage). Code lines 59-64 are listed below:

```
for(int i=0; i<all.size(); i++){
    UTXO ut = all.get(i);
    if(!map.containsKey(ut.getHashID())){
        unspent.add(ut);
    }
}
```

The final balance is calculated as *(gain - spending)*, where *gain* is the sum of all the funds ever transferred to the public key, and *spending* is the sum of all the funds ever spent by the public key. The last statement (shown below) returns the balance of a public key:

```
return (gain - spending);
```

Several other methods (lines 67-88) make use of this findRelatedUTXOs() method for their own specialized purposes. With the Blockchain class ready, we must update our Wallet class so that it can transfer funds. Five methods will be added to the Wallet class, but before that happens, we need to import ArrayList class into Wallet:

```
import java.util.ArrayList;
```

In addition, Wallet class needs another instance variable. Please include the following statement below the Wallet class header:

```
    private Blockchain localLedger = null;
```

The statement above is to let each wallet to have a local blockchain. The five to-be-added methods are explained below. Up first is the method getLocalLedger() which returns the local blockchain of this wallet. Remember that in a distributed system, it is assumed that a wallet has its own copy of the blockchain called ledger.

```
    public synchronized Blockchain getLocalLedger(){
        return this.localLedger;
    }
```

The method setLocalLedger() updates the wallet's ledger with the input ledger. (Later you will learn how to evaluate if a ledger needs to be updated). The method getCurrentBalance finds the balance of this public key (wallet) from a given blockchain. By default, we would want to find the balance of this wallet from the local ledger.

```
    public synchronized boolean setLocalLedger(Blockchain ledger){
        this.localLedger = ledger;
        return true;
    }

    public double getCurrentBalance(Blockchain ledger){
        return ledger.checkBalance(this.getPublicKey());
    }
```

To transfer fund, we must make sure that the sender has enough unspent UTXOs to cover the cost. The transferFund() method collects all available unspent UTXOs and the total value can be found in code line 3. Code lines 4-7 compute the total amount of funds needed as the sum of the fundToTransfer plus the transaction fee. Code lines 8-11 assess if the available funds can cover the expenses. If yes, code lines 12-18 collect enough UTXOs to serve as the input of the transaction being constructed in line 19. If not, the program displays an error message explaining the reason and return null. Here is an interesting detail though: how does the program decide which UTXOs become the input? A blockchain system can actually set preferences, such as spending the oldest UTXOs, small-bill UTXOs, or large-bill UTXOs first. In our algorithm, we have chosen to spend the oldest UTXOs first. But regardless, once the input is collected, a Transaction instance is created and signed by the wallet. If everything goes smoothly, the Transaction object should be returned, or otherwise null is returned (lines 19-26).

```
1   public Transaction transferFund(PublicKey[] receivers, double[] fundToTransfer){
2       ArrayList<UTXO> unspent = new ArrayList<UTXO>();
3       double available = this.getLocalLedger().findUnspentUTXOs(this.getPublicKey(),
                        unspent);
4       double totalNeeded = Transaction.TRANSACTION_FEE;
5       for(int i=0; i<fundToTransfer.length; i++){
6           totalNeeded += fundToTransfer[i];
7       }
8       if(available < totalNeeded){
9           System.out.println(this.walletName+" balance=" + available
                    + ", not enough to make the transfer of " + totalNeeded);
```

```
10              return null;
11          }
            // Create input for the transaction.
12          ArrayList<UTXO> inputs = new ArrayList<UTXO>();
13          available = 0;
14          for(int i=0; i<unspent.size() && available < totalNeeded; i++){
15              UTXO uxo = unspent.get(i);
16              available += uxo.getFundTransferred();
17              inputs.add(uxo);
18          }

            // Create the Transaction.
19          Transaction T = new Transaction(this.getPublicKey(),
                            receivers, fundToTransfer, inputs);
            // Prepare output UTXO.
20          boolean b = T.prepareOutputUTXOs();
21          if(b){
22              T.signTheTransaction(this.getPrivateKey());
23              return T;
24          }else{
25              return null;
26          }
27      }
```

Please also add the following overloaded method into your Wallet class.

```
public Transaction transferFund(PublicKey receiver, double fundToTransfer){
    PublicKey[] receivers = new PublicKey[1];
    double[] funds = new double[1];
    receivers[0] = receiver;
    funds[0] = fundToTransfer;
    return transferFund(receivers, funds);
}
```

And now the time has finally come where you have learned enough to be able to write the BlockchainPlatform class that culminates all the functionalities that we have covered in the past few chapters: how a blockchain system begins, how wallets/miners transfer funds and how to mine blocks. Moving forward, please note that miners are wallets. Therefore, when we say "wallet", we mean both wallets and miners. But if we just mention miners, we means miners only. Keep in mind also that currently, our wallets are not distributed and all share the same copy of blockchain. The system will be distributed when we apply networking architecture into this blockchain system. The codes of class BlockchainPlatform are listed below.

```
1   import java.util.ArrayList;
    // This class simulates a blockchain system.
2   public class BlockchainPlatform {
        // The blockchain.
3       private static Blockchain blockchain;
        // Use this variable to track how much transaction fee has been paid.
        // Currently no transaction fee has been collected by miners.
4       private static double transactionFee = 0.0;
5       public static void main(String[] args) throws Exception {
            // Set the mining difficult level. 25 is good for practice.
            // Depending on your computer, the mining might take tens
            // of seconds or a few minutes.
```

```
6              int difficultLevel = 25;
7              System.out.println("Blockchain platform starts ...");
8              System.out.println("creating genesis miner, "
                        + "genesis transaction and genesis block");
               // Create a genesis miner to start a blockchain.
9              Miner genesisMiner = new Miner("genesis", "genesis");
               // Create the genesis block. Its "previous block hash ID" is set "0" manually.
10             Block genesisBlock = new Block("0", difficultLevel);
               // Manually create two UTXOs as the input of the genesis transaction.
11             UTXO u1 = new UTXO("0", genesisMiner.getPublicKey(),
                                  genesisMiner.getPublicKey(), 10001.0);
12             UTXO u2 = new UTXO("0", genesisMiner.getPublicKey(),
                                  genesisMiner.getPublicKey(), 10000.0);
               // Prepare the input.
13             ArrayList<UTXO> inputs = new ArrayList<UTXO>();
14             inputs.add(u1);
15             inputs.add(u2);
               // Prepare the genesis transaction.
16             Transaction gt = new Transaction(genesisMiner.getPublicKey(),
                                  genesisMiner.getPublicKey(), 10000.0, inputs);
17             boolean b = gt.prepareOutputUTXOs();
               // Check if the output preparation is successful. If not, exit the system.
18             if(!b){
19                 System.out.println("genesis transaction failed.");
20                 System.exit(1);
21             }
               // The genesis miner signs the transaction.
22             gt.signTheTransaction(genesisMiner.getPrivateKey());
               // Add the genesis transaction into the genesis block.
23             genesisBlock.addTransaction(gt);
               // The genesis miner mines the genesis block.
24             System.out.println("genesis miner is mining the genesis block");
25             b = genesisMiner.mineBlock(genesisBlock);
               // Check if mining is successful.
26             if(b){
27                 System.out.println("genesis block is successfully mined. HashID:");
28                 System.out.println(genesisBlock.getHashID());
29             }else{
30                 System.out.println("failed to mine genesis block. System exit");
31                 System.exit(1);
32             }
               // Construct the blockchain.
33             blockchain = new Blockchain(genesisBlock);
34             System.out.println("blockchain genesis successful");
               // Genesis miner copies the blockchain to his local ledger.
               // It is not a real copy, though.
35             genesisMiner.setLocalLedger(blockchain);
               // Manually check the balance of the genesis miner. Please verify if
               // it is correct.
36             System.out.println("genesis miner balance: "
                        + genesisMiner.getCurrentBalance(genesisMiner.getLocalLedger()));
               // Create other wallets/miners.
37             Miner A = new Miner("Miner A", "miner A");
38             Wallet B = new Wallet("wallet B", "wallet B");
39             Miner C = new Miner("Miner C", "miner c");
               // Every wallet stores a local ledger. Please be aware that they
               // are in fact sharing the same blockchain as it is not distributed.
40             A.setLocalLedger(blockchain);
41             B.setLocalLedger(blockchain);
```

```
42          C.setLocalLedger(blockchain);

            // Create the second block.
43          Block b2 = new Block(blockchain.getLastBlock().getHashID(), difficultLevel);
44          System.out.println("\n\nBlock b2 created");
            // Let the genesis miner transfer 100 to A and 200 to B.
45          Transaction t1 = genesisMiner.transferFund(A.getPublicKey(), 100);
            // Make sure that the transaction is not null. If null, it means that
            // the transaction construction is not successful.
46          if(t1 != null){
                // Assume that someone is examining the transaction.
47              if(t1.verifySignature() && b2.addTransaction(t1)){
                    // Display the balance to show that everything works. At this
                    // moment, A, B, C, should have zero balance.
48                  System.out.println("t1 added to block b2. Before b2 is mined "
                            + "and added to the chain, the balances are:");
49                  double total = genesisMiner.getCurrentBalance(blockchain)
                            + A.getCurrentBalance(blockchain) + B.getCurrentBalance(blockchain)
                            + C.getCurrentBalance(blockchain);
50                  System.out.println("genesisMiner="
                            + genesisMiner.getCurrentBalance(blockchain) + ", A="
                            + A.getCurrentBalance(blockchain) + ", B="
                            + B.getCurrentBalance(blockchain) + ", C="
                            + C.getCurrentBalance(blockchain) + ", total="+total);
51              }else{
52                  System.out.println("t1 failed to add to b2");
53              }
54          }else{
55              System.out.println("t1 failed to create");
56          }
57          Transaction t2 = genesisMiner.transferFund(B.getPublicKey(), 200);
58          if(t2 != null){
59              if(t2.verifySignature() && b2.addTransaction(t2)){
60                  System.out.println("t2 added to block b2. Before b2 is mined "
                            + "and added to the chain, the balances are:");
61                  double total = genesisMiner.getCurrentBalance(blockchain)
                            + A.getCurrentBalance(blockchain) + B.getCurrentBalance(blockchain)
                            + C.getCurrentBalance(blockchain);
62                  System.out.println("genesisMiner="
                            + genesisMiner.getCurrentBalance(blockchain) + ", A="
                            + A.getCurrentBalance(blockchain) + ", B="
                            + B.getCurrentBalance(blockchain) + ", C="
                            + C.getCurrentBalance(blockchain) + ", total=" + total);
63              }else{
64                  System.out.println("t2 failed to add to block b2");
65              }
66          }else{
67              System.out.println("t2 failed to create");
68          }
            // Mine the block 2.
69          if(A.mineBlock(b2)){
70              System.out.println("A mined b2, hashID is:");
71              System.out.println(b2.getHashID());
72              blockchain.addBlock(b2);
73              System.out.println("After block b2 is added to the chain, the balances are:");
74              displayBalanceAfterBlock(b2, genesisMiner, A, B, C);
75          }

            // Another block.
```

```java
                Block b3 = new Block(blockchain.getLastBlock().getHashID(), difficultLevel);
                System.out.println("\n\nblock b3 created");
                // t3 should fail as A does not have enough fund.
                Transaction t3 = A.transferFund(B.getPublicKey(), 200.0);
                if(t3 != null){
                    if(t3.verifySignature() && b3.addTransaction(t3)){
                        System.out.println("t3 added to block b3");
                    }else{
                        System.out.println("t3 failed to add to block b3");
                    }
                }else{
                    System.out.println("t3 failed to create");
                }
                // t4 should fail as A does not have enough fund.
                Transaction t4 = A.transferFund(C.getPublicKey(), 300.0);
                if(t4 != null){
                    if(t4.verifySignature() && b3.addTransaction(t4)){
                        System.out.println("t4 added to block b3.");
                    }else{
                        System.out.println("t4 failed to add to block b3");
                    }
                }else{
                    System.out.println("t4 failed to create");
                }
                Transaction t5 = A.transferFund(C.getPublicKey(), 20.0);
                if(t5 != null){
                    if(t5.verifySignature() && b3.addTransaction(t5)){
                        System.out.println("t5 added to block b3.");
                    }else{
                        System.out.println("t5 failed to add to block b3");
                    }
                }else{
                    System.out.println("t5 failed to create");
                }
                Transaction t6 = B.transferFund(C.getPublicKey(), 80.0);
                if(t6 != null){
                    if(t6.verifySignature() && b3.addTransaction(t6)){
                        System.out.println("t6 added to block b3.");
                    }else{
                        System.out.println("t6 failed to add to block b3");
                    }
                }else{
                    System.out.println("t6 failed to create");
                }

                // Mine block 3.
                if(C.mineBlock(b3)){
                    System.out.println("C mined b3, hashID is:");
                    System.out.println(b3.getHashID());
                    blockchain.addBlock(b3);
                    System.out.println("After block b3 is added to the chain, the balances are:");
                    displayBalanceAfterBlock(b3, genesisMiner, A, B, C);
                }

                System.out.println("=========BlockChain platform shuts down=========");
        }

        // A method to display the balance of the wallets and miners.
        private static void displayBalanceAfterBlock(Block b, Wallet genesisMiner,
```

```
                                    Wallet A, Wallet B, Wallet C) {
128             double total = genesisMiner.getCurrentBalance(blockchain)
                    + A.getCurrentBalance(blockchain) + B.getCurrentBalance(blockchain)
                    + C.getCurrentBalance(blockchain);
129             transactionFee +=
                    b.getTotalNumberOfTransactions() * Transaction.TRANSACTION_FEE;
130             System.out.println("genesisMiner="
                    + genesisMiner.getCurrentBalance(blockchain) + ", A="
                    + A.getCurrentBalance(blockchain) + ", B=" + B.getCurrentBalance(blockchain)
                    + ", C="+C.getCurrentBalance(blockchain) + ", total cash =" + total
                    + ", transaction fee=" + transactionFee);
131             System.out.println("====>the length of the blockchain=" + blockchain.size());
132         }
133 }
```

You can certainly add more blocks in the above budding program. In fact, you should try creating a block whose previous block's hash ID is incorrect so that you can experience what will happen. When you download this chapter's programs at https://github.com/hhohho/Learning-Blockchain-in-Java-Edition-2, you will find that there is a class named BlockchainPlatform2 which we did not cover. Again, try it out! In BlockchainPlatform2, there is a block that cannot be properly added to the chain. Please experience it.

Please be advised that this primitive, initial version of blockchain still lacks many necessary features:
- Miners cannot collect mining rewards or transaction fees.
- When adding a block, currently we only examine if it is the right block after the last block of the blockchain. There should be some other types of verification. For example, we need to make sure that no UTXO is double spent, and no transaction is added twice, etc.

These features will be added in the next chapter.

# 6 BLOCKCHAIN IMPROVED

We're going to do things a bit differently this chapter. Instead of transferring all the programs from the previous chapter file, please go to: https://github.com/hhohho/Learning-Blockchain-in-Java-Edition-2 and download the programs of chapter 5 from there. Pick out the Block, Blockchain, LedgerList, Miner, Transaction, UtilityMethods, UTXO, and Wallet classes and place them in a folder (directory) dedicated for chapter 6. If you are using Eclipse, please start a new Java project named chapter6 and import the eight aforementioned programs into the source directory of Java project chapter6.

If you recall from what we covered in the last chapter, our current blockchain system lacks a few necessary features:
- Mining rewards cannot be collected.
- There is no validation process when a transaction is added to a block.
- Adding a block into the chain does not go through a complete validation process.
- Wallets currently share the same public blockchain instead of keeping local copies.

In this chapter, we will revise our programs to address these missing features.

The bitcoin white paper discusses memory management when blockchain grows enormously. One solution involves pruning spent transactions from blocks buried deep in the chain, but the caveat is that discarding spent transactions can break the block's hash. To bypass this complication, the algorithm Merkle Tree is applied to hash transactions. For a blockchain system as small as ours memory management shouldn't be a problem, we do not need to prune any transactions from any blocks. However, let's apply Merkle Hash Tree in block's hash computation as it is part of the blockchain technology. A Merkle tree can be a binary tree, a triple tree, or another type of tree. Let's construct a binary tree within the UtilityMethods class. In a binary Merkle hash tree, a node's hash is always constructed from hash values of the two tree nodes directly below it, the exception being the bottom nodes. Eventually, there will be only one hash left at the root, while the root hash is related to every bottom node. Figure 7 mimics the bitcoin white paper's illustration of the concept.

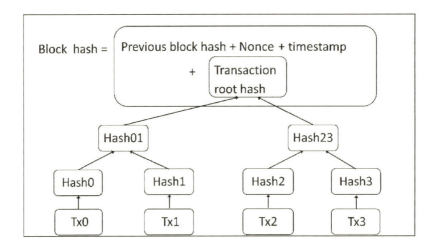

**Figure 7** Transactions are hashed into a root hash in a binary Merkle Tree. Those spent transactions can then be freely pruned without breaking a block's hash.

From Figure 7, we can understand that a block's hash is computed from previous block's hash, nonce, timestamp, and transactions' root hash which is computed via a Merkle Tree algorithm from all transactions' hashes. If transactions Tx0 and Tx1 have been spent and the block is buried deep in the blockchain, we then can remove Tx0 and Tx1 from the block. This can help save memory. Please be advised that our blockchain system never takes any action to remove any transactions from any blocks, however.

As usual, we will update our UtilityMethods class to include methods that compute Merkle Tree root hash. Please add the following four methods to your existing UtilityMethods class:

```
    // The method to be called by other classes. It applies a recursive algorithm to
    // generate the root hash starting from the tree leaves.
1   public static String computeMerkleTreeRootHash(String[] hashes){
2       return computeMerkleTreeRootHash(hashes, 0, hashes.length - 1);
3   }

    // The method recursively builds up root hash.
4   private static String computeMerkleTreeRootHash(String[] hashes, int from, int end) {
        // When there is only one hash string, return this string.
5       if(end - from + 1 == 1){
6           return hashes[end];
7       }else if(end - from + 1 == 2){
            // Compute the hashID from the two nodes below.
8           return messageDigestSHA256_toString(hashes[from] + hashes[end]);
9       }else{
            // We need continue dividing the array into two parts to reach the leaves.
10          int c = (from + end) / 2;
```

```
11              String mesg = computeMerkleTreeRootHash(hashes, from, c)
                         + computeMerkleTreeRootHash(hashes, c + 1, end);
12              return messageDigestSHA256_toString(mesg);
13         }
14     }

       // A method to display the content of a block.
15     public static void displayBlock(Block block, PrintStream out, int level){
16         displayTab(out, level, "Block{");
17         displayTab(out, level, "\tID: " + block.getHashID());
           // Display the transactions inside.
18         for(int i=0; i<block.getTotalNumberOfTransactions(); i++) {
19             displayTransaction(block.getTransaction(i), out, level + 1);
20         }
           // Display the reward transaction.
21         if(block.getRewardTransaction() != null) {
22             displayTab(out, level, "\tReward Transaction:");
23             displayTransaction(block.getRewardTransaction(), out, level + 1);
24         }
25         displayTab(out, level, "}");
26     }

       // A method to display the content of a blockchain.
27     public static void displayBlockchain(Blockchain ledger, PrintStream out, int level){
28         displayTab(out, level, "Blockchain{ number of blocks: " + ledger.size());
29         for(int i=0; i<ledger.size(); i++) {
30             Block block = ledger.getBlock(i);
31             displayBlock(block, out, level + 1);
32         }
33         displayTab(out, level,"}");
34     }
```

After adding these four methods, you may find error messages showing up if you are using an IDE (such as Eclipse) to edit your Java programs. This is because we are prematurely referencing a method called getRewardTransaction() (line 23) which will be added to the Block class below. The error messages should disappear once the update occurs. As you can imagine, the modification to the Block class will be significant, though some are arguably unnecessary. We will explain the rationale along the way by adding comments in the codes below.

```
1      import java.security.PublicKey;
2      import java.util.ArrayList;
3      public class Block implements java.io.Serializable{
4          private static final long serialVersionUID = 1L;
           // To limit the number of transactions inside a block. Note that is is not 2 any more.
5          public final static int TRANSACTION_UPPER_LIMIT = 100;
6          // Modification 1:
           // A new variable added to set a lower limit. This is to make sure that a block
           // can be started only after a certain number of valid transactions have been
           // collected. For demonstration purposes, it is set to be 1 so that there can
           // be enough blocks even when there are only a few transactions. This number should
           // always be greater than 0.
7          public final static int TRANSACTION_LOWER_LIMIT = 1;
8          private int difficultyLevel = 20;
9          private ArrayList<Transaction> transactions = new ArrayList<Transaction>();
10         private long timestamp;
11         private String previousBlockHashID;
```

```java
12          private int nonce = 0;
13          private String hashID;
            // Modification 2: may not be necessary.
            // To record the miner of each block. Doing so, we can enforce that any changes
            // to this block must be by this miner (creator).
14          private PublicKey creator;
            // Modification 3:
            // To mark if the block has been mined. Once a block has been mined,
            // no change is allowed any more. This is for tight secure coding.
15          private boolean mined = false;
            // Modification 4:
            // The miner must sign the block so that other miners can verify the signature.
16          private byte[] signature = null;
            // Modification 5:
            // The transaction to reward the miner.
17          private Transaction rewardTransaction = null;
            // Modification 6:
            // The constructor is revised.
18          public Block(String previousBlockHashID, int difficultyLevel, PublicKey creator){
19              this.previousBlockHashID = previousBlockHashID;
20              this.timestamp = UtilityMethods.getTimeStamp();
21              this.difficultyLevel = difficultyLevel;
22              this.creator = creator;
23          }

24          protected String computeHashID() {
25              StringBuilder sb = new StringBuilder();
26              sb.append(this.previousBlockHashID + Long.toHexString(this.timestamp));
                // Modification 7:
                // Transactions' hash values are converged into one root hash by means
                // of Merkle Tree.
27              sb.append(this.computeMerkleRoot());
28              sb.append("" + nonce);
29              byte[] b = UtilityMethods.messageDigestSHA256_toBytes(sb.toString());
30              return UtilityMethods.toBinaryString(b);
31          }

            // Modification 8:
            // A transaction can be added only before the block is mined and signed, and only
            // the creator of this block can add transaction(s) before this block is mined or
            // signed. The number of transactions cannot exceed the allowed limit.
32          public boolean addTransaction(Transaction t, PublicKey key){
33              if(this.getTotalNumberOfTransactions() >= Block.TRANSACTION_UPPER_LIMIT){
34                  return false;
35              }
36              if(key.equals(this.getCreator()) && !this.isMined() && !this.isSigned()){
37                  this.transactions.add(t);
38                  return true;
39              }else{
40                  return false;
41              }
42          }

43          public String getHashID(){
44              return this.hashID;
45          }

46          public int getNonce(){
47              return this.nonce;
```

```
48          }

49          public long getTimeStamp(){
50              return this.timestamp;
51          }

52          public String getPreviousBlockHashID(){
53              return this.previousBlockHashID;
54          }

            // Modification 9:
            // Only the creator of this block can mine the block and a block
            // can be mined for only once.
55          public boolean mineTheBlock(PublicKey key){
56              if(!this.mined && key.equals(this.getCreator())){
57                  this.hashID = this.computeHashID();
58                  while(!UtilityMethods.hashMeetsDifficultyLevel(
                                          this.hashID, this.difficultyLevel)){
59                      nonce++;
60                      this.hashID = this.computeHashID();
61                  }
62                  this.mined = true;
63              }
64              return this.mined;
65          }

66          public int getDifficultyLevel(){
67              return this.difficultyLevel;
68          }

69          public int getTotalNumberOfTransactions(){
70              return this.transactions.size();
71          }

72          public Transaction getTransaction(int index){
73              return this.transactions.get(index);
74          }

            // ---------- Methods added in chapter 6 -----------
            // Modification 10:
            // A block has only one reward transaction. It can be added only by the block
            // creator, i.e. the miner, and it cannot be changed once it has been added.
75          public boolean generateRewardTransaction(PublicKey pubKey,
                                          Transaction rewardTransaction){
76              if(this.rewardTransaction == null && pubKey.equals(this.creator)){
77                  this.rewardTransaction = rewardTransaction;
78                  return true;
79              }else{
80                  return false;
81              }
82          }

            // Modification 11:
83          public Transaction getRewardTransaction(){
84              return this.rewardTransaction;
85          }

            // Modification 12:
            // The transaction fee does not include the reward transaction.
```

```java
86      public double getTransactionFeeAmount(){
87          return this.transactions.size() * Transaction.TRANSACTION_FEE;
88      }

        // Modification 13:
        // When a wallet/miner needs to add this block into its local blockchain,
        // it is necessary to verify the signature. The verification requires
        // a public key, which is usually the block creator's public key.
89      public boolean verifySignature(PublicKey pubKey){
90          return UtilityMethods.verifySignature(pubKey,
                            this.signature, this.getHashID());
91      }
        // Modification 14:
        // A block must be signed. This is how it works:
        // the miner of this block generates a signature based on the block
        // hash ID, and calls this method to set the signature. This method
        // would examine if the signature is valid before accepting it.
        // Once the signature is set, no change is allowed.
92      public boolean signTheBlock(PublicKey pubKey, byte[] signature){
93          if(!isSigned()){
94              if(pubKey.equals(this.creator)){
95                  if(UtilityMethods.verifySignature(pubKey,
                                    signature, this.getHashID())){
96                      this.signature = signature;
97                      return true;
98                  }
99              }
100         }
101         return false;
102     }
        // Modification 15:
103     public PublicKey getCreator(){
104         return this.creator;
105     }
        // Modification 16:
106     public boolean isMined(){
107         return this.mined;
108     }
        // Modification 17:
109     public boolean isSigned(){
110         return this.signature != null;
111     }
        // Modification 18:
        // Compute the Merkle root hash.
112     private String computeMerkleRoot(){
113         String[] hashes;
            // Allowing underpay, i.e. the miner can mine a block
            // without accepting the reward, so the reward transaction
            // might be null.
114         if(this.rewardTransaction == null){
115             hashes = new String[this.transactions.size()];
116             for(int i=0; i<this.transactions.size(); i++){
117                 hashes[i] = this.transactions.get(i).getHashID();
118             }
119         }else{
120             hashes = new String[this.transactions.size() + 1];
121             for(int i=0; i<this.transactions.size(); i++){
122                 hashes[i] = this.transactions.get(i).getHashID();
123             }
```

```
124                hashes[hashes.length-1] = this.rewardTransaction.getHashID();
125            }
126            return UtilityMethods.computeMerkleTreeRootHash(hashes);
127        }
           // Modification 19:
           // Only the creator can delete a transaction before this block is mined and signed.
           // This method is never used.
128        public boolean deleteTransaction(Transaction ts, PublicKey key){
129            if(!this.mined && !this.isSigned() && key.equals(this.getCreator())){
130                return this.transactions.remove(ts);
131            }else{
132                return false;
133            }
134        }

           // Modification 20:
           // Only the creator can delete a transaction before this block is mined and signed.
           // This method is never used.
135        public boolean deleteTransaction(int index, PublicKey key){
136            if(!this.mined && !this.isSigned() && key.equals(this.getCreator())){
137                Transaction ts = this.transactions.remove(index);
138                return (ts != null);
139            }else{
140                return false;
141            }
142        }
143    }
```

Accordingly, the class Blockchain needs to be revised. All the modifications are marked by adding comments in the program below:

```
1     import java.security.PublicKey;
2     import java.util.ArrayList;
3     import java.util.HashMap;
4     public class Blockchain implements java.io.Serializable {
5         private static final long serialVersionUID = 1L;
6         public static final double MINING_REWARD = 100.0;
7         private LedgerList<Block> blockchain;

8         public Blockchain(Block genesisBlock){
9             this.blockchain = new LedgerList<Block>();
10            this.blockchain.add(genesisBlock);
11        }

12        public Block getGenesisBlock(){
13            return this.blockchain.getFirst();
14        }

15        public Block getLastBlock(){
16            return this.blockchain.getLast();
17        }

18        public int size(){
19            return this.blockchain.size();
20        }

21        public Block getBlock(int index){
```

```
22                return this.blockchain.findByIndex(index);
23            }

24        public double checkBalance(PublicKey key){
25            ArrayList<UTXO> all = new ArrayList<UTXO>();
26            ArrayList<UTXO> spent = new ArrayList<UTXO>();
27            ArrayList<UTXO> unspent = new ArrayList<UTXO>();
28            return findRelatedUTXOs(key, all, spent, unspent);
29        }

        // Modification 1:
        // Rewarding UTXOs are counted in this method now.
30        public double findRelatedUTXOs(PublicKey key, ArrayList<UTXO> all,
                    ArrayList<UTXO> spent, ArrayList<UTXO> unspent,
                    ArrayList<Transaction> sentTransactions, ArrayList<UTXO> rewards)
31        {
32            double gain = 0.0, spending = 0.0;
33            HashMap<String, UTXO> map = new HashMap<String, UTXO>();
34            int limit = this.size();
35            for(int a=0; a<limit; a++){
36                Block block = this.blockchain.findByIndex(a);
37                int size = block.getTotalNumberOfTransactions();
38                for(int i=0; i<size; i++){
39                    Transaction T = block.getTransaction(i);
40                    int N;
41                    if(a != 0 && T.getSender().equals(key)){
42                        N = T.getNumberOfInputUTXOs();
43                        for(int x=0; x<N; x++){
44                            UTXO ut = T.getInputUTXO(x);
45                            spent.add(ut);
46                            map.put(ut.getHashID(), ut);
47                            spending += ut.getFundTransferred();
48                        }
49                        sentTransactions.add(T);
50                    }
51                    N = T.getNumberOfOutputUTXOs();
52                    for(int x=0; x<N; x++){
53                        UTXO ux = T.getOuputUTXO(x);
54                        if(ux.getReceiver().equals(key)){
55                            all.add(ux);
56                            gain += ux.getFundTransferred();
57                        }
58                    }
59                }
                // Add reward transactions. The reward should never be null in our program.
                // In bitcoin, a miner might underpay himself, i.e. the reward transaction
                // can be null.
60                if(block.getCreator().equals(key)) {
61                    Transaction rt = block.getRewardTransaction();
62                    if(rt != null && rt.getNumberOfOutputUTXOs() > 0){
63                        UTXO ux = rt.getOuputUTXO(0);
                        // Double check again, so a miner can only reward himself.
                        // If he rewards others, this reward is not counted.
64                        if(ux.getReceiver().equals(key)){
65                            rewards.add(ux);
66                            all.add(ux);
67                            gain += ux.getFundTransferred();
68                        }
69                    }
```

```java
70              }
71          }
72          for(int i=0; i<all.size(); i++){
73              UTXO ut = all.get(i);
74              if(!map.containsKey(ut.getHashID())){
75                  unspent.add(ut);
76              }
77          }
78          return (gain - spending);
79      }

        // Modification 2:
        // This method calls the overloaded method in lines 38-79.
80      public double findRelatedUTXOs(PublicKey key, ArrayList<UTXO> all,
                            ArrayList<UTXO> spent, ArrayList<UTXO> unspent,
                            ArrayList<Transaction> sentTransactions)
81      {
82          ArrayList<UTXO> rewards = new ArrayList<UTXO>();
83          return findRelatedUTXOs(key, all, spent, unspent, sentTransactions, rewards);
84      }

85      public double findRelatedUTXOs(PublicKey key, ArrayList<UTXO> all,
                            ArrayList<UTXO> spent, ArrayList<UTXO> unspent){
86          ArrayList<Transaction> sendingTransactions = new ArrayList<Transaction>();
87          return findRelatedUTXOs(key, all, spent, unspent, sendingTransactions);
88      }

89      public ArrayList<UTXO> findUnspentUTXOs(PublicKey key){
90          ArrayList<UTXO> all = new ArrayList<UTXO>();
91          ArrayList<UTXO> spent = new ArrayList<UTXO>();
92          ArrayList<UTXO> unspent = new ArrayList<UTXO>();
93          findRelatedUTXOs(key, all, spent, unspent);
94          return unspent;
95      }

96      public double findUnspentUTXOs(PublicKey key, ArrayList<UTXO> unspent){
97          ArrayList<UTXO> all = new ArrayList<UTXO>();
98          ArrayList<UTXO> spent = new ArrayList<UTXO>();
99          return findRelatedUTXOs(key, all, spent, unspent);
100     }

        // Modification 3:
        // This method examines if a transaction already exists inside a blockchain.
        // This is necessary when collecting a transaction and when adding a block
        // into the blockchain.
101     protected boolean isTransactionExist(Transaction T){
102         int size = this.blockchain.size();
103         for(int i=size-1; i>0; i--){
104             Block b = this.blockchain.findByIndex(i);
105             int bs = b.getTotalNumberOfTransactions();
106             for(int j=0; j<bs; j++){
107                 Transaction t2 = b.getTransaction(j);
108                 if(T.equals(t2)){
109                     return true;
110                 }
111             }
112         }
113         return false;
114     }
```

```java
            // Modification 4:
            // The genesis miner is the miner who starts the blockchain by mining the genesis block.
115         public PublicKey getGenesisMiner(){
116             return this.getGenesisBlock().getCreator();
117         }

            // Modification 5:
            // This static method validates a given Blockchain. This method could be an
            // instance method. The reason why it is written as a static method is to let
            // wallets and miners use it. When a miner calls this method, it sounds more
            // like the miner is validating a blockchain. If written as an instance field,
            // it will look more like that the blockchain is validating itself.
118         public static boolean validateBlockchain(Blockchain ledger) {
119             int size = ledger.size();
120             for(int i = size - 1; i>0; i--){
121                 Block currentBlock = ledger.getBlock(i);
122                 boolean b = currentBlock.verifySignature(currentBlock.getCreator());
123                 if(!b){
124                     System.out.println("validateBlockChain(): block "
                            + (i + 1) + "  signature is invalid.");
125                     return false;
126                 }
127                 b = UtilityMethods.hashMeetsDifficultyLevel(currentBlock.getHashID(),
                            currentBlock.getDifficultyLevel()) &&
                            currentBlock.computeHashID().equals(currentBlock.getHashID());
128                 if(!b){
129                     System.out.println("validateBlockChain():  block "
                            + (i+1) + "  its hashing is bad");
130                     return false;
131                 }
132                 Block previousBlock = ledger.getBlock(i-1);
133                 b = currentBlock.getPreviousBlockHashID().equals(previousBlock.getHashID());
134                 if(!b){
135                     System.out.println("validateBlockChain():  block  "
                            + (i+1) + "  invalid previous block hashID");
136                     return false;
137                 }
138             }
139             Block genesisBlock = ledger.getGenesisBlock();
                // Confirm the genesis block is signed.
140             boolean b2 = genesisBlock.verifySignature(genesisBlock.getCreator());
141             if(!b2){
142                 System.out.println("validateBlockChain():   genesis block "
                            + "is tampered, signature bad");
143                 return false;
144             }

145             b2 = UtilityMethods.hashMeetsDifficultyLevel(
                        genesisBlock.getHashID(), genesisBlock.getDifficultyLevel())
                        && genesisBlock.computeHashID().equals(genesisBlock.getHashID());
146             if(!b2){
147                 System.out.println("validateBlockChain(): genesis block's "
                            + "hash value is bad");
148                 return false;
149             }
150             return true;
151         }

            // Modification 6:
```

```
            // It is a good idea to synchronize this method. In addition, this method makes sure
            // that the block is a valid successor of the last block in the chain.
152         public synchronized boolean addBlock(Block block){
153             if(this.size() == 0){
154                 this.blockchain.add(block);
155                 return true;
156             }else if(block.getPreviousBlockHashID().equals(this.getLastBlock().getHashID())){
157                 this.blockchain.add(block);
158                 return true;
159             }else{
160                 return false;
161             }
162         }

            // Modification 7:
            // A private constructor used by this class only for copying purpose.
163         private Blockchain(LedgerList<Block> chain){
164             this.blockchain = new LedgerList<Block>();
165             int size = chain.size();
166             for(int i=0; i<size; i++){
167                 this.blockchain.add(chain.findByIndex(i));
168             }
169         }

            // Modification 8:
            // This is not a deep copy, though it creates a different object of
            // blockchain. The blocks and their order are preserved.
170         public synchronized Blockchain copy_NotDeepCopy(){
171             return new Blockchain(this.blockchain);
172         }
173     }
```

Validating a blockchain would be a complicated task if we need to verify every single transaction. For example, suppose there are 10000 blocks in a chain. To validate transactions in block 5000, we would need to examine blocks 1-4999 to make sure that every transaction has proper UTXOs. A simple solution to this dilemma would be to provide a storage for all UTXOs and index each UTXO by its hash. A more challenging task would be, when a new blockchain comes in with a larger size, how to guarantee it is the legitimate one when it has a few blocks different from a local copy. A type of blockchain attack called Selfish Mining Attack is similar to this scenario. Large blockchain systems such as bitcoin are more immune to such an attack while a small size blockchain system can suffer from such an attack. We will discuss this in the last chapter. In our blockchain system, we need to make sure that every block 1) is built upon the last block of the blockchain (except for the genesis block), 2) has a valid hash ID; and 3) is signed properly. The method validateBlockchain() (code lines 118-151) only examines these three requirements. Code lines 127 and 145 specifically examine if the block hash meets the difficulty level and if the right nonce has been found.

To improve the current blockchain system, there are two more classes to update: Wallet and Miner. In addition, there is a new class to add. Miners must be able to collect mining rewards and transaction fees. Therefore, it is necessary to differentiate a normal UTXO from the UTXO of mining reward. Thus, we add a new class UTXOAsMiningReward which is a subclass of UTXO.

```
import java.security.PublicKey;
public class UTXOAsMiningReward extends UTXO{
```

```java
        private static final long serialVersionUID = 1L;
        public UTXOAsMiningReward(String parentTransactionID, PublicKey sender,
                                    PublicKey receiver, double fundToTransfer){
            super(parentTransactionID, sender, receiver, fundToTransfer);
        }

        public boolean isMiningReward(){
            return true;
        }
    }
```

For class Wallet, there are several new methods to include in addition to modifications that need to be performed on the existing method setLocalLedger(). Comments to document and explain these modifications can be found in the following code list.

```java
        // Modification 1:
        // When setting the local blockchain (ledger), if the wallet does not have a local
        // ledger, the wallet simply accepts the incoming ledger. If the wallet already
        // has a local ledger, then it is necessary to compare the existing ledger with
        // the incoming one. The wallet only accepts the incoming ledger if it 1) is validated;
        // 2) is longer than the existing one; 3) both the incoming one and local one
        // have the same genesis block.
1       public synchronized boolean setLocalLedger(Blockchain ledger){
            // Make sure that the incoming blockchain is valid first.
2           boolean b = Blockchain.validateBlockchain(ledger);
3           if(!b){
4               System.out.println(this.getName()
                        + "] Warning: the incoming blockchain failed validation");
5               return false;
6           }
            // If there is no current blockchain locally, accepts the incoming one.
7           if(this.localLedger == null){
8               this.localLedger = ledger;
9               return true;
10          }else{
                // The incoming blockchain must be longer.
                // Also make sure that both the incoming blockchain and the local
                // one have the same genesis miner.
11              if(ledger.size() > this.localLedger.size() &&
                        ledger.getGenesisMiner().equals(this.localLedger.getGenesisMiner())){
12                  this.localLedger = ledger;
13                  return true;
14              }else if(ledger.size() <= this.localLedger.size()){
15                  System.out.println(this.getName() + "] Warning: the incoming "
                            + "blockchain  is no longer than current local one"
                            +", local size=" + this.localLedger.size()
                            +", incoming size=" + ledger.size());
17                  return false;
18              }else{
19                  System.out.println(this.getName() + "] Warning: the incoming blockchain "
                            + "has a different genesis miner than current local one");
20                  return false;
21              }
22          }
23      }

        // Modification 2: a new method added in chapter 6.
```

```
        // This method is never used, but we should be prepared for the scenario: when
        // there are a number of incoming blockchains, how to select one to update the
        // local copy. There are two cases. Case 1, if the wallet has a local copy;
        // Case 2, if the wallet currently does not have a local copy.
24      public synchronized  boolean updateLocalLedger(ArrayList<Blockchain> chains){
            // If the array list is empty, no action is needed.
25          if(chains.size() == 0){
26              return false;
27          }
            // When there is already a local blockchain, let's find the longest
            // validated blockchain in the incoming blockchains.
28          if(this.localLedger != null){
29              Blockchain max = this.localLedger;
30              for(int i=0; i<chains.size(); i++){
31                  Blockchain bc = chains.get(i);
32                  boolean b = bc.getGenesisMiner().equals(this.localLedger.getGenesisMiner());
33                  if(b && bc.size() > max.size() && Blockchain.validateBlockchain(bc)){
34                      max = bc;
35                  }
36              }
                // It is possible that nothing changed, i.e. the max is the local one.
37              this.localLedger = max;
38              return true;
39          }else{
                // When there is no local one, then simply picks the longest one that
                // is validated. No need to check on the genesis miner.
40              Blockchain max = null;
41              int currentLength = 0;
42              for(int i=0; i<chains.size(); i++){
43                  Blockchain bc = chains.get(i);
44                  boolean b = Blockchain.validateBlockchain(bc);
45                  if(b && bc.size() > currentLength){
46                      max = bc;
47                      currentLength = max.size();
48                  }
49              }
50              if(max != null){
51                  this.localLedger = max;
52                  return true;
53              }else{
54                  return false;
55              }
56          }
57      }

        // Modification 3: a new method added in chapter 6.
        // When a new block comes, before accepting it and adding it to the local
        // blockchain, we must verify the block.
58      public synchronized boolean updateLocalLedger(Block block){
59          if(verifyGuestBlock(block)){
60              return this.localLedger.addBlock(block);
61          }
62          return false;
63      }

        // Modification 4:
        // This is a new method added in chapter 6.
        // Verify an incoming block against a blockchain. Some codes in this method
        // show repetition of codes in method Blockchain.validateBlockchain().
```

```
            // Please be aware of the difference between verifying a block and validating
            // a blockchain. Validating a blockchain in this implementation does not
            // validate each transaction. However, verifying a block must make sure that
            // each transaction in the block is validated against the local blockchain.
64          public boolean verifyGuestBlock(Block block, Blockchain ledger){
                // Verify the signature.
65              if(!block.verifySignature(block.getCreator())){
66                  System.out.println("\tWarning: block(" + block.getHashID() + ") signature tampered");
67                  return false;
68              }
                // Verify the proof-of-work including recomputing block hash.
69              if(!UtilityMethods.hashMeetsDifficultyLevel(block.getHashID(),
                            block.getDifficultyLevel())
                            || !block.computeHashID().equals(block.getHashID())){
70                  System.out.println("\tWarning: block(" + block.getHashID()
                            + ") mining is not successful!");
71                  return false;
72              }
                // Make sure that this block is built upon the last block.
73              if(!ledger.getLastBlock().getHashID().equals(block.getPreviousBlockHashID())){
74                  System.out.println("\tWarning: block(" + block.getHashID()
                            + ") is not linked to last block");
75                  return false;
76              }
                // Examine if all the transactions are valid.
77              int size = block.getTotalNumberOfTransactions();
78              for(int i=0; i<size; i++){
79                  Transaction T = block.getTransaction(i);
80                  if(!validateTransaction(T)){
81                      System.out.println("\tWarning: block(" + block.getHashID()
                                + ") transaction " + i + " is invalid either because of signature "
                                + " being tampered or already existing in the blockchain.");
82                      return false;
83                  }
84              }
                // Here, we do not examine if the transaction balance is in good standing.
                // However, we do scrutinize the rewarding transaction.
85              Transaction tr = block.getRewardTransaction();
86              if(tr.getTotalFundToTransfer() > Blockchain.MINING_REWARD
                            + block.getTransactionFeeAmount()){
87                  System.out.println("\tWarning: block(" + block.getHashID() + ") over rewarded");
88                  return false;
89              }
90              return true;
91          }

            // Modification 5: a new method added in chapter 6.
92          public boolean verifyGuestBlock(Block block){
93              return this.verifyGuestBlock(block, this.getLocalLedger());
94          }

            // Modification 6: a new method added in chapter 6.
            // A transaction must be validated before it is collected into a block.
95          public boolean validateTransaction(Transaction ts){
                // In case of a null.
96              if(ts == null){
97                  return false;
98              }
99              if(!ts.verifySignature()){
```

```
100                System.out.println("WARNING: transaction ID=" + ts.getHashID() + " from "
                            + UtilityMethods.getKeyString(ts.getSender())
                            + " is invalid. It has been tampered.");
101                return false;
102         }

            // Make sure that this transaction does not exist in the existing ledger.
            // This type of implementation is a time consuming process.
103         boolean exists;
104         if(this.getLocalLedger() == null){
105             exists = false;
106         }else{
107             exists = this.getLocalLedger().isTransactionExist(ts);
108         }
109         return !exists;
100    }
```

Code line 11 examines if the incoming blockchain has the same genesis miner with the existing local blockchain. The creation of another blockchain from scratch is prevented by enforcing the incoming blockchain to have the same genesis miner with the existing local blockchain.

The Miner class is significantly revised as well. The complete Miner class is presented below.

```
1     public class Miner extends Wallet{
2         public Miner(String minerName, String password){
3             super(minerName, password);
4         }

5         public Miner(String minerName){
6             super(minerName);
7         }

          // Modification 1:
          // After a miner mines a block, the miner signs the block.
8         public boolean mineBlock(Block block){
9             if((block.mineTheBlock(this.getPublicKey()))){
                  // The miner needs to sign the block.
10                byte[] signature = UtilityMethods.generateSignature(
                         this.getPrivateKey(), block.getHashID());
11                return block.signTheBlock(this.getPublicKey(), signature);
12            }else{
13                return false;
14            }
15        }

          // Modification 2:
          // A transaction must be validated before being added into a block.
16        public boolean addTransaction(Transaction ts, Block block){
17            if(this.validateTransaction(ts)){
18                return block.addTransaction(ts, this.getPublicKey());
19            }else{
20                return false;
21            }
22        }

          // Modification 3:
          // Only the block creator can delete a transaction before the block
```

```
             // is signed and mined.
23       public boolean deleteTransaction(Transaction ts, Block block){
24           return block.deleteTransaction(ts, this.getPublicKey());
25       }

         // Modification 4:
26       public boolean generateRewardTransaction(Block block){
27           double amount = Blockchain.MINING_REWARD + block.getTransactionFeeAmount();
28           Transaction T = new Transaction(this.getPublicKey(),
                       this.getPublicKey(), amount, null);
29           UTXO ut = new UTXOAsMiningReward(T.getHashID(), T.getSender(),
                       this.getPublicKey(), amount);
30           T.addOutputUTXO(ut);
31           T.signTheTransaction(this.getPrivateKey());
32           return block.generateRewardTransaction(this.getPublicKey(), T);
33       }

         // Modification 5:
         // A block is supposed to be created by a miner.
34       public Block createNewBlock(Blockchain ledger, int difficultLevel){
35           Block b = new Block(ledger.getLastBlock().getHashID(),
                       difficultLevel, this.getPublicKey());
36           return b;
37       }
38   }
```

With all relevant classes significantly updated, our blockchain system is improved and much more functional except that there is no network, i.e. all wallets or miners are still working inside the same environment (JVM). To experience how this blockchain system works, we can re-write the BlockchainPlatform class. The following is the example:

```
import java.security.PublicKey;
import java.util.ArrayList;
public class BlockchainPlatform {
    public static Blockchain ledger;
    public static void main(String[] args) {
        // Store all wallets/miners for later processing.
        ArrayList<Wallet> users = new ArrayList<Wallet>();
        int difficultLevel = 22;
        System.out.println("Blockchain platform starts ...");
        System.out.println("creating genesis miner, genesis transaction "
                + "and genesis block");
        // Create a genesis miner to start a blockchain.
        Miner genesisMiner = new Miner("genesis", "genesis");
        users.add(genesisMiner);
        // Create genesis block.
        Block genesisBlock =
                new Block("0", difficultLevel, genesisMiner.getPublicKey());
        UTXO u1 = new UTXO("0", genesisMiner.getPublicKey(),
                genesisMiner.getPublicKey(), 10001.0);
        UTXO u2 = new UTXO("0", genesisMiner.getPublicKey(),
                genesisMiner.getPublicKey(), 10000.0);
        // Manually prepare the input for the genesis transaction.
        ArrayList<UTXO> inputs = new ArrayList<UTXO>();
        inputs.add(u1);
        inputs.add(u2);
        // Create the genesis transaction, and then prepare its output.
```

```java
Transaction gt = new Transaction(genesisMiner.getPublicKey(),
            genesisMiner.getPublicKey(), 10000.0, inputs);
boolean b = gt.prepareOutputUTXOs();
if(!b){
    System.out.println("genesis transaction failed.");
    System.exit(1);
}
// Sign the transaction before adding it to the genesis block.
gt.signTheTransaction(genesisMiner.getPrivateKey());
b = genesisBlock.addTransaction(gt, genesisMiner.getPublicKey());
if(!b){
    System.out.println("failed to add the genesis transaction to "
            + "the genesis block. System quit");
    System.exit(1);
}
// The genesis miner mines the genesis block.
System.out.println("genesis miner is mining the genesis block");
b = genesisMiner.mineBlock(genesisBlock);
if(b){
    System.out.println("genesis block is successfully mined. HashID:");
    System.out.println(genesisBlock.getHashID());
}else{
    System.out.println("failed to mine genesis block. System exit");
    System.exit(1);
}
// Make a copy of the blockchain.
ledger = new Blockchain(genesisBlock);
System.out.println("block chain genesis successful");
// The genesis miner copies the blockchain to his local ledger.
genesisMiner.setLocalLedger(ledger);
System.out.println("genesis miner balance: "
        + genesisMiner.getCurrentBalance(genesisMiner.getLocalLedger()));

System.out.println("creating two miners and one wallet");
Miner A = new Miner("A", "A");
Wallet B = new Wallet("B", "B");
Miner C = new Miner("C", "C");
users.add(A); users.add(B); users.add(C);
// Everyone has a local ledger copy.
A.setLocalLedger(ledger.copy_NotDeepCopy());
B.setLocalLedger(ledger.copy_NotDeepCopy());
C.setLocalLedger(ledger.copy_NotDeepCopy());

// Start another block by miner A.
Block b2 = A.createNewBlock(A.getLocalLedger(), difficultlevel);
System.out.println("Block b2 created by A");
System.out.println("genesis miner sends B: 500+200, C: 300+100");
PublicKey[] receiver = {B.getPublicKey(), B.getPublicKey(),
                    C.getPublicKey(), C.getPublicKey()};
double[] funds = {500, 200, 300, 100};
Transaction t1 = genesisMiner.transferFund(receiver, funds);
System.out.println("A is collecting Transactions ...");
if(A.addTransaction(t1, b2)){
    System.out.println("t1 added into block b2");
}else{
    System.out.println("Warning: t1 cannot be added into b2");
}
System.out.println("A is generating reward transaction");
if(A.generateRewardTransaction(b2)){
```

```java
            System.out.println("rewarding transaction successfully added to b2");
        }else{
            System.out.println("rewarding transaction cannot be added to b2");
        }
        System.out.println("A is mining block b2");
        if(A.mineBlock(b2)){
            System.out.println("b2 is mined and signed by A");
        }
        // Let C verify this block b2.
        b = verifyBlock(C, b2, "b2");
        if(b){
            System.out.println("all blockchain users begin to update their "
                    + "local blockchain now with b2");
            allUpdateBlockchain(users, b2);
            System.out.println("after b2 is added to the blockchain, "
                    + "the balances are:");
            displayAllBalances(users);
        }
        // Display the balances for manual examination.
        System.out.println("total should=" + (20000 + Blockchain.MINING_REWARD)
                +". Adding all wallets, total="
                + (genesisMiner.getCurrentBalance(ledger) + A.getCurrentBalance(ledger)
                + B.getCurrentBalance(ledger) + C.getCurrentBalance(ledger)));
        
        // Start another block.
        Block b3 = A.createNewBlock(ledger, difficultLevel);
        System.out.println("Again, genesis miner sends B: 500+200, C: 300+100");
        Transaction t2 = genesisMiner.transferFund(receiver, funds);
        // Try to add t1 into b3. This effort should fail.
        if(A.addTransaction(t1, b3)){
            System.out.println("t1 added into block b3");
        }else{
            System.out.println("Warning: t1 cannot be added into b3, t1 already exists");
        }
        // Add the transaction t2 into block b3.
        if(A.addTransaction(t2, b3)){
            System.out.println("t2 added into block b3");
        }else{
            System.out.println("Warning: t2 cannot be added into b3");
        }
        System.out.println("A is collecting Transactions ...");
        System.out.println("A is generating reward transaction");
        if(A.generateRewardTransaction(b3)){
            System.out.println("rewarding transaction successfully added to b3");
        }else{
            System.out.println("rewarding transaction CANNOT be added to b3");
        }
        
        // Assume that miner C wants to mine the block. This should fail.
        if(C.mineBlock(b3)){
            System.out.println("b3 is mined and signed by C");
        }else{
            System.out.println("C cannot mine b3");
        }
        // Assume that miner C wants to change the block. This should fail.
        if(C.deleteTransaction(b3.getTransaction(0), b3)){
            System.out.println("C deleted the first transaction from b3");
        }else{
            System.out.println("C cannot delete the first transaction from b3");
```

```java
}
// Only A can mine block b3 as A is its creator.
if(A.mineBlock(b3)){
    System.out.println("b3 is mined and signed by A");
}else{
    System.out.println("ERROR: b3 is created by A, why A cannot mine it?");
}
// Assume that miner A wants to change the block after mining. This should fail.
if(A.deleteTransaction(b3.getTransaction(0), b3)){
    System.out.println("A deleted the first transaction from b3");
}else{
    System.out.println("A cannot delete the first transaction from b3,"
            + " block already signed");
}
// Let C verify this block b3.
b = verifyBlock(C, b3, "b3");
if(b){
    System.out.println("all blockchain users begin to update their "
            + "local blockchain now with b3");
    allUpdateBlockchain(users, b3);
    System.out.println("after b3 is added to the blockchain, "
            + "the balances are:");
    displayAllBalances(users);
}
System.out.println("total should=" + (20000 + Blockchain.MINING_REWARD*2)
    +". Adding all wallets, total=" + (genesisMiner.getCurrentBalance(ledger)
    + A.getCurrentBalance(ledger) + B.getCurrentBalance(ledger)
    + C.getCurrentBalance(ledger)));

Transaction t5 = C.transferFund(C.getPublicKey(), 20);
// Assume that miner A wants to add t5 into the b3 at this time. This should fail.
if(A.addTransaction(t5, b3)){
    System.out.println("A added t5 into b3");
}else{
    System.out.println("A cannot add t5 into b3, block already signed");
}
System.out.println();

// Start another block b4 by miner C.
Block b4 = C.createNewBlock(ledger, difficultLevel);
System.out.println("C created block b4");
if(C.addTransaction(t5, b4)){
    System.out.println("C added t5 into b4");
}else{
    System.out.println("C failed to add t5 into b4");
}
Transaction t6 = C.transferFund(A.getPublicKey(), 100);
Transaction t7 = B.transferFund(A.getPublicKey(), 100);
Transaction t8 = C.transferFund(B.getPublicKey(), 100);
if(C.addTransaction(t6, b4)){
    System.out.println("C added t6 into b4");
}else{
    System.out.println("C failed to add t6 into b4");
}
if(C.addTransaction(t7, b4)){
    System.out.println("C added t7 into b4");
}else{
    System.out.println("C failed to add t7 into b4");
}
```

```java
            if(C.addTransaction(t8, b4)){
                System.out.println("C added t8 into b4");
            }else{
                System.out.println("C failed to add t8 into b4");
            }
            if(C.generateRewardTransaction(b4)){
                System.out.println("C generated reward transaction in b4");
            }else{
                System.out.println("C CANNOT generat reward transaction in b4");
            }
            if(C.mineBlock(b4)){
                System.out.println("C mined b4, hashID:");
                System.out.println(b4.getHashID());
                b = verifyBlock(A, b4, "b4");
                if(b){
                    System.out.println("all blockchain users begin to update "
                        + "their local blockchain now with b4");
                    allUpdateBlockchain(users, b4);
                    System.out.println("after b4 is added to the blockchain, "
                        + "the balances are:");
                    displayAllBalances(users);
                }
            }
            // Let's try to add b4 twice, it should fail.
            b = ledger.addBlock(b4);
            if(b){
                System.out.println("ERROR: b4 is added again into the ledger.");
            }else{
                System.out.println("b4 CANNOT be added again into the ledger.");
            }
            // Assess the balance again.
            System.out.println("after b4, the balances are:");
            displayAllBalances(users);
            System.out.println("total should=" + (20000 + Blockchain.MINING_REWARD*3)
                + ". Adding all wallets, total="
                + (genesisMiner.getCurrentBalance(ledger) + A.getCurrentBalance(ledger)
                + B.getCurrentBalance(ledger) + C.getCurrentBalance(ledger)));
            
            System.out.println();
            System.out.println("=======================================");
            System.out.println("blockchain looks like:");
            System.out.println();
            UtilityMethods.displayBlockchain(ledger, System.out, 0);
            System.out.println("=========BlockChain platform shuts down=========");
    }
    public static boolean verifyBlock(Wallet w, Block b, String blockName){
        if(w.verifyGuestBlock(b)){
            System.out.println(w.getName() + " accepted block " + blockName);
            return true;
        }else{
            System.out.println(w.getName() + " rejected block " + blockName);
            return false;
        }
    }
    public static void allUpdateBlockchain(ArrayList<Wallet> users, Block b){
        for(int i=0; i<users.size(); i++){
            Wallet w = users.get(i);
```

```java
            w.updateLocalLedger(b);
            System.out.println(w.getName() + " updated its local blockchain.");
        }
    }

    public static void displayUTXOs(ArrayList<UTXO> us, int level){
        for(int i=0; i<us.size(); i++){
            UTXO xo = us.get(i);
            UtilityMethods.displayUTXO(xo, System.out, level);
        }
    }

    // A method to display a wallet's balance in order.
    public static void displayBalance(Wallet w){
        Blockchain ledger = w.getLocalLedger();
        ArrayList<UTXO> all = new ArrayList<UTXO>();
        ArrayList<UTXO> spent = new ArrayList<UTXO>();
        ArrayList<UTXO> unspent = new ArrayList<UTXO>();
        ArrayList<Transaction> sentT = new ArrayList<Transaction>();
        ArrayList<UTXO> rewards = new ArrayList<UTXO>();
        double balance = ledger.findRelatedUTXOs(w.getPublicKey(),
                    all, spent, unspent, sentT, rewards);
        int level = 0;
        UtilityMethods.displayTab(System.out, level, w.getName() + "{");
        UtilityMethods.displayTab(System.out, level + 1, "All UTXOs:");
        displayUTXOs(all, level + 2);
        UtilityMethods.displayTab(System.out, level + 1, "Spent UTXOs:");
        displayUTXOs(spent, level + 2);
        UtilityMethods.displayTab(System.out, level + 1, "unspent UTXOs:");
        displayUTXOs(unspent, level + 2);
        if(w instanceof Miner){
            UtilityMethods.displayTab(System.out, level + 1, "Mining Rewards:");
            displayUTXOs(rewards, level + 2);
        }
        UtilityMethods.displayTab(System.out, level + 1, "Balance=" + balance);
        UtilityMethods.displayTab(System.out, level, "}");
    }
    public static void displayAllBalances(ArrayList<Wallet> users){
        for(int i=0; i<users.size(); i++){
            displayBalance(users.get(i));
        }
    }
}
```

The BlockchainPlatform program simulates wallet and miner creation, blockchain genesis, transaction initiation, block mining, miner reward collection and the updating of a wallet's local blockchain copy. You should modify this program to experience firsthand the various blockchain concepts and techniques we have covered so far. Figure 8 shows what the output should look like when the BlockchainPlatform class starts, and Figure 9 illustrates the last output of the execution of class BlockchainPlatform.

You can download chapter 6 programs at: https://github.com/hhohho/Learning-Blockchain-in-Java-Edition-2. Among the downloaded programs, you will find a class named Simulator. This is a dynamic blockchain application simulator. It is an interactive program and is much more functional than the class BlockchainPlatform. The Simulator class allows you to 1) select the mining difficulty level; 2) transfer funds between wallets of your choices; and 3) pick individual miners for block mining. It displays the balance of each wallet after every block mining session so that you can manually examine if everything is working as expected. The program is highly recommended and you are encouraged to try it out.

```
Blockchain platform starts ...
creating genesis miner, genesis transaction and genesis block
A wallet exists with the same name and password. Loaded the existing wallet
genesis miner is mining the genesis block
genesis block is successfully mined. HashID:
00000000000000000000000100111011100011101010011001111001001100010011111001001000011001
01011110111110110010010000110001000101010111010000000100111001110101001001011000100
00100011101101001111101011001111101011011110001001110000110000001101100101010111001100
block chain genesis successful
genesis miner balance: 20000.0
creating two miners and one wallet
A wallet exists with the same name and password. Loaded the existing wallet
A wallet exists with the same name and password. Loaded the existing wallet
A wallet exists with the same name and password. Loaded the existing wallet
Block b2 created by A
genesis miner sends B: 500+200, C: 300+100
A is collecting Transactions ...
t1 added into block b2
A is generating reward transaction
rewarding transaction successfully added to b2
A is mining block b2
```

**Figure 8 The execution of BlockchainPlatform class.**

```
            Transaction{
                    ID: w6fB1b/50XLe4f4Y3bMspjkIkXk9HOFbjH+3WNseQ4U=
                    sender: MIIBIjANBgkqhkiG9w0BAQEFAAOCAQ8AMIIBCgKCAQEAkv/w9H39ZJJ2+T6h+KZ4l
                    fundToBeTransferred total: 100.0
                    Input:
                            fund: 300.0, receiver: MIIBIjANBgkqhkiG9w0BAQEFAAOCAQ8AMIIBCgKCAQE
                    Output:
                            fund: 100.0, receiver: MIIBIjANBgkqhkiG9w0BAQEFAAOCAQ8AMIIBCgKCAQE
                            change: 199.0
                    transaction fee: 1.0
                    signature verification: true
            }
            Reward Transaction:
            Transaction{
                    ID: lSLqgUL459up4HiqoMlbHjKsrEM9lDXP2cD28hZRGlg=
                    sender: MIIBIjANBgkqhkiG9w0BAQEFAAOCAQ8AMIIBCgKCAQEAkv/w9H39ZJJ2+T6h+KZ4l
                    fundToBeTransferred total: 104.0
                    Input:
                    Output:
                            change: 104.0
                    transaction fee: 1.0
                    signature verification: true
            }
    }
}
=========BlockChain platform shuts down=========
```

**Figure 9**  The last output of BlockchainPlatform execution. Information of senders and receivers are truncated.

# 7 NETWORK AND NETWORK MESSAGING

Please note that chapter 7 consists of stand-alone programs, and you do not need to copy any programs from chapter 6. However, you still need to create a dedicated directory for the source codes of the programs to be written. If you are using Eclipse, please start a new Java project named chapter7.

Though we have significantly improved our blockchain system in chapter 6, it is still missing a quintessential characteristic of the blockchain system. The current prototype can only be tested inside a single JVM environment, meaning it is yet distributed. To make it a distributed system, we must incorporate network components into the system. Java provides a network package with classes supporting TCP and UDP protocols, each, however, having their own pros and cons. TCP, or Transmission Control Protocol, requires establishing a connection before two entities can communicate. Once the connection is set up, communication is bidirectional and messages between the two entities are guaranteed to arrive and arrive in order. UDP, or User Datagram Protocol, requires no such connection and therefore is more efficient. That being said, it does not guarantee the arrival of messages. UDP wraps data into datagrams, and these datagrams can take different routes and arrive in different orders. If the order is important, then the application layer must take care of it instead.

Before we decide which protocol to adopt for our blockchain system, let us experiment with both. One thing common in both TCP and UDP is that data are sent and received in byte streams. To test out UDP, we mostly use three classes: DatagramPacket, DatagramSocket and InetAddress. DatagramPacket has two types of constructors: one for sending a datagram, and the other for receiving a datagram. In UDP, all data are wrapped inside datagrams. To send a datagram, the datagram must contain the following information: data, destination port and destination IP address. A datagram also contains the sender's IP address and listening port. Think of every datagram as an independent package that contains all the information necessary for routing service providers to send it to its final destination.

Next, let's write a simple chat program based on UDP that can be used as a mode of communication between two users. One user acts as the server, the other as the client. The server program is presented below:

```java
1   import java.net.DatagramPacket;
2   import java.net.DatagramSocket;
3   import java.net.SocketException;
4   import java.util.Scanner;
5   import java.io.IOException;

6   public class TestUDPServer {
7       private int serverPort;
8       private DatagramSocket serverUDPSocket;
9       private boolean forever = true;
10      private Scanner in;

11      public TestUDPServer(int serverPort){
12          this.serverPort = serverPort;
13          this.in = new Scanner(System.in);
14          try{
15              this.serverUDPSocket = new DatagramSocket(this.serverPort);
16          }catch(SocketException e){
17              throw new RuntimeException(e);
18          }
19          in = new Scanner(System.in);
20      }

21      public void start(){
22          System.out.println("UDP server starts at port " + this.serverPort);
23          while(forever){
24              byte[] buf = new byte[2048];
25              DatagramPacket dp = new DatagramPacket(buf, buf.length);
26              try{
27                  System.out.println("server listening to incoming messages ...");
28                  serverUDPSocket.receive(dp);
29                  System.out.println("client]: port=" + dp.getPort()
                            +", IP=" + dp.getAddress().getHostAddress());
30                  String r = (new String(dp.getData())).trim();
31                  if(r.startsWith("END")){
32                      System.out.println("ENDing now ...");
33                      forever = false;
34                      in.close();
35                      continue;
36                  }else{
37                      System.out.println("client]: " + r);
38                  }
39                  System.out.println("Please type your response below:");
40                  String m = in.nextLine();
41                  DatagramPacket rp = new DatagramPacket(m.getBytes(),
                            m.getBytes().length, dp.getAddress(), dp.getPort());
42                  serverUDPSocket.send(rp);
43                  if(m.startsWith("END")){
44                      forever = false;
45                  }
46              }catch(IOException e){
47                  forever = false;
48                  throw new RuntimeException(e);
49              }
50          }
51          this.serverUDPSocket.close();
52      }
```

```
53          public static void main(String[] args) {
54              TestUDPServer server = new TestUDPServer(8888);
55              server.start();
56              System.out.println("========= Server Ended ==========");
57          }
58      }
```

Code line 7 specifies an instance field for the port number that the server will be listening at. The concept of port is akin to a TV channel. TVs, however, usually have less than 1000 channels, while a computer can have tens of thousands of ports. Information targeting a specific port is sorted by the network card to the proper port, the same way a signal for a specific TV channel can be viewed only when you switch to that channel. Port numbers 1-1024 are reserved for special purposes, so applications should use other port numbers. In this UDP program, we declare an instance field to represent the port at which the UDP server is listening (expecting incoming messages).

Code line 8 declares a DatagramSocket variable by the statement "private DatagramSocket serverUDPSocket;". In Java UDP, both the server and the client make use of DatagramSocket to send and receive network messages. The only difference is that, a server DatagramSocket is always bound to a specific port, while a client DatagramSocket is not.

What is the instance variable *forever* for (code line 9)? While a network server should not stop providing services, there should be a mechanism to properly terminate the server when needed. Having a boolean variable to control the loop (lines 23-50) has its advantage – as long as we turn *forever* to be false, the program can exit from the loop. This is the purpose of the variable *forever*.

Code lines 11-20 define the constructor of the class. This constructor requires an input argument specifying the port number at which the server socket is listening. Inside this constructor, the serverUDPSocket is initialized with a port number and a Scanner object is prepared to take standard keyboard input for chat purposes.

Code lines 21-52 present the method start() which uses the following sequence to receive and send messages:
- Use a loop so that the program continuously runs until an END message is received (lines 23-50).
- Create a DatagramPacket to accept incoming message (lines 24-25).
- Upon receiving a message from the client (line 28), display the client's information including client socket's IP address and listening port number (line 29), and fetch the data from the DatagramPacket object (line 30). The statement "serverUDPSocket.receive(dp);" blocks the execution of the program until a datagram message is received.
- The server takes different actions depending on the message from the client. If it is an END message, the server quits; otherwise the server displays the message (lines 31-38).
- Ask the user for a message to respond the client (lines 39-40).
- Construct a DatagramPacket object to store the message. The destination port number and destination IP address are found from the client's DatagramPacket (lines 41).
- Send the response to the client (line 42).

- Code lines 43-45 evaluate if the user at the server side wants to exit. If the user enters "END", the server quits.

Code lines 53-57 present the main() method to execute the UDP server program.

The program for the client is presented below:

```
1    import java.net.DatagramPacket;
2    import java.net.DatagramSocket;
3    import java.net.InetAddress;
4    import java.net.UnknownHostException;
5    import java.net.SocketException;
6    import java.util.Scanner;
7    import java.io.IOException;

8    public class TestUDPClient {
9        private int serverPort;
10       private InetAddress serverAddress;
11       private boolean forever = true;
12       private Scanner in;
13       private DatagramSocket clientSocket;

14       public TestUDPClient(int serverPort, String serverAddress){
15           this.serverPort = serverPort;
16           in = new Scanner(System.in);
17           try{
18               this.serverAddress = InetAddress.getByName(serverAddress);
19               clientSocket = new DatagramSocket();
20           }catch(SocketException e){
21               throw new RuntimeException(e);
22           }catch(UnknownHostException uhe){
23               throw new RuntimeException(uhe);
24           }
25       }

26       public void start() throws IOException {
27           while(forever){
28               System.out.println("Please type your message to be sent: ");
29               String mesg = in.nextLine();
                 // Generate a sending datagram.
30               DatagramPacket dp = new DatagramPacket(mesg.getBytes(),
                         mesg.length(), this.serverAddress, serverPort);
                 // Send the datagram.
31               this.clientSocket.send(dp);
32               if(mesg.startsWith("END")){
33                   forever = false;
34                   continue;
35               }

                 // Wait for a message.
36               byte[] data = new byte[2048];
37               DatagramPacket rp = new DatagramPacket(data, data.length);
38               this.clientSocket.receive(rp);
39               String m = new String(rp.getData()).trim();
                 // If it is an END message, stop the program.
40               if(m.startsWith("END")){
41                   System.out.println("== ENDing now ==");
```

```
42                    forever = false;
43                    in.close();
44                }else{
45                    System.out.println("server]: " + m);
46                }
47            }
48            this.clientSocket.close();
49        }
50        public static void main(String[] args) throws IOException {
51            System.out.println("What is the IP address of the server?:");
52            Scanner in = new Scanner(System.in);
53            String ip = in.nextLine();
54            if(ip.trim().length() < 5){
55                ip = "localhost";
56            }
57            System.out.println("IP: " + ip);
58            TestUDPClient client = new TestUDPClient(8888, ip);
59            System.out.println("UDP client starts now, server is listening "
                                + "at port 8888");
60            client.start();
61            in.close();
62            System.out.println("===== Client Stopped =============="); }
63        }
```

The codes of the client program are very similar to those of the server program, but with two major differences. The first being that the client program's DatagramSocket does not need to bind to a port (code line 19). If you want to bind it to a port, the port should be different from the one the server is bound to. This is extremely important if you are testing your server and client programs on the same computer. The second difference lies in the method main(). The main method requires the server's IP address because the client needs to locate the server. However, in the TestUDPServer class, the DatagramSocket does not require any IP address. Why? Every computer has a loopback IP address called "localhost". This IP address is 127.0.0.1 for all computers. It represents this computer itself. If a computer is on a network, this computer must have at least another IP address uniquely assigned in the network. Other computers find this computer based on its network IP address. A network server starts automatically on the local computer with IP address 127.0.0.1 and can be found based on the computer's network address. Therefore, when a server starts, it does not need to be given an IP address. Code line 38 blocks the execution of this program until the client socket receives a message.

The execution the two programs above should be fairly straightforward, but regardless, the steps are posted below:
1) Open a terminal window on your computer A and start the program TestUDPServer. Keep in mind that a UDP server should be up and running before the client, so as to prevent the client's messages from getting lost.
2) If you are testing the client program on the same computer, please open another terminal window on computer A. From there, please start the TestUDPClient program. When you are prompted for an IP address, please type "127.0.0.1" or "localhost", and then hit "Enter".
3) If the client program is being run on another computer B, then the IP entered should be the IP address of computer A. Note that you can find the IP address with the command "ipconfig /all" on Windows, or the command "ifconfig" on a Linux or Mac computer.

4) To quit the chat at any time, enter "END" (either on the server side or the client side).

Another advantage of UDP is that it is naturally suitable for broadcasting and multicasting. The major weakness of UDP lies in the fact that it is not a message-guaranteed network model. The transmitted data can get lost, and even if the data are not lost, they must be divided into multiple packets if the data are larger than 64 Kb because UDP has the size limit of 64Kb per data packet. Packets can arrive in any order, forcing the application program to spend extra time and effort sorting through them. For these reasons, TCP is more commonly used than UDP, even though it is less efficient.

Java differentiates the socket for a server from the socket for a client in TCP. As mentioned before, servers run full time but client sockets can be on and off. When a server socket is on, it keeps listening for connection requests from clients and upon obtaining a request, the server socket forks a socket dedicated to that particular connection. From then on, all communication between the server and the client is facilitated through this socket-to-socket connection. The following sample program is an example of a TCP server. Note that this server in particular is meant to be a messaging system between two users, where one user is acting as a server, the other as a client.

```
1   import java.net.Socket;
2   import java.net.ServerSocket;
3   import java.io.IOException;
4   import java.util.Scanner;

5   public class TestTCPServer {
6       public static final int port = 8888;
7       public static void main(String[] args) throws IOException {
8           System.out.println("What you want to call your friend?");
9           Scanner in = new Scanner(System.in);
10          String friendName = in.nextLine();
11          ServerSocket server = new ServerSocket(port);
12          System.out.println("server is listening now");
13          Socket socket = server.accept();
14          System.out.println("Connected, start chat!");
15          MessageManagerTCP messageManager = new MessageManagerTCP(socket, friendName);
16          messageManager.start();
17          System.out.println("message manager started");
18          CommunicationChannel channel = new CommunicationChannel(messageManager);
19          channel.start();
20          System.out.println("communication channel is ready");
21          server.close();
22      }
23  }
```

You will run into errors if you copy and paste the above codes into your TestTCPServer class. This is because you are missing two required classes – MessageManagerTCP and CommunicationChannel – which we are about to cover.

Code line 6 makes use of the port 8888. Typically in software development, we should have a configuration file or something similar to control these settings, but we can just hardcode it for now.

Code line 9 creates a Scanner instance so that we can obtain the name of the client from the standard input. Note: do not close the Scanner instance after taking the input. Closing it also closes the System.in. This will cause errors when you need to obtain information from System.in later.

Code line 11 creates a ServerSocket. There should be only one ServerSocket in this case.

Code line 13 will block the program execution if there is no incoming connection. Once the server accepts an incoming connection request, it generates a socket to set up the connection.

Code line 15 creates a MessageManagerTCP instance which is dedicated to sending and receiving messages to and from the client. Note that MessageManagerTCP is a subclass of Thread, meaning that the MessageManagerTCP instance is a thread, which is why we need line 16 to start it.

Code line 18 creates a CommunicationChannel object, a thread dedicated to receiving inputs from System.in. The inputs are messages entered by users.

Code line 21 closes the server socket. But even if the server socket is closed and the TestTCPServer class terminates, the two threads created by lines 15 and 18 will continue running and provide a messaging service between the server and client. Shutting down the server is to allow only two users to chat with each other.

The codes for class MessageManagerTCP is presented below:

```
1     import java.io.IOException;
2     import java.io.ObjectInputStream;
3     import java.io.ObjectOutputStream;
4     import java.net.Socket;
5     public class MessageManagerTCP extends Thread {
6         private ObjectInputStream in;
7         private ObjectOutputStream out;
8         private boolean forever = true;
9         private String friendName;
10        public MessageManagerTCP(Socket socket, String friendName) throws IOException {
              // In TCP socket, you must create the outputstream before
              // the inputstream. The order is critical.
11            this.out = new ObjectOutputStream(socket.getOutputStream());
12            this.in = new ObjectInputStream(socket.getInputStream());
13            this.friendName = friendName;
14        }

15        public void sendMessage(String mesg){
16            try{
17                this.out.writeObject(mesg);
18            }catch(IOException ioe){
19                System.out.println("Error: writing message runs into exception.");
20                ioe.printStackTrace();
21            }
22        }

23        public void run() {
24            System.out.println("Message manager is up ...");
25            while(forever){
26                try{
```

```
27                    String m = (String)(this.in.readObject());
28                    System.out.println(this.friendName + "]: " + m);
29                    if(m.trim().startsWith("END")){
30                        forever = false;
31                    }
32                }catch(Exception e){
33                    System.out.println("Error: This is only for text messaging.");
34                    System.exit(1);
35                }
36            }
37            System.out.println("message manager retired");
38            System.exit(1);
39        }
40    }
```

Code line 5 marks that this class is a subclass of Thread. A thread instance can live and continue executing independently. If you do not have any experience with Java thread, it is a good time to learn about it as it is thread that enables multiprocessing in Java. The efficient and secure use of multi-threads is both a science and an art. When we talked about UDP programs, you may have noticed that the programs worked like a walkie-talkie: one user sends a message and must wait for an incoming message before the user can send another. Things wouldn't have to be so rigid and linear if threads were effectively applied in the programs. In this TCP example, threads can make our programs more powerful.

Code lines 10-14 present the constructor of this class. The constructor requires an argument of Socket and an argument of String. The string is intended for the name of the user as we need the name to properly display the chat messages. The socket is needed to create the network IO. Its OutputStream is wrapped to produce an ObjectOutputStream, and the Socket's InputStream is wrapped to create an ObjectInputStream. If you recall, in Chapter 4 we encountered both the ObjectOutputStream and ObjectInputStream. They take care of the serialization and deserialization of objects. Important note that the order here matters – the ObjectOutputStream must be created first. This is kind of like taking a bus. We need passengers on the bus to leave before outside passengers can board.

Code lines 15-22 define a method for sending messages using the output stream.

Code lines 23-39 override the run() method of Thread. The run() method represents the task that the thread is programmed to carry out. Exiting from the run() method signals the termination of the thread. It is critical to understand that we do not call this run() method directly, instead we start a thread by calling its method start(). In the Java Thread class, the method start() calls the run() method internally. However, calling the start() method starts the thread as a new and independent process, calling the run() method, instead, executes the thread inside the current calling process. Line 27 waits for an incoming message and it will block the thread if there is none coming. Lines 29-31 set up a proper way to terminate the thread: whenever "END" is entered, the thread will exit from the loop and finish its lifespan.

Now let us write the CommunicationChannel class. Just as the MessageManagerTCP class allows users to continuously receive messages without interruption, this class allows you to continuously type messages without interruption.

```
1    import java.util.Scanner;
2    public class CommunicationChannel extends Thread {
3        private Scanner in;
4        private MessageManagerTCP messageManager;
5        private boolean forever = true;
6        public CommunicationChannel(MessageManagerTCP messageManager){
7            this.messageManager = messageManager;
8            in = new Scanner(System.in);
9        }
10       public void run() {
11           System.out.println("Communication channel is up, please type below:");
12           while(forever){
13               try{
14                   String mesg = in.nextLine();
15                   messageManager.sendMessage(mesg);
16                   if(mesg.trim().startsWith("END")){
17                       forever = false;
18                   }
19               }catch(Exception e){
20                   forever = false;
21               }
22           }
23           System.out.println("Channel closed");
24           System.exit(1);
25       }
26   }
```

This class is constructed with a MessageManagerTCP object embedded. In the run() method, whenever a message is entered from standard input (line 14), the MessageManagerTCP object is called to send the message. Lines 16-18 dictate when "END" is the input, the chat is over. Note that the server sends the END message to the client first per proper closing of the network connection, to ensure that the client also knows to quit the chat.

The client side of the program is relatively simple and makes use of the MessageManagerTCP and CommunicationChannel classes as well.

```
1    import java.net.Socket;
2    import java.io.IOException;
3    import java.util.Scanner;
4    public class TestTCPClient{
5        private static int port = 8888;
6        public static void main(String[] args) throws IOException {
7            Scanner keyboard = new Scanner(System.in);
8            System.out.println("Please enter the server's IP address");
9            String ip = keyboard.nextLine();
10           Socket socket = new Socket(ip, port);
11           System.out.println("What is your friend's name");
12           String name = keyboard.nextLine();
13           System.out.println("connected, ready to go");
14           MessageManagerTCP manager = new MessageManagerTCP(socket, name);
15           manager.start();
16           System.out.println("manager started");
17           CommunicationChannel channel = new CommunicationChannel(manager);
```

```
18                channel.start();
19                System.out.println("channel ready for you");
20          }
21    }
```

Code lines 7-9 creates a Scanner object called *keyboard* to fetch the IP address of the server. If the server is on the same computer, please enter "127.0.0.1" or "localhost". Again, do not close the Scanner instance *keyboard*, otherwise you also shutdown System.in.

The statement "`Socket socket = new Socket(ip, port);`" in line 10 shows how to construct a socket connection. It needs the IP address of the server and the port number at which the server is listening. If the connection fails, an IOException is thrown. If this statement is successful, a network connection between the client and the server has been established.

Code lines 11-12 obtain the name of another user (the user on the server side). We need the user name to display more readable messages.

Code lines 14-15 start a MessageManagerTCP thread dedicated to receiving and sending messages.

Code lines 17-18 start a CommunicationChannel thread dedicated to taking user input.

To run the TCP chat program, please follow the instructions below:
1) Open a terminal window on computer A and execute the Java program TestTCPServer. Note that for TCP, the server must start up first. A client cannot initiate a connection request if the server is down.
2) If the TCP chat program is being tested on a single computer, open another terminal window on computer A. If it is being tested on two different computers, open the second terminal window on computer B. Don't forget to also import the necessary Java programs into computer B.
3) The second terminal window, whether appearing on computer A or B, will execute the TestTCPClient program. When prompted for a server IP address, enter "127.0.0.1" if you are testing on one computer; otherwise enter the network IP address of computer A.
4) If all goes well, the messaging network should be up and running. Feel free to send as many messages as you desire without waiting in between. To stop the chat at any time, remember to enter "END".

Having reviewed both messaging techniques, we will be applying TCP in our distributed blockchain system. Once you have learned how to build a blockchain application using TCP, you can try building another with UDP. However, please bear in mind that TCP is chosen because it is the better choice when conducting business transactions with zero fault tolerance. That being said, blockchain can implement both TCP and UDP, just for different functions. Bitcoin, for example, started with TCP, but bitcoin's Fast Internet Bitcoin Relay Engine (FIBRE) is a UDP-based relay network.

Bitcoin is built upon a peer-to-peer (P2P) network. It is time for us to experience a little bit about P2P. In a P2P environment, each peer is a server and a client. In the following simple example of two-users

P2P chat program, each server is dedicated to message receiving and each client is dedicated to sending messages. You may think it weird at this moment. Please not worry, we will implement two more complicated P2P networks later and then you will experience the true power of P2P: completely decentralization, i.e. the network works without a central server. Note that the following class PeerTCP has two inner classes, both extend Thread.

```
1   import java.io.IOException;
2   import java.io.ObjectInputStream;
3   import java.io.ObjectOutputStream;
4   import java.net.InetAddress;
5   import java.net.ServerSocket;
6   import java.net.Socket;
7   import java.util.Scanner;
8   public class PeerTCP {
9       public static final int port = 8888;
10      public static void main(String[] args) throws IOException {
11          Scanner keyboard = new Scanner(System.in);
12          System.out.println("What you want to call your friend?");
13          String friendName = keyboard.nextLine();
14          System.out.println("What is your own name?");
15          String self = keyboard.nextLine().trim();
16          PeerTCPOutgoingMessageManager outgoing
                = new PeerTCPOutgoingMessageManager(friendName, self);
17          outgoing.start();
18          ServerSocket server = new ServerSocket(port);
19          System.out.println("server is listening now");
20          Socket socket = server.accept();
21          InetAddress clientAddress = socket.getInetAddress();
22          System.out.println(friendName + " is from " + clientAddress.getHostAddress());
23          System.out.println("Incoming connection established, receiving messages now.");
24          PeerTCPIncomingMessageManager pi
                = new PeerTCPIncomingMessageManager(socket, friendName);
25          pi.start();
26          server.close();
27      }
28  }


29  class PeerTCPIncomingMessageManager extends Thread {
30      private ObjectInputStream in;
31      private ObjectOutputStream out;
32      private boolean forever = true;
33      private String friendName;
34      public PeerTCPIncomingMessageManager(Socket socket, String friendName) throws IOException
35      {
            //In TCP socket, you must create the outputstream first
            //then the inputstream. The order is critical
36          this.out = new ObjectOutputStream(socket.getOutputStream());
37          this.in = new ObjectInputStream(socket.getInputStream());
38          this.friendName = friendName;
39      }

40      public void run() {
41          System.out.println("PeerIncomingMessageManager is up ...");
42          while(forever){
43              try{
44                  String m = (String)(this.in.readObject());
```

```
45                    System.out.println(this.friendName+"]: " + m);
46                    if(m.trim().startsWith("END")){
47                        forever = false;
48                    }
49                }catch(Exception e){
50                    System.out.println("Error: This is only for text messaging.");
51                    forever = false;
52                }
53            }
54            System.out.println("PeerIncomingMessageManager retired");
55            try{
56                this.out.close();
57                this.in.close();
58            }catch(IOException ioe){
                    // Do nothing
59            }
60            System.exit(1);
61        }
62    }

63    class PeerTCPOutgoingMessageManager extends Thread {
64        private ObjectInputStream in;
65        private ObjectOutputStream out;
66        private boolean forever = true;
67        private String friendName;
68        private String self;
69        private Scanner keyboard;
70        public PeerTCPOutgoingMessageManager(String friendName, String self) {
71            this.friendName = friendName;
72            this.self = self;
73            keyboard = new Scanner(System.in);
74        }

75        public void run() {
76            System.out.println("Outgoing connection has not established. "
                    + "please enter your peer friend's IP address:");
77            String ip = keyboard.nextLine();
78            try{
79                Socket socket = new Socket(ip, PeerTCP.port);
                    //In TCP socket, you must create the outputstream first
                    //then the inputstream. The order is critical
80                this.out = new ObjectOutputStream(socket.getOutputStream());
81                this.in = new ObjectInputStream(socket.getInputStream());
82            }catch(IOException ioe){
83                ioe.printStackTrace();
84                System.exit(1);
85            }
86            System.out.println("Outgoing connection established. Feel free to send "
                    + friendName+" messages.");
87            while(forever){
88                try{
89                    Thread.sleep(500);
90                    try{
91                        String mesg = keyboard.nextLine();
92                        System.out.println(self+"]: " + mesg);
93                        this.out.writeObject(mesg);
94                        if(mesg.trim().startsWith("END")){
95                            forever = false;
96                        }
```

```
97                    }catch(Exception e){
98                        forever = false;
99                    }
100               }catch(InterruptedException ie){
                       // Do nothing
101               }
102           }
103           try{
104               this.out.close();
105               this.in.close();
106           }catch(IOException ioe){
                   // Do nothing
107           }
108           System.out.println("PeerIncomingMessageManager retired");
109           System.exit(1);
110       }
111   }
```

The class PeerTCP contains three parts: the driver class PeerTCP itself, the two inner classes PeerTCPIncomingMessageManager and PeerTCPOutgoingMessageManager. PeerTCP starts a an instance of PeerTCPOutgoingMessageManager before creating a TCP server socket. This is to avoid being blocked by the server socket. PeerTCPOutgoingMessageManager wraps around a client socket and is dedicated to sending messages. PeerTCPIncomingMessageManager wraps a server side socket connection to manage incoming messages. Note that PeerTCPIncomingMessageManager does not send messages and PeerTCPOutgoingMessageManager does not receive messages.

Code lines 11-15 fetch from standard input the names of the two users.

Code lines 16-17 creates an instance of PeerTCPIncomingMessageManager and starts it.

Code line 18 creates an instance of ServerSocket with the given port.

Code line 20 blocks the driver class execution if there is no incoming connection. Once the server socket accepts an incoming connection request, it generates a socket to set up the connection.

Code line 21 obtains the network address of the incoming network request and code line 21 displays the IP address of another user. In case you do not know the IP address of another user, you should know it by now.

Code lines 22-23 create an instance of PeerTCPIncomingMessageManager and starts it.

Code line 26 terminates the server socket so that there can only be two users in this program. Note that even the server socket is terminated, because both PeerTCPIncomingMessageManager and PeerTCPOutgoingMessageManager are independent threads, they will continue executing.

Code lines 29-62 depict the inner class PeerTCPIncomingMessageManager, a thread that accepts incoming messages at the server side. Line 29 specifies that this class is a thread, which requires the implementation of the method run() specified by lines 40-61.

Code lines 34-39 present the constructor of PeerTCPIncomingMessageManager.

Code lines 40-61 describe the function of this thread. Note the use of the variable *forever* which allows the thread to live until an exception happens or the users desires the quit (by entering the "END"). A loop is critical to let the thread live.

Code lines 55-59 release network resources if the program is properly terminated.

Code line 60, "System.exit(1)", can force the release of all resources taken by this Java application.

Thread PeerTCPOutgoingMessageManager's function is presented by its method run() defined by code lines 75-110. Inside the method run(), the IP address of another peer is demanded at line 77. Code line 77 blocks the thread until the IP address is given. Note that if the IP address is not correct, an exception will be thrown and the program will halt. At this moment, our program does not handle unexpected conditions. Later, we will.

Code line 79 creates a Socket instance connecting to another peer's server.

Code lines 80-81 obtains the IO of the socket. Note that the ObjectInputStream inside this thread is not used at all as this thread is dedicated to sending messages only.

The while loop allows this thread live until it is terminated. Code line 89 inside the loop is important: since the user may be idle, it is necessary to let the thread sleep time to time so that other programs on your computer can use some CPU time.

Code line 91 fetches the user input from standard input.

Code line 93 sends the user input to another peer.

If the user input is to quit the chat, code lines 94-96 turns the variable *forever* to be false. The execution of this thread will then exit from the loop and terminate.

Code lines 103-107 releases network resources taken by this thread.

To run the PeerTCP chat program, please follow the instructions below:
1) You need two computers to test this program. You cannot test it on a single computer.
2) Open a terminal window on computer A and execute the Java program PeerTCP.
3) Open a second terminal window on computer B and execute the Java program PeerTCP.
4) In both terminal windows, enter proper information prompted by the program. Note you need to know the IP addresses of both computer A and computer B. On a Windows computer, please use the command "ipconfig" to obtain the IP address. On a linux or mac computer, please issue the command "ifconfig" to find its IP address.
5) To stop the chat at any time, remember to enter "END".

The two chat programs we coded above have the disadvantage of only allowing messaging between two users. Since blockchain has a prominent broadcasting feature, we need to write another chat program in which more than two users can share their messages on a discussion board. For this multi-user chat program, we will have a central server that acts like a message routing center, accepting multiple connections simultaneously and forwarding messages to all users. The central server is critical. Without it, no communication among the users is available. Figure 10 shows a network star model which we will adopt for our multi-users chat application.

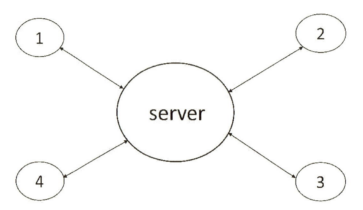

Figure 10  A network star model.  Server is the center star while clients 1, 2, 3, and 4 are nodes connected to the server individually.

Users must be differentiated by their names on a public chat board. Let's assume in our case that every user has a unique name, keeping in mind that this does not hold true in reality. Blockchain identifies wallets by their public keys instead of names. Is there a chance for a public key to be repeated? Theoretically speaking, there is a chance. But the probability is much smaller than the probability of that you got hit twice by lightning and won a jackpot lottery all in one day. Therefore, it is safe to consider every public and private key pair is unique.

On the public chat board, messages should appear with the name of the user first, followed by the body of his/her message. The following class wraps every text message for proper formatting:

```java
public class SimpleTextMessage implements java.io.Serializable {
    private static final long serialVersionUID = 1L;
    private String name;
    private String message;

    public SimpleTextMessage(String senderName, String message){
        this.name = senderName;
        this.message = message;
    }
```

```
        public String getSenderName(){
            return this.name;
        }

        public String getMessage(){
            return this.message;
        }
    }
```

This class unifies the messages in the network. Every message received and sent is a SimpleTextMessage containing the name of the sender and the message from the sender.

Three classes are needed on the server side. One is the driver class which is also responsible for accepting incoming connection requests. Upon accepting a connection, a socket is forked to establish the connection. This socket is wrapped into class UserChannelInfo which implements Runnable. Once a socket is created, a thread is created based on UserChannelInfo to manage all socket-to-socket communication. Upon receiving messages, this UserChannelInfo thread fetches the messages and leave them into a queue shared by all threads. Another thread, ServerMessageManager polls the queue from time to time. If messages are found in the queue, the ServerMessageManager will forward the messages to participating clients, i.e. broadcasting the messages. The server program is presented below, notice that it has two inner classes.

```
1   import java.net.Socket;
2   import java.net.ServerSocket;
3   import java.io.IOException;
4   import java.util.Hashtable;
5   import java.util.Enumeration;
6   import java.util.concurrent.ConcurrentLinkedQueue;
7   import java.io.ObjectInputStream;
8   import java.io.ObjectOutputStream;

9   public class TestTCPServerCenter {
10      public static final int port = 8888;
11      private static boolean forever = true;
        // The message queue. A thread keeps polling this queue to check messages.
12      private static ConcurrentLinkedQueue<SimpleTextMessage> messageQueue =
                            new ConcurrentLinkedQueue<SimpleTextMessage>();
        // A Hashtable storing all connections. Please notice that Hashtable is used
        // instead of HashMap because Hashtable is thread safe.
13      private static Hashtable<String, UserChannelInfo> users =
                            new Hashtable<String, UserChannelInfo>();
        // The main method.
14      public static void main(String[] args) throws IOException, ClassNotFoundException {
            // The server socket starts.
15          ServerSocket server = new ServerSocket(port);
            // Create a message manager that continuously polls the message queue. Upon
            // finding available messages, the messagae manager forwards them to
            // all network connections.
16          ServerMessageManager smm = new ServerMessageManager(messageQueue, users);
            // ServerMessageManager implements Runnable interface. To make it an
            // independent running thread, a thread instance needs to be instantiated
            // with an ServerMessageManager instance.
17          Thread ts = new Thread(smm);
```

```
18                ts.start();
                  // A server should be on forever.
                  // However, for demonstration purposes, we set a timeout on the server so
                  // that it will quit after some time. The timeout is set to be 1 hour.
                  // If you do not want the server to time out, please delete the statement.
19                server.setSoTimeout(1000 * 60 * 60);
20                while(forever){
21                    try{
22                        System.out.println("server is listening now");
23                        Socket socket = server.accept();
24                        System.out.println("got a connection, identifying name");
                          // Create a channel dedicated for this connection.
25                        UserChannelInfo channel = new UserChannelInfo(socket, messageQueue);
26                        System.out.println("user is: " + channel.getName());
                          // Store this connection's information.
                          // Assume that everyone has a unique name.
27                        users.put(channel.getName(), channel);
28                        Thread t = new Thread(channel);
29                        t.start();
30                    }catch(java.net.SocketTimeoutException te){
31                        System.out.println("server time out. Byebye");
32                        forever = false;
33                    }
34                }
35                server.close();
36                System.out.println("server closed");
                  // Calling System.exit(0) is important to clean all resources used by JVM.
37                System.exit(0);
38            }

          // This method removes a UserChannelInfo from storage. When a user leaves,
          // this method is called to remove its dedicated UserChannelInfo.
39        public static synchronized UserChannelInfo removeUserChannel(String name){
40            return users.remove(name);
41        }
42    }

      // An inner class. Please notice that this class does not extend Thread instead
      // it implements Runnable.
43    class UserChannelInfo implements Runnable {
44        private ObjectInputStream input;
45        private ObjectOutputStream output;
46        private Socket socket;
47        private String name = null;
48        private ConcurrentLinkedQueue<SimpleTextMessage> messageQueue;
49        private boolean forever = true;
          // The purpose of this variable errors is to count how many times exceptions
          // have happened in the execution. If it is over a limit, we need to shutdown
          // the server.
50        private int errors = 0;
          // This class wraps the Socket to take care of the task of receiving
          // and sending messages for this connection. The argument messageQueue
          // is supposed to be the server's message queue.
51        public UserChannelInfo(Socket socket,
                                 ConcurrentLinkedQueue<SimpleTextMessage> messageQueue)
                                       throws IOException, ClassNotFoundException
52        {
53            this.socket = socket;
54            this.output = new ObjectOutputStream(socket.getOutputStream());
```

```
55              this.input = new ObjectInputStream(socket.getInputStream());
                // When a connection is built up, we assume that the client-side socket
                // must send in the name of the user first.
56              this.name = (String)(this.input.readObject());
57              this.messageQueue = messageQueue;
                // Broadcast the message to let everyone know that this user is in.
58              this.messageQueue.add(new SimpleTextMessage("System", this.name+" joined."));
59          }

            // Since this class implements Runnable, we must write this run() method. We will
            // explain the difference between Thread and Runnable later. Whatever this class
            // needs to accomplish should be included in this method run().
60          public void run() {
61              System.out.println("The communication channel for " + this.name + " is up.");
62              while(forever){
                    // Sleep this thread so that other processes can use some CPU time.
63                  try{
64                      Thread.sleep(500);
65                  }catch(Exception e2){
66                      errors++;
67                  }
68                  try{
69                      String mesg = (String)input.readObject();
                        // Upon receiving END message, close this connection.
70                      if(mesg.startsWith("END")){
71                          forever = false;
72                      }else{
                            // Add this message to the queue.
73                          SimpleTextMessage sm = new SimpleTextMessage(this.getName(), mesg);
74                          this.messageQueue.add(sm);
75                      }
                    // There are two types of Exceptions to catch. Let's just catch
                    // the general Exception for simplicity.
76                  }catch(Exception e){
77                      errors++;
                        // If Exceptions happened too many times, let's close this channel.
78                      if(errors>=5){
                            // Close this channel.
79                          System.out.println("server is closing the channel for "
                                    + this.name + " because of error: " + e.getMessage());
80                          forever = false;
                            // Inform the client side socket to close connection.
81                          sendMessage(new SimpleTextMessage("Server", "END"));
82                      }
83                  }
84              }
                // Remove self from the Hashtable.
85              UserChannelInfo U = TestTCPServerCenter.removeUserChannel(this.getName());
86              if(U != null){
                    // Let everyone know that U left.
87                  SimpleTextMessage sm =
                            new SimpleTextMessage("System", U.getName() + " left.");
88                  this.messageQueue.add(sm);
89              }
90          }

            // This method sends out a message.
91          public void sendMessage(SimpleTextMessage message){
92              try{
```

```
 93                    this.output.writeObject(message);
 94             }catch(Exception e){
 95                 errors++;
 96                 if(errors >= 5){
 97                     throw new RuntimeException(e);
 98                 }
 99             }
100         }

         // Return the name of the user this channel dedicated to.
101      public String getName(){
102          return this.name;
103      }
104  }

     // Another inner class that polls the message queue to broadcast messages.
105  class ServerMessageManager implements Runnable {
106      private ConcurrentLinkedQueue<SimpleTextMessage> messageQueue = null;
107      private Hashtable<String, UserChannelInfo> users = null;
108      private boolean forever = true;

         // This manager needs to have access to the server's message queue and instances
         // of UserChannelInfo. When it has fetched messages from the queue, it request
         // all the UserChannelInfo instances to send the messages to their
         // clients (users) which they are dedicated to.
109      public ServerMessageManager(ConcurrentLinkedQueue<SimpleTextMessage> messageQueue,
                                     Hashtable<String, UserChannelInfo> users){
110          this.messageQueue = messageQueue;
111          this.users = users;
112      }

113      public void run(){
114          System.out.println("ServerMessageManager is up, "
                                 + "waiting for incoming messages");
             // Polling is not the most efficient approaoch. Let's use it, though.
115          while(forever){
                 // Put into sleep so other processes can use some CPU time.
116              try{
117                  Thread.sleep(100);
118              }catch(Exception e){ }
                 // Process the messages in the queue by broadcasting them
                 // to all users (clients).
119              while(!messageQueue.isEmpty()){
                     // The message sent to users must be a SimpleTextMessage instance.
120                  SimpleTextMessage sm = messageQueue.poll();
                     // Send the message to other users.
121                  Enumeration<UserChannelInfo> all = users.elements();
122                  while(all.hasMoreElements()){
123                      UserChannelInfo user = all.nextElement();
124                      user.sendMessage(sm);
125                  }
126              }
127          }
128      }
129  }
```

There are a couple more concepts requiring extra explanation from the program above:

- Thread vs Runnable. In our first TCP program, we let class MessageManagerTCP extend

Thread. This means MessageManagerTCP is a subclass of Thread inheriting every available method and field from Thread, many of which our class does not need at all. Runnable, however, is an interface with only the method run() to be implemented. Implementing Runnable is certainly a cleaner approach than extending Thread. More importantly, Runnable is like a task while Thread acts like a task runner. It is a good programming practice to separate the task from the task runner, while a class extending Thread would make the class the task and the task runner at the same time. That is why in this program both UserChannelInfo and ServerMessageManager are implementing the Runnable interface.

- Code lines 17-18 and 28-29 demonstrate how threads are created based on Runnable objects. To let a thread run as an independent process, we must start it by calling its start() method.
- Letting a thread sleep for some time is important (line 117) as it allows other processes on the computer to get some CPU time.
- Polling is not the best practice for multithreading in Java. The wait-notify mechanism is more efficient. Polling is adopted in class `ServerMessageManager` because our blockchain system has no efficiency concerns.

We would like to have a graphic user interface (GUI) on the client side, therefore we are going to connect network programming with Java graphics. The client side program is illustrated below:

```
1   import java.awt.GridBagConstraints;
2   import java.awt.GridBagLayout;
3   import java.awt.Container;
4   import java.awt.Color;
5   import java.awt.event.KeyListener;
6   import java.awt.event.KeyEvent;
7   import javax.swing.JOptionPane;
8   import javax.swing.JFrame;
9   import javax.swing.JTextArea;
10  import javax.swing.JButton;
11  import javax.swing.JLabel;
12  import javax.swing.JScrollPane;
13  import javax.swing.ScrollPaneConstants;
14  import java.io.ObjectInputStream;
15  import java.io.ObjectOutputStream;
16  import java.io.IOException;
17  import java.net.Socket;

    // Use a Frame to be our GUI.
18  public class TestTCPClientFrame extends JFrame{
        // This is for user to enter text.
19      private JTextArea textInput;
        // Click this button to send text message.
20      private JButton sentButton;
        // For message board.
21      private JTextArea displayArea;
        // GridBagLayout is probably the most powerful layout in Java.
22      private GridBagLayout mgr = null;
23      private GridBagConstraints gcr = null;
        // Dedicated to receiving messages.
24      private MessageManagerTCP_x messenger;
        // Network communication IO.
25      private ObjectOutputStream out;
```

```
26          private ObjectInputStream in;

            // The constructor needs the user name and server IP.
27          public TestTCPClientFrame(String name, String ip) throws Exception{
28              super(name);
29              setUp();
                // Construct a socket connection.
30              Socket socket = new Socket(ip, 8888);
                // The output stream must be created before the input stream.
31              this.out = new ObjectOutputStream(socket.getOutputStream());
32              this.in = new ObjectInputStream(socket.getInputStream());
                // Must send the user name first.
33              this.sendMessage(name);
34              MessageManagerTCP_x messenger = new MessageManagerTCP_x(in, this.displayArea);
35              Thread t = new Thread(messenger);
36              t.start();
                // When window (Frame) is closed, we should close the network
                // connection if it has not been closed.
37              this.addWindowListener(new java.awt.event.WindowAdapter(){
38                  public void windowClosing(java.awt.event.WindowEvent e){
                        // Close the thread.
39                      try{
40                          messenger.close();
41                      }catch(Exception e1){}
                        // Let the server know that the user is leaving.
42                      try{
43                          sendMessage("END");
44                      }catch(Exception ee){}
45                      dispose();
46                      System.exit(2);
47                  }
48              });
49          }

            // This method is dedicated to sending messages.
50          protected void sendMessage(String mesg){
51              try{
52                  this.out.writeObject(mesg);
53              }catch(Exception e){
54                  e.printStackTrace();
55              }
56          }

            // Set up the GUI.
57          private void setUp(){
                // Specify the size of the frame.
58              this.setSize(500, 400);
                // Obtain the container of the frame. All graphic components are added
                // into the container.
59              Container c = getContentPane();
                // Make use of GridBagLayout.
60              mgr = new GridBagLayout();
                // Layout constraints are used to specify how graphic components
                // are arranged in the container (canvas).
61              gcr = new GridBagConstraints();
                // Let the container apply this constraints instance.
62              c.setLayout(mgr);
                // A label is read-only.
63              JLabel lblInput = new JLabel("Message Board");
```

```
64                  // Make use of a textarea as the message board.
                    this.displayArea = new JTextArea(50, 100);
                    // For entering text messages.
65                  this.textInput = new JTextArea(5, 100);
66                  this.sentButton = new JButton("Click me or hit enter to send the message below");
                    // Define what the program will do when the button is clicked: sending a message.
67                  this.sentButton.addActionListener(new java.awt.event.ActionListener(){
68                      public void actionPerformed(java.awt.event.ActionEvent e){
69                          try{
70                              sendMessage(textInput.getText());
71                          }catch(Exception e2){
72                              System.out.println("Error: " + e2.getMessage());
73                          }
                            // After sending message, reset the message-entering box.
74                          textInput.setText("");
75                      }
76                  });

77                  this.gcr.fill = GridBagConstraints.BOTH;
78                  this.gcr.weightx = 1;
79                  this.gcr.weighty = 0.0;
80                  this.gcr.gridx = 0;
81                  this.gcr.gridy = 0;
82                  this.gcr.gridwidth = 1;
83                  this.gcr.gridheight = 1;
84                  this.mgr.setConstraints(lblInput, this.gcr);
85                  c.add(lblInput);

86                  this.gcr.weighty = 0.9;
87                  this.gcr.gridx = 0;
88                  this.gcr.gridy = 1;
89                  this.gcr.gridheight = 9;
                    // Make the textarea vertically scrollable.
90                  JScrollPane scroll = new JScrollPane(this.displayArea);
91                  scroll.setVerticalScrollBarPolicy(ScrollPaneConstants.VERTICAL_SCROLLBAR_ALWAYS);
92                  scroll.setHorizontalScrollBarPolicy(
                                    ScrollPaneConstants.HORIZONTAL_SCROLLBAR_NEVER);
93                  this.mgr.setConstraints(scroll, this.gcr);
                    // Add the scroll into the container.
94                  c.add(scroll);
                    // Make the message board read-only.
95                  this.displayArea.setEditable(false);
96                  this.displayArea.setBackground(Color.LIGHT_GRAY);

97                  this.gcr.weighty = 0.0;
98                  this.gcr.gridx = 0;
99                  this.gcr.gridy = 11;
100                 this.gcr.gridheight = 1;
101                 this.mgr.setConstraints(this.sentButton, this.gcr);
102                 c.add(this.sentButton);

103                 this.gcr.weighty = 0.1;
104                 this.gcr.gridx = 0;
105                 this.gcr.gridy = 12;
106                 this.gcr.gridheight = 2;
107                 JScrollPane scroll2 = new JScrollPane(this.textInput);
108                 scroll2.setVerticalScrollBarPolicy(
                                    ScrollPaneConstants.VERTICAL_SCROLLBAR_AS_NEEDED);
109                 scroll2.setHorizontalScrollBarPolicy(
```

```
                            ScrollPaneConstants.HORIZONTAL_SCROLLBAR_NEVER);
110         this.mgr.setConstraints(scroll2, this.gcr);
111         c.add(scroll2);
            // Add a key listener to the textarea such that hitting Enter can
            // also send the message, while CTRL + Enter or Shift + Enter insert
            // a line separator.
112         this.textInput.addKeyListener(new KeyListener(){
113             public void keyTyped(KeyEvent e) {}
114             public void keyReleased(KeyEvent e) {}
115             public void keyPressed(KeyEvent e) {
116                 int key = e.getKeyCode();
117                 if (key == KeyEvent.VK_ENTER) {
                        // Allow using shift + Enter or control + Enter to get a
                        // line separator.
118                     if(e.isShiftDown() || e.isControlDown()){
119                         textInput.append(System.getProperty("line.separator"));
120                     }else{
121                         try{
122                             sendMessage(textInput.getText());
123                         }catch(Exception e2){
124                             System.out.println("Error: " + e2.getMessage());
125                             throw new RuntimeException(e2);
126                         }
                        // Consume the Enter so that the cursor will stay
                        // at the beginning.
127                     e.consume();
128                     textInput.setText("");
129                     }
130                 }
131             }
132         });
133         this.setVisible(true);
134     }

        // The main method.
135     public static void main(String[] args){
136         String name = JOptionPane.showInputDialog(
                                "Please enter your unique name. Thanks:");
137         String ip = JOptionPane.showInputDialog(
                                "Please enter the server IP address here:");
            // If no valid input, assume it is the localhost.
138         if(ip.length() < 5){
139             ip = "localhost";
140         }
141         TestTCPClientFrame clientFrame = null;
            // The following try-catch clause makes sure when the network
            // connection is not successful, the GUI is disposed.
142         try{
143             clientFrame= new TestTCPClientFrame(name, ip);
144         }catch(Exception e){
145             System.exit(2);
146         }
147         clientFrame.setVisible(true);
148     }
149 }

    // An inner class dedicated to message receiving.
    // Please note that this class implements Runnable instead of extending Thread.
150 class MessageManagerTCP_x implements Runnable {
```

```
151        private ObjectInputStream in;
152        private boolean forever = true;
153        private JTextArea pane;
154        private int errors = 0;
155        public MessageManagerTCP_x(ObjectInputStream in,  JTextArea pane) throws IOException {
156            this.in= in;
157            this.pane = pane;
158        }

           // When this method is called, the instance variable forever is set to be false.
           // This gives the thread a chance to exit from the loop in the method run().
159        public void close(){
160            forever = false;
161        }

           // Implement the run() method.
162        public void run(){
163            System.out.println("Message manager is up ...");
164            while(forever){
165                try{
                       // This statement will block the execution until a message
                       // is received.
166                    SimpleTextMessage m = (SimpleTextMessage)(this.in.readObject());
                       // Upon receiving an END message, exit from the loop.
167                    if(m.getMessage().startsWith("END")){
168                        forever = false;
169                    }else{
                           // Properly display the message.
170                        pane.append(m.getSenderName() + "] " + m.getMessage() + "\n");
171                        pane.setCaretPosition(pane.getText().length());
172                    }
173                }catch(Exception e){
174                    errors++;
175                    System.out.println("Error: This is only for text messaging.");
176                    e.printStackTrace();
                       // If exceptions happened too many times, let's quit.
177                    if(errors >= 5){
178                        forever = false;
179                    }
180                }
181            }
182            System.out.println("message manager retired");
183            System.exit(1);
184        }
185    }
```

To test the TCP multiple-users chat program coded above, please take the following steps:
1) Compile the TestTCPServerCenter and TestTCPClientFrame classes.
2) Execute the TestTCPServerCenter on a computer A.
3) Copy and paste the programs to multiple computers and execute the TestTCPClientFrame program on those computers.
4) Start chatting with others.

And that concludes yet another chapter. You can download the programs from chapter 7 at: https://github.com/hhohho/Learning-Blockchain-in-Java-Edition-2. In the next chapter we will combine the knowledge learned in chapters 6 and 7 so as to develop a blockchain system that can run seamlessly across multiple computers.

# 8 DISTRIBUTED BLOCKCHAIN SYSTEM

This will be a relatively long chapter because we will be assembling our distributed blockchain system. We will start with programs from chapter 6, so please copy all of them into a directory (folder) for chapter 8. If you are using Eclipse or other IDE tools, please create a Java project named chapter8 and import the chapter 6 source codes. All chapter 6 and chapter 8 programs can be found and downloaded from: https://github.com/hhohho/Learning-Blockchain-in-Java-Edition-2.

In an ideal peer-to-peer (P2P) network, all nodes are equal. This is why nodes are also called peers. In reality, peers are not absolutely equal. Some peers carry more functions, such as relaying network traffics. The crucial concept of P2P is to decentralization, i.e. there should not be a central server that controls everything. Two peers may not connect to each other directly, but their connection is not gorverned by a central server. In an ideal P2P environment, each peer is a server and a client. Individuals can share their resources as a "server" and access the resources of others as a "client". Hence, the concepts of "server" and "client" are negligible and unnecessary in P2P networks. Instead, the proper terminologies would be "outgoing/outbound" connections and "incoming/inbound" connections. Depending on the architecture and implementation of the P2P network, an incoming connection could be a TCP client socket connection, or it could be the responding socket connection from the server socket. The latter choice is not common, however.

Bitcoin network is built upon a collection of nodes running the bitcoin P2P protocol. These peer nodes maintain the network routing function. Each node is supposed to have eight outgoing connections and can accept around one hundred incoming connections. These connections are in constant revision because nodes can go online or offline at any time. These nodes and their connections make up the "backbone" of bitcoin, but the extended bitcoin network also involves nodes running the P2P protocol and other specialized protocols.

Bitcoin P2P protocol is very sophisticated, so much so that for demonstration purposes, we will not be simulating a real P2P protocol. We will, however, in the next chapter, develop a simple but completely decentralized P2P network. In this chapter, instead, we are going to adopt the star network model shown in Figure 10 in chapter 7. Once we understand how a blockchain system can be implemented via the network star model, we can then start implementing our P2P network.

The core of the star model is the server. Our server starts with two components: a genesis miner and a message routing service provider. The genesis miner begins by constructing a genesis block and jumpstarting the blockchain. Having formed the genesis blockchain, the genesis miner hands it over to the message routing service provider and ceases direct contact. From now on, the genesis miner behaves like any other wallet, forming a normal network connection with the message routing service provider. Certainly, by now the message routing service provider becomes the only component in the server. The message routing service provider (or just message service provider for short) is in charge of managing all incoming messages. It is composed of a network server, a collection of network connections and a message task manager. After setting up, the genesis miner has an additional task of providing sign-in bonuses for a number of wallets. In our simulation, we need wallets to have funds to initiate transactions, and the genesis miner will provide some wallets with initial sign-in bonuses to get things started. The genesis miner will also mine a few blocks so as to make sure that the blockchain is functional. Once the number of wallets and miners reach a certain quota, the genesis miner will shut down and leave the blockchain system in the hands of miners. This simulates bitcoin's origins when Satoshi Nakamoto quit and left bitcoin after mining a number of blocks.

The message service provider is very similar to the TestTCPServerCenter class explained in chapter 7. The primary role of the message service provider is to route requests and responses from participating wallets. Its second role is to provide every wallet a sign-in genesis blockchain containing only the genesis block. This guarantees that every wallet's blockchain is built upon the genesis block. To fulfill its secondary function, the message service provider must be synchronized with the genesis miner in the beginning so that it can fetch the genesis block directly. The message service provider also has to be fully functional and running before the first wallet – the genesis miner – attempts a network connection. Every node in this blockchain system is either a wallet or a miner and each connects to the message service provider through the network. The architecture of our blockchain application system can be explained by Figure 11.

Except for the genesis miner, each wallet (remember, miners are also wallets) has three major components: an agent dedicated to network connection, a task manager dedicated to processing messages, and a GUI that facilitates contact between the user and the connection agent or the message task manager. Both the network connection agent and the message processing task manager are independent working threads.

With the aforementioned system architecture in mind, let's proceed by developing our blockchain system step-by-step. The very first step is to define what messages should be available in our blockchain system. For a blockchain with minimum functionalities, the network messages should include:
- Private and broadcast chat messages.
- Block broadcast messages (broadcast a mined block).
- Transaction broadcast messages (broadcast a transaction).
- Private blockchain messages upon request.

- Private messages paging available participants (addresses).
- Private messages containing available addresses upon request.
- Private messages asking to close network connection.

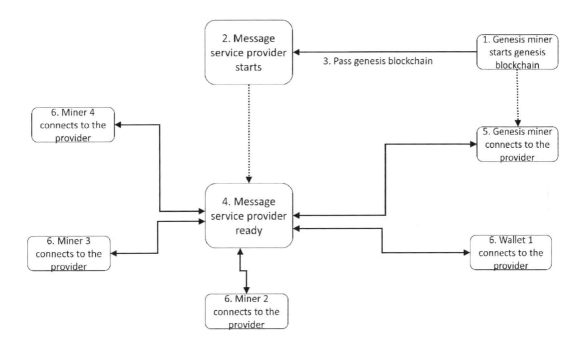

Figure 11  The architecture of the book's blockchain application system. 1. Genesis miner starts by generating the genesis blockchain; 2. Message service provider starts; 3. Message service provider fetches the genesis blockchain from the genesis miner directly; 4. Message service provider is ready to accept connections; 5. Genesis miner is the first to connect to the service provider via network; 6. All other wallets connect to the service provider through the network.

Ideally, all messages should be encrypted and password-protected. Chapter 3 explained how to encrypt messages via the AES algorithm. The general method consists of utilizing public and private key technology so multiple nodes can agree on an AES secret key, and then applying a password-based AES algorithm to encrypt all messages. The most challenging part is to make the key dynamic. It must keep evolving the way passwords should be changed from time to time, so as not to compromise security. Given that there are likely a large number of nodes, synchronizing the key updating process seamlessly across the entire network can be a challenge. For simplicity's sake, we will not encrypt messages; however, messages will be signed. The following Java classes represent all the different types of messages used in the basic blockchain system we are developing. Note that all messages must implement the java.io.Serializable interface because they need to be serialized into bytes and then deserialized from bytes back into objects during network transportation.

```
1    public abstract class Message implements java.io.Serializable{
2        private static final long serialVersionUID = 1L;
3        public static final int ID = 0;
         // The following defines different types of messages.
4        public static final int TEXT_BROADCAST = 1;
5        public static final int TEXT_PRIVATE = 2;
6        public static final int TRANSACTION_BROADCAST = 10;
7        public static final int BLOCK_BROADCAST = 20;
8        public static final int BLOCK_PRIVATE = 21;
9        public static final int BLOCK_ASK_PRIVATE = 22;
10       public static final int BLOCK_ASK_BROADCAST = 23;
11       public static final int BLOCKCHAIN_BROADCAST = 3;
12       public static final int BLOCKCHAIN_PRIVATE = 31;
13       public static final int BLOCKCHAIN_ASK_BROADCAST = 33;
14       public static final int ADDRESS_BROADCAST = 4;
15       public static final int ADDRESS_PRIVATE = 41;
         // A text string used to testify if the message transportation is tampered.
16       public static final String JCOIN_MESSAGE = "This package is from mdsky.";
17       public abstract int getMessageType();
         // A text phrase asking the server to close the connection.
18       public static final String TEXT_CLOSE = "CLOSE_me";
19       public static final String TEXT_ASK_ADDRESSES = "TEXT_QUERY_ADDRESSES";
         // The message body.
20       public abstract Object getMessageBody();
         // To differentiate between broadcast and private messages.
21       public abstract boolean isForBroadcast();
22   }
```

All messages in this system are a subclass of the Message class. They all need to implement the three abstract methods: getMessageType(), getMessageBody() and isForBroadcast(). The Message class is an abstract class, meaning objects cannot be directly created from it, and instead they can only be constructed from its subclasses. The Message class is to define a standard applying to all message types used within the system. You may be wondering why we select the Java abstract class instead of the Java interface. Both the abstract class and the interface allow polymorphisms in object-oriented programming. However, an interface only defines methods that are to be implemented but has no object states or other implemented methods. An abstract class, on the other hand, is a perfect choice for the super class which is partially completed except for the part that different subclasses can have different implementations. This is the case for our Message class. The following class, MessageSigned, extends Message to add one another function that examines if a message is valid.

```
public abstract class MessageSigned extends Message{
    private static final long serialVersionUID = 1L;
    public abstract boolean isValid();
}
```

The following class, MessageID, is used to send the name and public key of a wallet to the message service provider. In blockchain, a wallet's name does not appear in a transaction or a block. However, for demonstration purposes, it is easier to follow along with names rather than public keys which are "meaningless" codes at best. In this system, we associate each public key with a name. Thus, we need an additional KeyNamePair class which is presented below:

```
1     import java.security.PublicKey;
2     public class KeyNamePair implements java.io.Serializable {
3         private static final long serialVersionUID = 1L;
4         private PublicKey key;
5         private String name;
6         public KeyNamePair(PublicKey key, String name){
7             this.key = key;
8             this.name = name;
9         }

10        public String getName(){
11            return this.name;
12        }

13        public PublicKey getKey(){
14            return this.key;
15        }
16    }
```

The following codes list the class MessageID:

```
1     import java.security.PrivateKey;
2     import java.security.PublicKey;
3     public class MessageID extends MessageSigned {
4         private static final long serialVersionUID = 1L;
5         private String info = null;
6         private byte[] signature = null;
7         private PublicKey sender = null;
8         private String name = null;
9         public MessageID(PrivateKey pk, PublicKey sender, String name){
10            this.info = Message.JCOIN_MESSAGE;
11            signature = UtilityMethods.generateSignature(pk, this.info);
12            this.sender = sender;
13            this.name = name;
14        }

15        public String getMessageBody(){
16            return this.info;
17        }

18        public boolean isValid(){
19            return UtilityMethods.verifySignature(this.getPublicKey(), signature, this.info);
20        }

21        public int getMessageType(){
22            return Message.ID;
23        }

24        protected PublicKey getPublicKey() {
25            return this.sender;
26        }

27        public boolean isForBroadcast(){
28            return false;
29        }

30        public String getName(){
31            return this.name;
```

```
32          }

33          public KeyNamePair getKeyNamePair(){
34              KeyNamePair kp = new KeyNamePair(this.getPublicKey(), this.getName());
35              return kp;
36          }
37      }
```

For private chat, a class named MessageTextPrivate is defined. When the message service provider forwards a private chat message, it needs to know who is the receiver, and the receiver needs to know the identity of the sender. Therefore, MessageTextPrivate must include the following information: the text message, the sender's public key and name, and the receiver's public key.

```
1    import java.security.PrivateKey;
2    import java.security.PublicKey;
3    public class MessageTextPrivate extends MessageSigned{
4        private static final long serialVersionUID = 1L;
5        private String info = null;
6        private byte[] signature = null;
7        private PublicKey senderKey = null;
8        private String senderName;
9        private PublicKey receiver = null;

10       public MessageTextPrivate(String text, PrivateKey prikey,
                 PublicKey senderKey, String senderName, PublicKey receiver){
11           this.info = text;
12           signature = UtilityMethods.generateSignature(prikey, this.info);
13           this.senderKey = senderKey;
14           this.receiver = receiver;
15           this.senderName = senderName;
16       }

17       public String getMessageBody(){
18           return this.info;
19       }

20       public boolean isValid(){
21           return UtilityMethods.verifySignature(senderKey, signature, this.info);
22       }

23       public int getMessageType(){
24           return Message.TEXT_PRIVATE;
25       }

26       public PublicKey getReceiver(){
27           return this.receiver;
28       }

29       public PublicKey getSenderKey(){
30           return this.senderKey;
31       }

32       public String getSenderName(){
33           return this.senderName;
34       }

35       public KeyNamePair getSenderKeyNamePair(){
```

```
36            return new KeyNamePair(this.getSenderKey(), this.senderName);
37        }

38        public boolean isForBroadcast(){
39            return false;
40        }
41    }
```

The class MessageTextBroadcast is for public chat. It is similar to the MessageTextPrivate class, but since MessageTextBroadcast is for public chat, it only needs to be broadcast. Therefore, the method isForBroadcast() returns true.

```
1     import java.security.PublicKey;
2     import java.security.PrivateKey;
3     public class MessageTextBroadcast extends MessageSigned {
4         private static final long serialVersionUID = 1L;
5         private String info = null;
6         private byte[] signature = null;
7         private PublicKey pubkey = null;
8         private String name = null;

9         public MessageTextBroadcast(String text, PrivateKey key,
                                       PublicKey pubkey, String name){
10            this.info = text;
11            this.signature = UtilityMethods.generateSignature(key, text);
12            this.pubkey = pubkey;
13            this.name = name;
14        }

15        public String getMessageBody(){
16            return this.info;
17        }

18        public boolean isValid(){
19            return UtilityMethods.verifySignature(this.pubkey, this.signature, this.info);
20        }

21        public int getMessageType(){
22            return Message.TEXT_BROADCAST;
23        }

24        public boolean isForBroadcast(){
25            return true;
26        }

27        public PublicKey getSenderKey(){
28            return this.pubkey;
29        }

30        public String getSenderName(){
31            return this.name;
32        }
33    }
```

Every node in the blockchain system is a wallet. When a wallet starts a transaction, this transaction is broadcast to all other nodes as a public message. The class MessageTransactionBroadcast is listed as the following:

```
1    public class MessageTransactionBroadcast extends Message {
2         private static final long serialVersionUID = 1L;
3         private Transaction transaction = null;
4         public MessageTransactionBroadcast(Transaction transaction){
5              this.transaction = transaction;
6         }
7         public int getMessageType(){
8              return Message.TRANSACTION_BROADCAST;
9         }
10        public Transaction getMessageBody(){
11             return this.transaction;
12        }
13        public boolean isForBroadcast(){
14             return true;
15        }
16   }
```

A transaction message does not need to be signed because the transaction itself is signed and it is broadcast publicly across the network. The same logic applies to block messages.

```
1    public class MessageBlockBroadcast extends Message{
2         private static final long serialVersionUID = 1L;
3         private Block block = null;
4         public MessageBlockBroadcast(Block block){
5              this.block = block;
6         }
7         public int getMessageType(){
8              return Message.BLOCK_BROADCAST;
9         }
10        public Block getMessageBody(){
11             return this.block;
12        }
13        public boolean isForBroadcast(){
14             return true;
15        }
16   }
```

The blockchain, the ledger itself, should not be broadcast, but only sent to wallets who request it. Broadcasting a blockchain is actually very inefficient and difficult because the chain can grow to fairly large sizes. Though this book provides a message for broadcasting a blockchain, broadcasting a blockchain does not happen in this implementation at all. The two classes for blockchain messages are listed together below:

```
1    import java.security.PublicKey;
2    public class MessageBlockchainPrivate extends Message implements java.io.Serializable{
3         private static final long serialVersionUID = 1L;
```

```
4         private Blockchain ledger = null;
5         private PublicKey sender = null;
6         private PublicKey receiver = null;
7         private int initialSize = 0;

8         public MessageBlockchainPrivate(Blockchain ledger, PublicKey sender, PublicKey receiver){
9             this.ledger = ledger;
10            this.receiver = receiver;
11            this.sender = sender;
12            this.initialSize = this.ledger.size();
13        }

14        public int getInfoSize(){
15            return this.initialSize;
16        }

17        public int getMessageType(){
18            return Message.BLOCKCHAIN_PRIVATE;
19        }

20        public PublicKey getReceiver(){
21            return this.receiver;
22        }

23        public Blockchain getMessageBody(){
24            return this.ledger;
25        }

26        public boolean isForBroadcast(){
27            return false;
28        }

29        public PublicKey getSender(){
30            return this.sender;
31        }
32    }


1     import java.security.PublicKey;
2     public class MessageBlockchainBroadcast extends Message{
3         private static final long serialVersionUID = 1L;
4         private Blockchain ledger = null;
5         private PublicKey sender = null;
6         private int initialSize = 0;

7         public MessageBlockchainBroadcast(Blockchain ledger, PublicKey sender){
8             this.ledger = ledger;
9             this.sender = sender;
10            this.initialSize = ledger.size();
11        }

12        public int getInfoSize(){
13            return this.initialSize;
14        }

15        public int getMessageType(){
16            return Message.BLOCKCHAIN_BROADCAST;
17        }
```

```
18      public Blockchain getMessageBody(){
19          return this.ledger;
20      }

21      public boolean isForBroadcast(){
22          return true;
23      }

24      public PublicKey getSender(){
25          return this.sender;
26      }
27  }
```

The class MessageBlockchainPrivate has an instance variable named initialSize. This variable is added to double check if the blockchain is truncated in the process of transportation. Its presence is not mandatory, but doesn't hurt either.

The MessageAskForBlockchainBroadcast message is used when a wallet needs to update its local blockchain. When a wallet returns to the blockchain system after a substantial hiatus, the first thing it should do is to update its blockchain copy. This message is a broadcast message sent to other miners so someone can send over their local copies of the blockchain.

```
1   import java.security.PrivateKey;
2   import java.security.PublicKey;
3   public class MessageAskForBlockchainBroadcast extends MessageTextBroadcast{
4       private static final long serialVersionUID = 1L;
5       public MessageAskForBlockchainBroadcast(String text, PrivateKey prikey,
                                                PublicKey sender, String name){
6           super(text, prikey, sender, name);
7       }

8       public int getMessageType(){
9           return Message.BLOCKCHAIN_ASK_BROADCAST;
10      }
11  }
```

The last message type in this book is MessageAddressPrivate. A wallet that wants a list of all participating wallets (including the genesis miner) in the blockchain system can send a private query for this message. In most cases this action is not necessary. This is because each wallet is constantly and automatically updating its local wallet list whenever it receives a message from other wallets.

```
1   import java.util.ArrayList;
2   public class MessageAddressPrivate extends Message {
3       private static final long serialVersionUID = 1L;
4       private ArrayList<KeyNamePair> addresses;
5       public MessageAddressPrivate(ArrayList<KeyNamePair> addresses){
6           this.addresses = addresses;
7       }

8       public int getMessageType(){
9           return Message.ADDRESS_PRIVATE;
10      }
```

```
11      public ArrayList<KeyNamePair> getMessageBody(){
12          return this.addresses;
13      }
14      public boolean isForBroadcast(){
15          return false;
16      }
17  }
```

A wallet node is composed of three classes: WalletSimulator for the graphic user interface (GUI), WalletConnectionAgent for network connection including message receiving and sending, and WalletMessageTaskManager that processes incoming messages including updating local blockchain and displaying chat messages. The GUI accepts user instructions to display wallet balances and blockchain content, start transactions, update local wallet list and blockchain, and communicate with other wallets via public or private message channels.

To properly display blockchain content on GUI, we need to update our UtilityMethods class once again. We already have methods that display blockchain content through standard output via the PrintStream class. Those methods do not allow displaying blockchain content on GUI, however. To mend that, we need to store blockchain content as string by means of the Java StringBuilder class. Strings have the advantage and flexibility to be displayed in various ways. The following methods are similar to the existing content-displaying methods except that they store blockchain content in a StringBuilder object. These methods present another example of how software is gradually improved.

```
1   public static void displayTab(StringBuilder out, int level, String s){
2       for(int i=0; i<level; i++){
3           out.append("\t");
4       }
5       out.append(s + System.getProperty("line.separator"));
6   }

7   public static void displayUTXO(UTXO ux, StringBuilder out, int level){
8       displayTab(out, level, "fund: " + ux.getFundTransferred()
                + ", receiver: " + UtilityMethods.getKeyString(ux.getReceiver()));
9   }

10  public static void displayTransaction(Transaction T, StringBuilder out, int level) {
11      displayTab(out, level, "Transaction{");
12      displayTab(out, level + 1, "ID: " + T.getHashID());
13      displayTab(out, level + 1, "sender: " + UtilityMethods.getKeyString(T.getSender()));
14      displayTab(out, level + 1, "fundToBeTransferred total: " + T.getTotalFundToTransfer());
15      displayTab(out, level + 1, "Input:");
16      for(int i=0; i<T.getNumberOfInputUTXOs(); i++){
17          UTXO ui = T.getInputUTXO(i);
18          displayUTXO(ui, out, level + 2);
19      }
20      displayTab(out, level+1, "Output:");
21      for(int i=0; i<T.getNumberOfOutputUTXOs() - 1; i++){
22          UTXO ut = T.getOuputUTXO(i);
23          displayUTXO(ut, out, level+2);
24      }
25      UTXO change = T.getOuputUTXO(T.getNumberOfOutputUTXOs()-1);
26      displayTab(out, level + 2, "change: " + change.getFundTransferred());
27      displayTab(out, level + 1, "transaction fee: " + Transaction.TRANSACTION_FEE);
```

```java
28          boolean b = T.verifySignature();
29          displayTab(out, level + 1, "signature verification: " + b);
30          displayTab(out, level, "}");
31      }

32      public static void displayBlockchain(Blockchain ledger, StringBuilder out, int level){
33          displayTab(out, level, "Blockchain{ number of blocks: " + ledger.size());
34          for(int i=0; i<ledger.size(); i++) {
35              Block block = ledger.getBlock(i);
36              displayBlock(block, out, level+1);
37          }
38          displayTab(out, level,"}");
39      }

40      public static void displayBlock(Block block, StringBuilder out, int level){
41          displayTab(out, level, "Block{");
42          displayTab(out, level, "\tID: " + block.getHashID());
43          for(int i=0; i<block.getTotalNumberOfTransactions(); i++) {
44              displayTransaction(block.getTransaction(i), out, level+1);
45          }
            // Display the reward transaction.
46          if(block.getRewardTransaction() != null) {
47              displayTab(out, level, "\tReward Transaction:");
48              displayTransaction(block.getRewardTransaction(), out, level + 1);
49          }
50          displayTab(out, level, "}");
51      }

52      public static int guaranteeIntegerInputByScanner(java.util.Scanner in,
                                                        int lowerBound, int upperBound){
53          int x = -1;
54          try{
55              x = in.nextInt();
56          }catch(java.util.InputMismatchException ee){
57              x = lowerBound - 1;
58          }
59          while(x < lowerBound || x > upperBound){
60              System.out.println("You selected " + x
                        + ", please only enter an integer beteween " + lowerBound
                        + " and " + upperBound + " inclusively");
61              try{
62                  x = in.nextInt();
63              }catch(java.util.InputMismatchException e){
64                  in.nextLine();
65                  x = lowerBound-1;
66              }
67          }
            // Digest the "Enter" so that the scanner object can read a text input later.
68          in.nextLine();
69          return x;
70      }
```

Code lines 52-70 delineate the method `guaranteeIntegerInputByScanner()` which benefits from some additional explanation. Its purpose is to guarantee that an integer in a defined range is entered as an input. If an invalid input is given, the method will insist on asking for a valid input. With this method, it is assured that no exception or runtime error will occur when standard input is entered.

In chapter 7, we mentioned that some settings should be placed in a configuration file or something similar for easy configuration. It is good practice to have central control over certain application settings and to keep a log message manager to supervise log messages displayed through standard output. So far, settings have all been hardcoded. For demonstration purposes, let's control some settings through our Configuration class.

```java
    public final class Configuration{
         private static String KEY_LOCATION = "keys";
         public static final String keyLocation(){
              return Configuration.KEY_LOCATION;
         }

         private static String HASH_ALGORITHM = "SHA-256";
         public static final String hashAlgorithm(){
              return Configuration.HASH_ALGORITHM;
         }

         private static final String SIGNATURE_ALGORITHM = "SHA256withRSA";
         public static final String signatureAlgorithm(){
              return Configuration.SIGNATURE_ALGORITHM;
         }

         private static final String KEYPAIR_ALGORITHM = "RSA";
         public static final String keyPairAlgorithm(){
              return Configuration.KEYPAIR_ALGORITHM;
         }

         private static final int PORT = 1117;
         public static final int networkPort(){
              return Configuration.PORT;
         }

         private static final int BLOCK_MINING_DIFFICULTY_LEVEL = 20;
         public static final int blockMiningDifficultyLevel(){
              return Configuration.BLOCK_MINING_DIFFICULTY_LEVEL;
         }
    }
```

When downloading chapter 8 programs, be aware that certain classes have already been modified to make use of this Configuration class, though these changes were not explicitly walked through. For example, the Wallet class has been slightly modified to make use of the Configuration class.

The class WalletConnectionAgent controls a wallet's network connection. It is responsible for:
1) constructing a network connection between the wallet and the message service provider;
2) accepting messages from the message service provider and placing them in a queue for the WalletMessageTaskManager to process;
3) sending messages out;
4) properly closing the network connection.

Please examine the following codes of the WalletConnectionAgent class:

```
1    import java.security.PublicKey;
2    import java.io.ObjectOutputStream;
```

```java
3     import java.io.ObjectInputStream;
4     import java.util.ArrayList;
5     import java.util.Hashtable;
6     import java.util.Iterator;
7     import java.util.concurrent.ConcurrentLinkedQueue;
8     import java.net.Socket;

9     public class WalletConnectionAgent implements Runnable {
10        private Wallet wallet;
11        private Socket socket;
12        private ObjectInputStream in;
13        private ObjectOutputStream out;
          // The message service provider has a pair of public and private key.
          // The message service provider is represented by its public key, too.
14        private PublicKey serverAddress;
          // The queue to store unprocessed messages.
15        private ConcurrentLinkedQueue<Message> messageQueue =
                              new ConcurrentLinkedQueue<Message>();
          // The local list of wallets in the system is stored in a Hashtable.
16        private Hashtable<String, KeyNamePair> allAddresses =
                              new Hashtable<String, KeyNamePair>();
17        private boolean forever = true;
18        public final long sleepTime = 100;
          // The constructor.
19        public WalletConnectionAgent(String host, int port, Wallet wallet){
20            this.wallet = wallet;
21            System.out.println("Begin to create agent for network communication");
22            try{
23                socket = new Socket(host, port);
24                out = new ObjectOutputStream(socket.getOutputStream());
25                in = new ObjectInputStream(socket.getInputStream());
                  // The agent gets a MessageForID from the message service provider.
26                MessageID fromServer = (MessageID)in.readObject();
                  // Make sure that the message is in good standing.
27                if(fromServer.isValid()){
28                    this.serverAddress = fromServer.getPublicKey();
29                }else{
30                    throw new Exception("MessageID from service provider is invalid.");
31                }
                  // If everything works well, the agent sends the server a responding
                  // MessageForID because the server is waiting for a MessageForID.
32                System.out.println("obtained server address and stored it, "
                              + "now sending wallet public key to server");
33                System.out.println("name=" + this.wallet.getName());
34                MessageID mid = new MessageID(this.wallet.getPrivateKey(),
                              this.wallet.getPublicKey(), this.wallet.getName());
35                out.writeObject(mid);
                  // Expecting for the genesis blockchain.
36                MessageBlockchainPrivate mbcp = (MessageBlockchainPrivate)in.readObject();
37                this.wallet.setLocalLedger(mbcp.getMessageBody());
38                System.out.println("The genesis block chain set, everything ready ...");
39            }catch(Exception e){
40                System.out.println("WalletConnectionAgent: creation failed "
                              + "because|" + e.getMessage());
41                System.out.println("Please restart");
42                System.exit(1);
43            }
44        }
```

```
              // Must implement this method to include all tasks this class is meant to accomplish.
45            public void run(){
46                try{
47                    Thread.sleep(this.sleepTime);
48                }catch(Exception er){
                  // Do nothing.
49                }
50                while(forever){
51                    try{
                          // Accepts a message and then stores it in the queue.
52                        Message m = (Message)in.readObject();
53                        this.messageQueue.add(m);
54                        Thread.sleep(this.sleepTime);
55                    }catch(Exception e){
56                        forever = false;
57                    }
58                }
59            }

              // Synchronize this method so that a message is sent out one by one.
60            public synchronized boolean sendMessage(Message m){
                  // Double ensure that no null message is sent.
61                if(m == null){
62                    System.out.println("message is null, cannot send");
63                    return false;
64                }
65                try{
66                    this.out.writeObject(m);
67                    return true;
68                }catch(Exception e){
69                    System.out.println("failed to send message [" + e.getMessage());
70                    return false;
71                }
72            }

              // Actively close this connection, i.e. the wallet initiates
              // the closing of this connection.
73            public void activeClose(){
74                MessageTextPrivate mc = new MessageTextPrivate(Message.TEXT_CLOSE,
                                  this.wallet.getPrivateKey(),this.wallet.getPublicKey(),
                                  this.wallet.getName(), this.getServerAddress());
75                this.sendMessage(mc);
76                try{
77                    Thread.sleep(this.sleepTime);
78                }catch(Exception ee){
                      // Do nothing.
79                }
80                this.close();
81            }

              // A normal closing action.
82            public void close(){
83                this.forever = false;
84                try{
85                    this.in.close();
86                    this.out.close();
87                }catch(Exception e){
                      // Do nothing.
88                }
```

```java
89          }

            // Obtain the list of wallets stored locally.
90          public ArrayList<KeyNamePair> getAllStoredAddresses(){
91              Iterator<KeyNamePair> E = this.allAddresses.values().iterator();
92              ArrayList<KeyNamePair> A = new ArrayList<KeyNamePair>();
93              while(E.hasNext()){
94                  A.add(E.next());
95              }
96              return A;
97          }

            // Add one address into the local list.
98          public void addAddress(KeyNamePair address){
99              this.allAddresses.put(UtilityMethods.getKeyString(address.getKey()), address);
100         }

            // Find the matched name based on a public key. If not found, return the address.
101         public String getNameFromAddress(PublicKey key){
102             if(key.equals(this.wallet.getPublicKey())){
103                 return this.wallet.getName();
104             }
105             String address = UtilityMethods.getKeyString(key);
106             KeyNamePair kp = this.allAddresses.get(address);
107             if(kp != null){
108                 return kp.getName();
109             }else{
110                 return address;
111             }
112         }

            // Return the server's address. Please remember that the server is
            // represented by its public key, too.
113         public PublicKey getServerAddress(){
114             return this.serverAddress;
115         }

            // Fetch the message queue.
116         protected ConcurrentLinkedQueue<Message> getMessageQueue(){
117             return this.messageQueue;
118         }

            // Initiate a transaction, prepare and send it.
119         protected boolean sendTransaction(PublicKey receiver, double fundToTransfer){
120             Transaction T = this.wallet.transferFund(receiver, fundToTransfer);
121             if(T != null && T.verifySignature()){
122                 MessageTransactionBroadcast m = new MessageTransactionBroadcast(T);
123                 this.sendMessage(m);
124                 return true;
125             }
126             return false;
127         }

            // Send a private chat message to a receiver.
128         protected boolean sendPrivateMessage(PublicKey receiver, String text){
129             MessageTextPrivate m = new MessageTextPrivate(text,
                        this.wallet.getPrivateKey(), this.wallet.getPublicKey(),
                        this.wallet.getName(), receiver);
130             this.sendMessage(m);
```

```
131                return true;
132            }
133    }
```

The WalletMessageTaskManager's major task is to poll the queue for available messages. If messages exist, the task manager will process them based on the message types. There is a method written specifically for every message type except for MessageBlockchainBroadcast. The reason is that WalletMessageTaskManager is a super class with two subclasses: MinerMessageTaskManager and MinerGenesisMessageTaskManager. These two subclasses need to take different actions upon some messages, which require them to override corresponding methods.

```
1    import java.util.ArrayList;
2    import java.util.concurrent.ConcurrentLinkedQueue;
3    import java.util.HashMap;

4    public class WalletMessageTaskManager implements Runnable{
5        private boolean forever = true;
6        private WalletConnectionAgent agent;
7        private Wallet wallet;
8        private ConcurrentLinkedQueue<Message> messageQueue;
9        private HashMap<String, String> thankYouTransactions = new HashMap<String, String>();
10       private WalletSimulator simulator = null;

         // The constructor. The agent is a WalletConnectionAgent that this manager
         // is working with for the wallet.
11       public WalletMessageTaskManager(WalletConnectionAgent agent, Wallet wallet,
                           ConcurrentLinkedQueue<Message> messageQueue){
12           this.agent = agent;
13           this.wallet = wallet;
14           this.messageQueue = messageQueue;
15       }

         // This message task manager needs to have access to the WalletSimulator
         // for proper message displaying on the GUI.
16       public void setSimulator(WalletSimulator simulator){
17           this.simulator = simulator;
18       }

         // Specifically for the message type: MessageAskForBlockchainBroadcast.
19       protected void askForLatestBlockchain(){
20           MessageAskForBlockchainBroadcast forLedger =
                   new MessageAskForBlockchainBroadcast("Thank you",
                   this.wallet.getPrivateKey(), this.wallet.getPublicKey(),
                   this.wallet.getName());
21           boolean b = this.agent.sendMessage(forLedger);
22           if(b){
23               System.out.println("sent a message for latest blockchain");
24           }else{
25               System.out.println("Error!!!! failed to send a message "
                           + "for latest blockchain");
26           }
27       }

         // This method specifies what this task manager should do when there is
         // no available messages to process. This method will be overridden by
         // MinerGenesisMessageTaskManager.
```

```java
28      public void whatToDo() {
            // Do nothing.
29      }

        // Must implement this method to include all tasks this class needs to accomplish.
30      public void run(){
31          try{
                // Sleep a while to free CPU time.
32              Thread.sleep(agent.sleepTime*2);
33          }catch(Exception ee){
                // Do nothing.
34          }
            // The first thing is to update the local blockchain.
35          askForLatestBlockchain();
36          while(forever){
37              if(this.messageQueue.isEmpty()){
38                  try{
39                      Thread.sleep(this.agent.sleepTime);
40                      whatToDo();
41                  }catch(Exception e){
42                      System.out.println("Error in sleep");
43                      e.printStackTrace();
44                      this.close();
45                      this.agent.activeClose();
46                  }
47              }else{
48                  Message m = this.messageQueue.poll();
49                  if(m == null){
50                      System.out.println("message  is null, impossible!");
51                  }else{
                        // The method processMessage() does not throw an exception.
                        // The reason why using try-catch here is to make sure if
                        // something unexpected happens, the network connection
                        // should be properly closed.
52                      try{
53                          processMessage(m);
54                      }catch(Exception e){
55                          System.out.println("Error when processing message");
56                          e.printStackTrace();
57                          this.close();
58                          this.agent.activeClose();
59                      }
60                  }
61              }
62          }
63      }

        // Different message types are processed differently in this method.
64      protected void processMessage(Message message) {
65          if(message == null){
66              return;
67          }
68          if(!message.isForBroadcast()){
                // If this is a private text message for this wallet.
69              if(message.getMessageType() == Message.TEXT_PRIVATE){
70                  MessageTextPrivate m = (MessageTextPrivate)message;
                    // Got to confirm the message is valid.
71                  if(!m.isValid()){
72                      System.out.println("text private message tampered");
```

```java
73                      return;
74                  }
                    // Check if the message is really for this wallet.
75                  if(!m.getReceiver().equals(this.wallet.getPublicKey())){
76                      System.out.println("text private is not for me, ignore it.");
77                      return;
78                  }
                    // Examine if it is a CLOSE connection message.
79                  String text = m.getMessageBody();
80                  if(m.getSenderKey().equals(agent.getServerAddress())
                            && text.equals(Message.TEXT_CLOSE)){
81                      System.out.println("Server is asking to close the connection.");
82                      this.close();
83                      agent.close();
84                  }else{
85                      receivePrivateChatMessage(m);
86                  }
87              }else if(message.getMessageType() == Message.ADDRESS_PRIVATE){
88                  MessageAddressPrivate mp = (MessageAddressPrivate)message;
89                  receiveMessageAddressPrivate(mp);
90              }else if(message.getMessageType() == Message.BLOCKCHAIN_PRIVATE){
91                  MessageBlockchainPrivate mbcb = (MessageBlockchainPrivate)message;
92                  receiveMessagaeBlockchainPrivate(mbcb);
93              }else{
94                  System.out.println("");
95                  System.out.println("....weird private message, not supported");
96                  System.out.println("");
97              }
98          }else if(message.getMessageType() == Message.BLOCK_BROADCAST){
                // Upon receiving a block, a wallet will validate the block first and then
                // try to update the local blockchain.
99              System.out.println("it is a block broadcast message, "
                        + "check if it is necessary to update it");
100             MessageBlockBroadcast mbb = (MessageBlockBroadcast)message;
101             this.receiveMessageBlockBroadcast(mbb);
102         }else if(message.getMessageType() == Message.BLOCKCHAIN_BROADCAST){
103             System.out.println("It is a blockchain broadcast message, "
                        + "check if it is necessary to update the blockchain");
104             MessageBlockchainBroadcast mbcb = (MessageBlockchainBroadcast)message;
105             boolean b = this.wallet.setLocalLedger(mbcb.getMessageBody());
106             if(b){
107                 System.out.println("blockchain is updated!");
108             }else{
109                 System.out.println("rejected the new blockchain");
110             }
111         }else if(message.getMessageType() == Message.TRANSACTION_BROADCAST){
                // As a wallet does not collect transaction or mine a block, a wallet
                // will just pay attention to transactions that have
                // payment to herself/himself.
112             System.out.println("It is a transaction broadcast message");
113             MessageTransactionBroadcast mtb =
                                (MessageTransactionBroadcast)message;
114             this.receiveMessageTransactionBroadcast(mtb);
115         }else if(message.getMessageType() == Message.BLOCKCHAIN_ASK_BROADCAST){
116             MessageAskForBlockchainBroadcast mabcb =
                                (MessageAskForBlockchainBroadcast)message;
117             if(!(mabcb.getSenderKey().equals(myWallet().getPublicKey()))
                                && mabcb.isValid()){
118                 receiveQueryForBlockchainBroadcast(mabcb);
```

```
119                    }
120                }else if(message.getMessageType() == Message.TEXT_BROADCAST){
121                    MessageTextBroadcast mtb = (MessageTextBroadcast)message;
122                    receiveMessageTextBroadcast(mtb);
123                }
124            }

           // Process a MessageTextBroadcast message.
125            protected void receiveMessageTextBroadcast(MessageTextBroadcast mtb){
126                String text = mtb.getMessageBody();
127                String name = mtb.getSenderName();
128                this.simulator.appendMessageLineOnBoard(name + "]: " + text);
                   // Automatically store the user information (can be self).
129                agent.addAddress(new KeyNamePair(mtb.getSenderKey(), mtb.getSenderName()));
130            }

           // Process a MessageAddressPrivate by updating the local wallet list.
           // In this implementation, the message must be from the message service provider.
131            protected void receiveMessageAddressPrivate(MessageAddressPrivate mp){
132                ArrayList<KeyNamePair> all = mp.getMessageBody();
133                System.out.println("There are these many addresses (users) "
                                   + "available (in addition to yourself): ");
134                for(int z=0; z<all.size(); z++){
135                    KeyNamePair pk = all.get(z);
136                    if(!pk.getKey().equals(wallet.getPublicKey())){
137                        agent.addAddress(pk);
138                        System.out.println(pk.getName() + "|key="
                                           + UtilityMethods.getKeyString(pk.getKey()));
139                    }
140                }
141            }

           // Process a private chat message. Display it on GUI.
142            protected void receivePrivateChatMessage(MessageTextPrivate m){
143                String text = m.getMessageBody();
144                String name = m.getSenderName();
145                this.simulator.appendMessageLineOnBoard("private<--" + name + "]: " + text);
                   // Automatically store the user information.
146                agent.addAddress(new KeyNamePair(m.getSenderKey(), m.getSenderName()));
147            }

           // A wallet does not respond to such a query.
148            protected void receiveQueryForBlockchainBroadcast(
                               MessageAskForBlockchainBroadcast mabcb){
149                System.out.println("I am just a wallet, ignore query for blockchain");
150            }

           // When a wallet receives a transaction broadcast message, either the
           // wallet can ignore it, or the wallet can send a THANK YOU message to
           // the transaction publisher if the transaction contains UTXO(s) paid
           // to this wallet. A better option is to send the THANK YOU message to the
           // transaction publisher when a block is published and accepted.
           // Anyhow, this method can be overridden if there is no need to do so.
151            protected void receiveMessageTransactionBroadcast(MessageTransactionBroadcast mtb){
152                Transaction ts = mtb.getMessageBody();
153                if(!this.thankYouTransactions.containsKey(ts.getHashID())){
154                    int n = ts.getNumberOfOutputUTXOs();
155                    int total = 0;
156                    for(int i=0; i<n; i++){
```

```
157                        UTXO ut = ts.getOuputUTXO(i);
158                        if(ut.getReceiver().equals(this.wallet.getPublicKey())){
159                            total += ut.getFundTransferred();
160                        }
161                    }
                       // If the UTXO sender is self, do not display this message.
162                    if(total > 0 && !ts.getSender().equals(myWallet().getPublicKey())){
163                        this.thankYouTransactions.put(ts.getHashID(), ts.getHashID());
164                        System.out.println("in the transaction, there is payment of "
                                    + total + " to me. Sending THANK YOU to the payer");
165                        MessageTextPrivate mtp = new MessageTextPrivate("Thank you "
                                    + "for the fund of " + total
                                    + ", waiting for its publishing.",
                                    this.wallet.getPrivateKey(), this.wallet.getPublicKey(),
                                    this.wallet.getName(), ts.getSender()));
166                        this.agent.sendMessage(mtp);
167                    }
168                }
169            }

               // When a block is rejected, transactions in the block must be broadcast again
               // if they haven't been successfully published to prevent them from being lost.
170            protected void receiveMessageBlockBroadcast(MessageBlockBroadcast mbb){
171                Block block = mbb.getMessageBody();
172                boolean b = this.wallet.updateLocalLedger(block);
173                if(b){
174                    System.out.println("new block is added to the local blockchain");
175                }else{
176                    int size = block.getTotalNumberOfTransactions();
177                    int counter = 0;
178                    for(int i=0; i<size; i++){
179                        Transaction T = block.getTransaction(i);
180                        if(!myWallet().getLocalLedger().isTransactionExist(T)){
181                            MessageTransactionBroadcast mt =
                                        new MessageTransactionBroadcast(T);
182                            this.agent.sendMessage(mt);
183                            counter++;
184                        }
185                    }
186                    System.out.println("new block is rejected, released "
                                + counter + " unpublished transactions into the pool");
187                }
188            }

               // A private message of blockchain must be for this wallet only.
               // If not, discard it. Else, examine whether or not this wallet
               // should update its local blockchain copy.
189            protected void receiveMessagaeBlockchainPrivate(MessageBlockchainPrivate mbcb){
190                System.out.println("It is a blockchain private message, check "
                            + "if it is for me and if necessary to update the blockchain");
191                if(mbcb.getReceiver().equals(myWallet().getPublicKey())){
192                    boolean b = this.myWallet().setLocalLedger(mbcb.getMessageBody());
193                    if(b){
194                        System.out.println("blockchain is updated!");
195                    }else{
196                        System.out.println("rejected the new blockchain");
197                    }
198                }else{
199                    System.out.println("ERROR!!! weird, it is a blockchain "
```

```
                                + "private message, but it is sent to me!");
200             }
201         }

            // Return the wallet that this task manager is working for.
202         protected Wallet myWallet(){
203             return this.wallet;
204         }

205         public void close(){
206             forever = false;
207         }
208 }
```

The method receiveMessageBlockBroadcast() is of special importance. Rejected blocks could still contain unpublished transactions that must be broadcast again so that they can be added to new blocks. Otherwise these transactions are lost. The code for this protocol can be found in lines 170-188. However, if every wallet needs to re-broadcast the unpublished transactions in blocks they rejected, significant network bandwidth can be wasted. To better understand this scenario, assuming there are blocks A, B, C mined by different miners and block A wins. Blocks B and C will then be rejected by every wallet in the blockchain system. Blocks B and C may contain some transactions different from what are inside block A, and these transactions need to be re-broadcast. Certainly it is not necessary for every wallet to re-broadcast these transactions. Instead, there should be a mechanism to minimize the network traffic while ensuring that those unpublished transactions are re-broadcast. For the sake of simplicity, our blockchain system does not provide such a mechanism to minimize network traffic.

The method receiveMessageTransactionBroadcast() (lines 151-169) can be left empty for a wallet. It sends a "Thank You" message to the sender of a transaction that contains a payment to the wallet. Alternatively, this "Thank You" message can be sent after the block containing the transaction has been successfully accepted and published.

The WalletSimulator is the driver class for a wallet. It makes use of the WalletConnectionAgent and WalletMessageTaskManager to mimic a Wallet's functions. If it has the MinerMessageTaskManager instance, it will simulate a miner instead. The WalletSimulator class contains four inner classes, each displaying a unique graphic user interface.

```
1   import java.awt.GridBagConstraints;
2   import java.awt.GridBagLayout;
3   import java.awt.GridLayout;
4   import java.awt.Container;
5   import java.awt.Color;
6   import java.awt.event.KeyListener;
7   import java.awt.event.WindowAdapter;
8   import java.awt.event.WindowEvent;
9   import java.awt.event.ActionListener;
10  import java.awt.event.ActionEvent;
11  import java.security.PublicKey;
12  import java.awt.event.KeyEvent;
13  import java.util.Scanner;
14  import javax.swing.JFrame;
15  import javax.swing.JTextArea;
16  import javax.swing.JTextField;
```

```java
17   import javax.swing.JTextPane;
18   import javax.swing.JButton;
19   import javax.swing.JComboBox;
20   import javax.swing.JLabel;
21   import javax.swing.JMenu;
22   import javax.swing.JMenuBar;
23   import javax.swing.JMenuItem;
24   import javax.swing.JScrollPane;
25   import javax.swing.ScrollPaneConstants;
26   import java.util.ArrayList;
27   import java.util.Random;
28   import java.util.Calendar;

29   public class WalletSimulator extends JFrame{
         // MessageFrame is an inner class to display balance or blockchain content.
30       protected static MessageFrame messageFrame = new MessageFrame();
         // FrameHelp is an inner class to display help messages only.
31       protected static FrameHelp help = new FrameHelp();
         // This variable controls if public key should be displayed when
         // wallet balance is displayed. It is a good idea to let it be false.
32       private boolean balanceShowPublicKey = false;
33       private JTextArea textInput;
34       private JButton sentButton;
         // This is the board displaying chat messages.
35       private JTextArea displayArea;
36       private GridBagLayout mgr = null;
37       private GridBagConstraints gcr = null;
         // The wallet that this GUI represents.
38       private Wallet wallet = null;
         // The agent dedicated to network connection.
39       private WalletConnectionAgent connectionAgent = null;
         // The manager dedicated to message processing.
40       private WalletMessageTaskManager taskManager = null;
         // This is for proper message display: we need to show the date and time.
41       private Calendar calendar = Calendar.getInstance();

         // The constructor.
42       public WalletSimulator(Wallet wallet, WalletConnectionAgent agent,
                                  WalletMessageTaskManager manager){
43           super(wallet.getName());
44           this.wallet = wallet;
45           this.connectionAgent = agent;
46           this.taskManager = manager;
47           setUpGUI();
             // When the GUI window is closed, close the network connection
             // after informing the network server.
48           this.addWindowListener(new java.awt.event.WindowAdapter(){
49               public void windowClosing(java.awt.event.WindowEvent e){
50                   try{
51                       connectionAgent.sendMessage(
                             new MessageTextPrivate(Message.TEXT_CLOSE,
                             wallet.getPrivateKey(), wallet.getPublicKey(),
                             wallet.getName(), connectionAgent.getServerAddress())));
52                   }catch(Exception e1){
                         // Do nothing.
53                   }
54                   try{
55                       connectionAgent.activeClose();
56                       taskManager.close();
```

```
57                    }catch(Exception ee){}
58                        dispose();
59                        System.exit(2);
60                    }
61                });
62            }

              // This method sets up the GUI. It sets up the menu bar first, however.
              // The main GUI is similar to what chapter 7 has. The major difference
              // lies in the menu bar.
63            private void setUpGUI(){
                  // The default size of the frame.
64                this.setSize(500, 600);
                  // Set the menu bar first.
65                setBar();
66                Container c = getContentPane();
                  // Make use of GridBagLayout manager.
67                mgr = new GridBagLayout();
68                gcr = new GridBagConstraints();
69                c.setLayout(mgr);
70                JLabel lblInput = new JLabel("                           Message Board");
71                lblInput.setForeground(Color.GREEN);
72                this.displayArea = new JTextArea(50, 100);
73                this.textInput = new JTextArea(5, 100);
74                this.sentButton = new JButton("Click me or hit Enter "
                          + "to send the message below");
75                this.sentButton.addActionListener(new java.awt.event.ActionListener(){
76                    public void actionPerformed(java.awt.event.ActionEvent e){
77                        try{
78                            MessageTextBroadcast m = new MessageTextBroadcast(
                                  textInput.getText(), wallet.getPrivateKey(),
                                  wallet.getPublicKey(), wallet.getName());
79                            connectionAgent.sendMessage(m);
80                        }catch(Exception e2){
81                            throw new RuntimeException(e2);
82                        }
83                        textInput.setText("");
84                    }
85                });
86                this.gcr.fill = GridBagConstraints.BOTH;
87                this.gcr.weightx = 1;
88                this.gcr.weighty = 0.0;
89                this.gcr.gridx = 0;
90                this.gcr.gridy = 0;
91                this.gcr.gridwidth = 1;
92                this.gcr.gridheight = 1;
93                this.mgr.setConstraints(lblInput, this.gcr);

94                c.add(lblInput);
95                this.gcr.weighty = 0.9;
96                this.gcr.gridx = 0;
97                this.gcr.gridy = 1;
98                this.gcr.gridheight = 9;
                  // Make the message area scrollable
99                JScrollPane scroll = new JScrollPane(this.displayArea);
100               scroll.setVerticalScrollBarPolicy(
                          ScrollPaneConstants.VERTICAL_SCROLLBAR_ALWAYS);
101               scroll.setHorizontalScrollBarPolicy(
                          ScrollPaneConstants.HORIZONTAL_SCROLLBAR_NEVER);
```

```
102                this.mgr.setConstraints(scroll, this.gcr);
103                c.add(scroll);

104                this.displayArea.setEditable(false);
105                this.displayArea.setBackground(Color.LIGHT_GRAY);
106                this.displayArea.setLineWrap(true);
107                this.displayArea.setWrapStyleWord(true);
108                this.gcr.weighty = 0.0;
109                this.gcr.gridx = 0;
110                this.gcr.gridy = 11;
111                this.gcr.gridheight = 1;
112                this.mgr.setConstraints(this.sentButton, this.gcr);
113                c.add(this.sentButton);

114                this.gcr.weighty = 0.1;
115                this.gcr.gridx = 0;
116                this.gcr.gridy = 12;
117                this.gcr.gridheight = 2;
                   // Make the text input area scrollable.
118                JScrollPane scroll2 = new JScrollPane(this.textInput);
119                scroll2.setVerticalScrollBarPolicy(
                       ScrollPaneConstants.VERTICAL_SCROLLBAR_AS_NEEDED);
120                scroll2.setHorizontalScrollBarPolicy(
                       ScrollPaneConstants.HORIZONTAL_SCROLLBAR_NEVER);
121                this.mgr.setConstraints(scroll2, this.gcr);
122                c.add(scroll2);
123                this.textInput.setLineWrap(true);
124                this.textInput.setWrapStyleWord(true);
                   // Add a key listener to the textarea. Allowing hitting Enter
                   // to send the message, too.
125                this.textInput.addKeyListener(new KeyListener(){
126                    public void keyTyped(KeyEvent e) {}
127                    public void keyReleased(KeyEvent e) {}
128                    public void keyPressed(KeyEvent e) {
129                        int key = e.getKeyCode();
130                        if (key == KeyEvent.VK_ENTER) {
131                            if(e.isShiftDown() || e.isControlDown()){
132                                textInput.append(System.getProperty("line.separator"));
133                            }else{
134                                try{
135                                    MessageTextBroadcast m =
                                           new MessageTextBroadcast(
                                           textInput.getText(),
                                           wallet.getPrivateKey(),
                                           wallet.getPublicKey(), wallet.getName());
136                                    connectionAgent.sendMessage(m);
137                                }catch(Exception e2){
138                                    throw new RuntimeException(e2);
139                                }
                                   // Consume the ENTER so that the cursor will stay
                                   // at the beginning.
140                                e.consume();
141                                textInput.setText("");
142                            }
143                        }
144                    }
145                }
146                );
147            this.setVisible(true);
```

```
148         }

            // If set true, then public key is displayed to represent a wallet.
            // Suggest to keep it false.
149         private void setBalanceShowPublicKey(boolean yesno){
150             this.balanceShowPublicKey = yesno;
151         }

152         public boolean showPublicKeyInBalance(){
153             return this.balanceShowPublicKey;
154         }

            // Set up the menu bar.
155         private void setBar(){
156             JMenuBar bar = new JMenuBar();
157             setJMenuBar(bar);
                // One menu is "Ask For", i.e. asking for information.
158             JMenu askMenu = new JMenu("Ask For");
                // Add an item to display help message.
159             JMenuItem helpItem = new JMenuItem("Click me for help");
160             helpItem.addActionListener(new ActionListener(){
161                 public void actionPerformed(ActionEvent e){
162                     showHelpMessage("1. When you 'update blockchain', "
                            + "a broadcast message is sent for the latest "
                            + "blockchain so as to update the local copy. "
                            + "This becomes necessary if your local copy "
                            + "is out of date.\n"
                            + "2. When you click 'update users', "
                            + "the service provider will update your user list.\n"
                            + "3. Clicking 'show balance' will display your "
                            + "balance on the display board.\n"
                            + "4. Clicking 'display blockchain' will display "
                            + "your local blockchain on the display board.");
163                 }
164             });

                // Add an item to allow updating local blockchain copy. Clicking
                // this item will send a message asking for the latest blockchain.
165             JMenuItem askBlockchainItem = new JMenuItem("update blockchain");
166             askBlockchainItem.addActionListener(new ActionListener(){
167                 public void actionPerformed(ActionEvent e){
168                     MessageAskForBlockchainBroadcast m =
                            new MessageAskForBlockchainBroadcast("please",
                                wallet.getPrivateKey(), wallet.getPublicKey(),
                                wallet.getName());
169                     connectionAgent.sendMessage(m);
170                 }
171             });

                // Add an item to allow updating the list of wallets. Clicking
                // this item will send a message asking for wallets online.
172             JMenuItem askAddressesItem = new JMenuItem("update users");
173             askAddressesItem.addActionListener(new ActionListener(){
174                 public void actionPerformed(ActionEvent e){
175                     MessageTextPrivate m =
                            new MessageTextPrivate(Message.TEXT_ASK_ADDRESSES,
                                wallet.getPrivateKey(), wallet.getPublicKey(),
                                wallet.getName(), connectionAgent.getServerAddress());
176                     connectionAgent.sendMessage(m);
```

```java
177                }
178            });

               // Add an item to allow showing the balance of this wallet.
179            JMenuItem askBalanceItem = new JMenuItem("show balance");
180            askBalanceItem.addActionListener(new ActionListener(){
181                public void actionPerformed(ActionEvent e){
182                    displayBalance(wallet);
183                }
184            });

               // Add an item to allow showing the content of local blockchain copy.
185            JMenuItem displayBlockchain = new JMenuItem("display blockchain");
186            displayBlockchain.addActionListener(new ActionListener(){
187                public void actionPerformed(ActionEvent e){
188                    displayBlockchain(wallet);
189                }
190            });

191            askMenu.add(helpItem);
192            askMenu.add(askBlockchainItem);
193            askMenu.add(askAddressesItem);
194            askMenu.add(askBalanceItem);
195            askMenu.add(displayBlockchain);
196            bar.add(askMenu);

               // Add another menu "To Send", i.e. to send messages.
197            JMenu sendMenu = new JMenu("To Send");
               // Add an item to display help message.
198            JMenuItem helpItem2 = new JMenuItem("Click me for help");
199            helpItem2.addActionListener(new ActionListener(){
200                public void actionPerformed(ActionEvent e){
201                    showHelpMessage("1. When you start a transaction, "
                            + "you need to choose the recipient(s) and "
                            + "the amount to each recipient.\n"
                            + "2. The private message you send to a "
                            + "user will be displayed on the message "
                            + "board, but only the recipient will be "
                            + "able to see it.");
202                }
203            });

               // Add an item to initiate and broadcast a transaction.
204            JMenuItem sendTransactionItem = new JMenuItem("start a transaction");
205            sendTransactionItem.addActionListener(new ActionListener(){
206                public void actionPerformed(ActionEvent e){
207                    FrameTransaction ft = new FrameTransaction(
                            connectionAgent.getAllStoredAddresses(), connectionAgent);
208                }
209            });

               // Add an item to send a private message to another wallet.
210            JMenuItem sendPrivateMessageItem = new JMenuItem("to send a private message");
211            sendPrivateMessageItem.addActionListener(new ActionListener(){
212                public void actionPerformed(ActionEvent e){
213                    FramePrivateMessage fpm = new FramePrivateMessage(
                            connectionAgent.getAllStoredAddresses(),
                            connectionAgent, WalletSimulator.this);
214                }
```

```
215             });
216             sendMenu.add(helpItem2);
217             sendMenu.add(sendTransactionItem);
218             sendMenu.add(sendPrivateMessageItem);
219             bar.add(sendMenu);
220         }

            // This method automatically adds new line at the end on the GUI.
221         protected void appendMessageLineOnBoard(String s){
222             String time = calendar.getTime().toString();
223             this.displayArea.append("(" + time + ") "
                            + s + System.getProperty("line.separator"));
224             this.displayArea.setCaretPosition(this.displayArea.getText().length());
225         }

            // Display the content of the wallet's local blockchain on the MessageFrame.
226         protected void displayBlockchain(Wallet w){
227             StringBuilder sb = new StringBuilder();
228             UtilityMethods.displayBlockchain(w.getLocalLedger(), sb, 0);
229             messageFrame.setMessage(sb.toString());
230         }

            // Display the balance of a wallet on the MessageFrame.
231         protected void displayBalance(Wallet w){
232             StringBuilder sb = new StringBuilder();
233             Blockchain ledger = w.getLocalLedger();
234             ArrayList<UTXO> all = new ArrayList<UTXO>();
235             ArrayList<UTXO> spent = new ArrayList<UTXO>();
236             ArrayList<UTXO> unspent = new ArrayList<UTXO>();
237             ArrayList<Transaction> sentT = new ArrayList<Transaction>();
238             ArrayList<UTXO> rewards = new ArrayList<UTXO>();
239             double balance = ledger.findRelatedUTXOs(w.getPublicKey(), all,
                                            spent, unspent, sentT, rewards);
240             int level = 0;
241             displayTab(sb, level, w.getName() + "{");
242             displayTab(sb, level + 1, "All UTXOs:");
243             displayUTXOs(sb, all, level + 2);
244             displayTab(sb, level + 1, "Spent UTXOs:");
245             displayUTXOs(sb, spent, level + 2);
246             displayTab(sb, level + 1, "unspent UTXOs:");
247             displayUTXOs(sb, unspent, level + 2);
248             if(w instanceof Miner){
249                 displayTab(sb, level + 1, "Mining Rewards:");
250                 displayUTXOs(sb, rewards, level + 2);
251             }
252             displayTab(sb, level + 1, "Balance=" + balance);
253             displayTab(sb, level, "}");
254             String s = sb.toString();
255             messageFrame.setMessage(s);
256         }

            // Prepare the content of UTXOs into a text storage: StringBuilder.
257         private void displayUTXOs(StringBuilder sb, ArrayList<UTXO> uxs, int level){
258             for(int i=0; i<uxs.size(); i++){
259                 UTXO ux = uxs.get(i);
260                 if(showPublicKeyInBalance()){
261                     displayTab(sb, level, "fund: "
                                + ux.getFundTransferred() +", receiver: "
                                + UtilityMethods.getKeyString(ux.getReceiver())
```

```
                        + ", sender: " + UtilityMethods.getKeyString(ux.getSender()));
262             }else{
263                 String ss = "fund: " + ux.getFundTransferred() + ", receiver: "
                        + connectionAgent.getNameFromAddress(ux.getReceiver())
                        + ", sender: "
                        + connectionAgent.getNameFromAddress(ux.getSender()));
264                 displayTab(sb, level, ss);
265             }
266         }
267     }

        // Prepare a text message into a text storage: StringBuilder.
268     private void displayTab(StringBuilder sb, int level, String mesg){
269         for(int i=0; i<level; i++){
270             sb.append("\t");
271         }
272         sb.append(mesg);
273         sb.append(System.getProperty("line.separator"));
274     }

        // Show the help message in a frame.
275     protected static void showHelpMessage(String message){
276         help.setMessage(message);
277     }

        // The main method. Please pay close attention.
278     public static void main(String[] args) throws Exception{
279         Random rand = new Random();
            // Let's make the probability of being a miner is 3 out 4,
            // and the probability of being a wallet is 1 out of 4.
280         int chance = rand.nextInt(4);
281         Scanner in = new Scanner(System.in);
282         System.out.println("please provide a name:");
283         String wname = in.nextLine();
284         System.out.println("Please provide your password:");
285         String wpassword = in.nextLine();
286         System.out.println("When showing balance, "
                    + "by default the public key is not shown as the address.\n"
                    + "This is for simplicity. "
                    + "Do you like to show the public key as address (Yes/No)??");
287         String yesno = in.nextLine();
288         boolean show = false;
289         if(yesno.toUpperCase().startsWith("Y")){
290             show = true;
291         }
292         System.out.println("To join the blockchain network, "
                    + "please present the service provider IP address:");
293         String ipAddress = in.nextLine();
            // If no input, let's assume that it is localhost.
294         if(ipAddress.length() < 5){
295             ipAddress = "localhost";
296         }
297         if(chance == 0){
298             System.out.println("===== Congratulation, you are a wallet, "
                    + "i.e. a general user =====");
299             Wallet wallet = new Wallet(wname, wpassword);
300             System.out.println("Welcome " + wname
                    + ", blockchain wallet created for you.");
301             WalletConnectionAgent agent = new WalletConnectionAgent(
```

```
                          ipAddress, Configuration.networkPort(), wallet);
302                 Thread agentThread = new Thread(agent);
303                 WalletMessageTaskManager manager = new WalletMessageTaskManager(
                          agent, wallet, agent.getMessageQueue());
304                 Thread managerThread = new Thread(manager);
305                 WalletSimulator simulator = new WalletSimulator(
                                          wallet, agent, manager);
306                 manager.setSimulator(simulator);
307                 agentThread.start();
308                 System.out.println("wallet connection agent started");
309                 managerThread.start();
310                 System.out.println("wallet task manager started");
311                 simulator.setBalanceShowPublicKey(show);
312             }else{
313                 System.out.println("===== Congratulation, you are a miner, "
                          + "i.e. a full-power user who mine blocks =====");
314                 Miner miner = new Miner(wname, wpassword);
315                 System.out.println("Welcome " + wname
                          + ", blockchain miner created for you.");
316                 WalletConnectionAgent agent = new WalletConnectionAgent(
                          ipAddress, Configuration.networkPort(), miner);
317                 Thread agentThread = new Thread(agent);
318                 MinerMessageTaskManager manager = new MinerMessageTaskManager(
                          agent, miner, agent.getMessageQueue());
319                 Thread managerThread = new Thread(manager);
320                 WalletSimulator simulator = new WalletSimulator(miner, agent, manager);
321                 manager.setSimulator(simulator);
322                 agentThread.start();
323                 System.out.println("miner connection agent started");
324                 managerThread.start();
325                 System.out.println("miner task manager started");
326                 simulator.setBalanceShowPublicKey(show);
327             }
328         }
329 }
    // Inner class 1, for displaying the wallet balance or the blockchain content.
330 class MessageFrame extends javax.swing.JFrame{
331     Container c = this.getContentPane();
332     javax.swing.JTextArea msg = new JTextArea();
333     JScrollPane pane = new JScrollPane();
334     public MessageFrame() {
335         super("Information Board");
336         this.setBounds(0, 0, 600, 450);
337         JScrollPane pane = new JScrollPane(this.msg);
338         pane.setVerticalScrollBarPolicy(JScrollPane.VERTICAL_SCROLLBAR_AS_NEEDED);
339         pane.setHorizontalScrollBarPolicy(JScrollPane.HORIZONTAL_SCROLLBAR_ALWAYS);
340         c.add(pane);
341         msg.setLineWrap(false);
342         msg.setRows(100);
343         msg.setColumns(80);
344         this.addWindowListener(new WindowAdapter(){
345             public void windowClosing(WindowEvent e){
                    // Do nothing.
346             }
347         });
348     }

349     public void setMessage(String message){
350         msg.setText(message);
```

```
351             this.validate();
352             this.setVisible(true);
353         }

354     public void appendMessage(String message){
355             msg.append(message);
356             this.validate();
357             this.setVisible(true);
358         }
359 }

    // Inner class 2, for displaying the help messages.
360 class FrameHelp extends javax.swing.JFrame{
361     javax.swing.JTextPane msg = new JTextPane();
362     public FrameHelp() {
363             super("Help Message");
364             Container c = this.getContentPane();
365             this.setBounds(500, 500, 300, 220);
366             msg.setBounds(0, 0, this.getWidth(), this.getHeight());
367             c.add(msg);
368         }

369     public void setMessage(String message){
370             msg.setText(message);
371             this.validate();
372             this.setVisible(true);
373         }
374 }

    // Inner class 3, for initiating a transaction.
375 class FrameTransaction extends javax.swing.JFrame implements ActionListener{
376     private ArrayList<KeyNamePair> users = null;
377     private WalletConnectionAgent agent = null;
378     public FrameTransaction(ArrayList<KeyNamePair> users, WalletConnectionAgent agent){
379             super("Prepare Transaction");
380             this.users = users;
381             this.agent = agent;
382             setUp();
383         }

384     private void setUp(){
385             Container c = this.getContentPane();
386             this.setSize(300, 120);
387             GridLayout layout = new GridLayout(3, 2, 5, 5);
388             JLabel je = new JLabel("Please select a user");
389             JLabel jf = new JLabel("The transaction amount");
390             JButton js = new JButton("Submit");
391             JButton jc = new JButton("Cancel");
392             c.setLayout(layout);
393             c.add(je);
394             c.add(jf);
395             JComboBox<String> candidates = new JComboBox<String>();
396             for(int i=0; i<users.size(); i++){
397                 candidates.addItem(users.get(i).getName());
398             }
399             c.add(candidates);
400             JTextField input = new JTextField();
401             c.add(input);
402             c.add(js);
```

```java
403                c.add(jc);
404                js.addActionListener(new ActionListener(){
405                    public void actionPerformed(ActionEvent e){
406                        int selectedIndex = candidates.getSelectedIndex();
407                        double amount = -1.0;;
408                        String text = input.getText();
409                        if(text != null && text.length() > 0){
410                            try{
411                                amount = Double.parseDouble(text);
412                            }catch(Exception pe){
413                                amount = -1;
414                            }
                            // The transaction amount must be positive.
                            // This is important.
415                            if(amount <= 0.0){
416                                input.setText("must be a positive number");
417                                return;
418                            }
419                            boolean b = agent.sendTransaction(
                                users.get(selectedIndex).getKey(), amount);
420                            if(!b){
421                                input.setText("Failed to send");
422                            }else{
423                                input.setText("Transaction sent");
424                            }
425                        }
426                    }
427                });
428            jc.addActionListener(this);
429            this.setVisible(true);
430        }
431        
431        public void actionPerformed(ActionEvent e){
432            this.dispose();
433        }
434    }

    // Inner class 4, for sending private chat messages.
435    class FramePrivateMessage extends javax.swing.JFrame implements ActionListener{
436        private ArrayList<KeyNamePair> users = null;
437        private WalletConnectionAgent agent = null;
438        private JTextArea board = null;
439        private WalletSimulator simulator;
440        public FramePrivateMessage(ArrayList<KeyNamePair> users,
                    WalletConnectionAgent agent, WalletSimulator simulator){
441            super("Send a private message");
442            this.users = users;
443            this.agent = agent;
444            this.simulator = simulator;
445            setUp();
446        }
447        
447        private void setUp(){
448            Container c = getContentPane();
449            this.setSize(300, 200);
450            GridBagLayout mgr = new GridBagLayout();
451            GridBagConstraints gcr = new GridBagConstraints();
452            c.setLayout(mgr);
453            JLabel ja = new JLabel("Please select:");
```

```java
454            gcr.fill = GridBagConstraints.BOTH;
455            gcr.weightx = 0.5;
456            gcr.weighty = 0.0;
457            gcr.gridx = 0;
458            gcr.gridy = 0;
459            gcr.gridwidth = 1;
460            gcr.gridheight = 1;
461            mgr.setConstraints(ja, gcr);
462            c.add(ja);
463            JComboBox<String> candidates = new JComboBox<String>();
464            for(int i=0; i<users.size(); i++){
465                candidates.addItem(users.get(i).getName());
466            }
467            gcr.weightx = 0.5;
468            gcr.weighty = 0.0;
469            gcr.gridx = 1;
470            gcr.gridy = 0;
471            gcr.gridwidth = 1;
472            gcr.gridheight = 1;
473            mgr.setConstraints(candidates, gcr);
474            c.add(candidates);
475            gcr.weighty = 0.9;
476            gcr.weightx = 1.0;
477            gcr.gridx = 0;
478            gcr.gridy = 1;
479            gcr.gridheight = 2;
480            gcr.gridwidth = 2;
481            JTextArea input = new JTextArea(2, 30);
482            input.setLineWrap(true);
483            input.setWrapStyleWord(true);
484            mgr.setConstraints(input, gcr);
485            c.add(input);
486            gcr.weighty = 0.0;
487            gcr.gridx = 0;
488            gcr.gridy = 3;
489            gcr.gridheight = 1;
490            gcr.gridwidth = 1;
491            JButton js = new JButton("Send");
492            mgr.setConstraints(js, gcr);
493            c.add(js);
494            js.addActionListener(new ActionListener(){
495                public void actionPerformed(ActionEvent e){
496                    int selectedIndex = candidates.getSelectedIndex();
497                    String text = input.getText();
498                    if(text != null && text.length() > 0){
499                        PublicKey key = users.get(selectedIndex).getKey();
500                        boolean b = agent.sendPrivateMessage(key, text);
501                        if(b){
502                            input.setText("message sent");
503                            simulator.appendMessageLineOnBoard("private-->"
                                    + agent.getNameFromAddress(key) + "]: " + text);
504                        }else{
505                            input.setText("ERROR: message failed");
506                        }
507                    }
508                }
509            });
510            gcr.weighty = 0.0;
511            gcr.gridx = 1;
```

```
512             gcr.gridy = 3;
513             gcr.gridheight = 1;
514             gcr.gridwidth = 1;
515             JButton jc = new JButton("Cancel");
516             mgr.setConstraints(jc, gcr);
517             c.add(jc);
518             jc.addActionListener(this);
519             this.setVisible(true);
520         }

521         public void actionPerformed(ActionEvent e){
522             this.dispose();
523         }
524     }
```

The WalletSimulator class references the MinerMessageTaskManager class which is a subclass of the WalletMessageTaskManager class (code line 318). MinerMessageTaskManager delineates the actions a miner should take upon receiving various message types – actions different from those of the wallets. However, both miners and wallets use the same WalletSimulator to start the application. When mining a block, the miner should simultaneously be able to manage incoming messages, for example, continue with collecting transactions. Thus, the mining process should be an independent thread, and therefore we need to have the following MinerTheWorker class that is dedicated to block mining only.

```
1   import java.util.ArrayList;
2   public class MinerTheWorker implements Runnable{
3       private Miner miner;
4       private WalletConnectionAgent agent;
5       private MinerMessageTaskManager manager;
6       private boolean goon = true;
7       private ArrayList<Transaction> existingTransactions = null;

        // The constructor. MinerTheWorker needs to have access to the miner it works for,
        // the message task manager, the netework connection agent, and the queue
        // containing the transactions for a block.
8       public MinerTheWorker(Miner miner, MinerMessageTaskManager manager,
                WalletConnectionAgent agent, ArrayList<Transaction> existingTransactions)
9       {
10          this.miner = miner;
11          this.agent = agent;
12          this.existingTransactions = existingTransactions;
13          this.manager = manager;
14      }

        // Implement the run() method in which the task of the class is defined.
15      public void run() {
16          final long breakTime = 2;
17          System.out.println("Miner " + miner.getName()
                    + " begins to mine a block. Competition starts.");
18          Block block = miner.createNewBlock(miner.getLocalLedger(),
                            Configuration.blockMiningDifficultyLevel());
19          for(int i=0; i<this.existingTransactions.size(); i++){
20              miner.addTransaction(this.existingTransactions.get(i), block);
21          }

            // Reward the miner.
22          miner.generateRewardTransaction(block);
```

```
23              try{
24                  Thread.sleep(breakTime);
25              }catch(Exception e1){
                    // Do nothing.
26              }
                // Check if it should abort the mining task.
27              if(!goon){
28                  manager.resetMiningAction();
29                  return;
30              }
31              // Mine the block.
32              boolean b = miner.mineBlock(block);
33              if(b){
34                  System.out.println(miner.getName() + " mined and signed the block, hashID is:");
35                  System.out.println(block.getHashID());
36              }else{
37                  System.out.println(miner.getName()
                            + " failed to mine the block, mission aborted");
38                  manager.resetMiningAction();
39                  return;
40              }
41              try{
42                  Thread.sleep(breakTime);
43              }catch(Exception e2){
                    // Do nothing.
44              }
                // Check if it should abort the mining task.
45              if(!goon){
46                  manager.resetMiningAction();
47                  return;
48              }
                // To make it fair, the miner needs to announce the block first.
                // The miner should not just go ahead to update his local ledger.
                // He needs to send this block into the public pool to compete.
                // He only updates his local ledger with this block if this block
                // comes back first from the public pool.
49              MessageBlockBroadcast mbbc = new MessageBlockBroadcast(block);
50              this.agent.sendMessage(mbbc);
51              manager.resetMiningAction();
52          }

            // To provide a mechanism to abort the mining. In this class, there are two check
            // points at line 27 and line 45 respectively. If this method is called on an instance
            // of MinerTheWorker, then the instance will abort when the execution reaches
            // either line 27 or line 45. However, if the execution has already passed line 45
            // when this method is called, the execution will finish.
53          protected void abort(){
54              this.goon = false;
55          }
56      }
```

The class MinerTheWorker has two check points (lines 27 and 45) to decide whether to continue or terminate the mining. These check points are to simulate this scenario: in the middle of mining, the miner finds out that someone else has already won the mining competition. At this point, the mining process should stop right away so that the miner can move on to a new mining process. As we know, the real CPU-consuming process is in code line 32: miner.mineBlock(block). To really save time, there should theoretically be check points inside the method mineBlock() (a method of the class Miner). In this implementation, there are no such check points set up inside the method mineBlock(). In fact, the above check points in the MinerTheWorker class are never used either, they exist for demonstration purpose only.

It is reasonable to mandate that a miner is only allowed to mine one block at a time. Therefore, when a miner is mining a block, a flag must be raised to prevent the miner from starting on another block. After the mining process concludes, the flag should be reset in order for the miner to start another block mining. In the following MinerMessageTaskManager program, the variable *miningAction* is used for this purpose. A MinerTheWorker thread is created to mine a block only after two conditions have been met: 1) that there are enough transactions to construct a block, and 2) that *miningAction* is true. When the MinerMessageTaskManager receives a valid transaction, it first checks to see if there are enough transactions. If so, then it goes on to test whether *miningAction* is true. If the second condition fails, it will halt and wait. But if the condition is also met, it sets *miningAction* to false before creating a MinerTheWorker thread.

```
1     import java.security.PublicKey;
2     import java.util.ArrayList;
3     import java.util.concurrent.ConcurrentLinkedQueue;

4     public class MinerMessageTaskManager extends WalletMessageTaskManager implements Runnable{
5         private boolean miningAction = true;
6         private ArrayList<Transaction> existingTransactions = new ArrayList<Transaction>();
7         private WalletConnectionAgent agent;

          // The constructor.
8         public MinerMessageTaskManager(WalletConnectionAgent agent, Miner miner,
                              ConcurrentLinkedQueue<Message> messageQueue){
9             super(agent, miner, messageQueue);
10            this.agent = agent;
11        }

12        protected synchronized void resetMiningAction(){
13            this.miningAction = true;
14        }

15        protected synchronized boolean getMiningAction(){
16            return this.miningAction;
17        }

18        protected synchronized void raiseMiningAction(){
19            this.miningAction = false;
20        }

          // A miner must respond to a query for blockchain.
21        protected void receiveQueryForBlockchainBroadcast(
                              MessageAskForBlockchainBroadcast mabcb){
22            PublicKey receiver = mabcb.getSenderKey();
23            Blockchain bc = myWallet().getLocalLedger().copy_NotDeepCopy();
24            MessageBlockchainPrivate message = new MessageBlockchainPrivate(bc,
                              myWallet().getPublicKey(), receiver);
25            boolean b = this.agent.sendMessage(message);
26            if(b){
27                System.out.println(myWallet().getName()
                          + ": sent local blockchain to the requester, chain size="
```

```
                            + message.getMessageBody().size() + "|" + message.getInfoSize());
28          }else{
29              System.out.println(myWallet().getName()
                            + ": failed to send local blockchain to the requester");
30          }
31      }

        // A miner needs to collect the transactions for block mining.
32      protected void receiveMessageTransactionBroadcast(MessageTransactionBroadcast mtb){
33          Transaction ts = mtb.getMessageBody();
            // This transaction should not exist in the current transaction pool.
34          for(int i=0; i<this.existingTransactions.size(); i++){
35              if(ts.equals(this.existingTransactions.get(i))){
36                  return;
37              }
38          }
            // Add this transaction into the existing storage if it is valid.
            // If it is not valid, ignore it.
39          if(!myWallet().validateTransaction(ts)){
40              System.out.println("Miner " + myWallet().getName()
                            + " found an invalid transaction. Should broadcast it though");
41              return;
42          }
43          this.existingTransactions.add(ts);
            // Assess if it is good to start building a block.
44
45          if(this.existingTransactions.size() >= Block.TRANSACTION_LOWER_LIMIT
                                        && this.getMiningAction()){
46              this.raiseMiningAction();
47              System.out.println(myWallet().getName() + " has enough transactions "
                        + "to mine the block now, miningAction requirement met. "
                        + "Start mining a new block");
                // Create a MinerTheWorker to mine the block.
48              MinerTheWorker worker = new MinerTheWorker(myWallet(),
                                    this, this.agent, this.existingTransactions);
49              Thread miningThread = new Thread(worker);
50              miningThread.start();
                // Once the mining starts, pool new incoming Transactions.
51              this.existingTransactions = new ArrayList<Transaction>();
52          }
53      }

        // Override this method so that a Miner is returned when called.
54      protected Miner myWallet(){
55          return (Miner)(super.myWallet());
56      }
57  }
```

Code lines 21-31 override a method so that a miner can respond to a query for blockchain. In line 23 the local blockchain is copied and this copy is used to construct a MessageBlockchainPrivate instance in line 24.

Code lines 32-53 overrides another method to define how a miner should respond to a transaction message. A wallet can ignore a transaction message, but a miner needs to collect the transaction for block mining. When every transaction is broadcast to all blockchain participants including both wallets and miners, the same transaction can be collected by all miners for their respective block mining. This is not always a fair design. Consider a scenario where A, B, C are three miners. All three work on the same transactions, but A having superior block-mining power and will always win. If this were the case, miners B and C may never be able to mine any blocks. A fairer design could disallow a miner to collect transactions temporarily if this miner is currently mining a block and has won a number of consecutive mining competitions.

Code lines 54-56 override the method myWallet() to guarantee that this method returns a Miner instead of a Wallet.

At this point, let us review the similarities and differences between wallet and miner nodes. They are constructed in the same way: both are composed of WalletSimulator, WalletConnectionAgent, and WalletMessageTaskManager. The only main difference is that miner nodes make use of a subclass of WalletMessageTaskManager called MinerMessageTaskManager.

Class MinerGenesisMessageTaskManager is a subclass of MinerMessageTaskManager (it could be designed as a subclass of WalletMessageTaskManager instead). It overrides some methods so that a genesis miner can act differently than a common miner. For example, a genesis miner does not chat, collect public transactions, or participate in mining competition. As aforementioned, the genesis miner has the added function of sending out sign-in bonuses.

```
1     import java.util.ArrayList;
2     import java.util.HashMap;
3     import java.util.concurrent.ConcurrentLinkedQueue;
4     public final class MinerGenesisMessageTaskManager extends
                    MinerMessageTaskManager implements Runnable{
          // Specify the number of sign-in bonus blocks that the genesis miner will mine.
          // Additional sign-in bonus transactions are collected by other miners.
5         public static final int SELF_BLOCKS_TO_MINE_LIMIT = 2;
          // Record how many sign-in bonus blocks have been mined.
6         private int blocksMined = 0;
          // The maximum sign-in bonuses the genesis miner will send out.
7         public static final int SIGN_IN_BONUS_USERS_LIMIT = 1000;
          // The list of wallets that the genesis miner has collected.
8         private HashMap<String, KeyNamePair> users = new HashMap<String, KeyNamePair>();
9         private WalletConnectionAgent agent;
10        private final int signInBonus = 1000;
          // The list of wallets to which the genesis miner needs to send sign-in bonus
11        private ArrayList<KeyNamePair> waitingListForSignInBonus = new ArrayList<KeyNamePair>();

12        public MinerGenesisMessageTaskManager(WalletConnectionAgent agent,
                      Miner miner, ConcurrentLinkedQueue<Message> messageQueue){
13            super(agent, miner, messageQueue);
14            this.agent = agent;
15        }

          // The genesis miner polls the message service provider for new users by sending
          // a MessageTextPrivate until it has enough new users for sign-in bonuses.
16        public void whatToDo(){
17            try{
18                Thread.sleep(agent.sleepTime*10);
19                if(waitingListForSignInBonus.size() == 0
                          && users.size() < SIGN_IN_BONUS_USERS_LIMIT){
20                    MessageTextPrivate mp =
                          new MessageTextPrivate(Message.TEXT_ASK_ADDRESSES,
```

```
                        myWallet().getPrivateKey(), myWallet().getPublicKey(),
                        myWallet().getName(), this.agent.getServerAddress());
21                  agent.sendMessage(mp);
22                  Thread.sleep(agent.sleepTime*10);
23              }else{
24                  sendSignInBonus();
25              }
26          }catch(Exception e){}
27      }

        // This method instantiates an instance of MinerTheWorker to construct
        // and mine a block that is a sign-in bonus for a new coming blockchain
        // participant. However, if the genesis miner has mined enough
        // sign-in bonus blocks, the sign-in bonus will be broadcast as
        // a transaction such that other miners can collect it.
28      private void sendSignInBonus(){
29          if(waitingListForSignInBonus.size() <= 0){
30              return;
31          }
32          KeyNamePair pk = waitingListForSignInBonus.remove(0);
33          Transaction T = myWallet().transferFund(pk.getKey(), signInBonus);
34          if(T != null && T.verifySignature()){
35              System.out.println(myWallet().getName() + " is sending "
                        + pk.getName() + " sign-in bonus of " + signInBonus);
36              if(blocksMined < SELF_BLOCKS_TO_MINE_LIMIT && this.getMiningAction()){
37                  blocksMined++;
38                  this.raiseMiningAction();
39                  System.out.println(myWallet().getName() + " is mining the "
                            + "sign-in bonus block for " + pk.getName() + " by himself");
40                  ArrayList<Transaction> tss = new ArrayList<Transaction>();
41                  tss.add(T);
42                  MinerTheWorker worker = new MinerTheWorker(myWallet(),
                                            this, this.agent, tss);
43                  Thread miningThread = new Thread(worker);
44                  miningThread.start();
45              }else{
                    // broadcast this transaction.
46                  System.out.println(myWallet().getName() + " is broadcasting "
                            + "the transaction of sign-in bonus for " + pk.getName());
47                  MessageTransactionBroadcast mtb = new MessageTransactionBroadcast(T);
48                  this.agent.sendMessage(mtb);
49              }
50          }else{
                // Got to redo. Theoretically, this is impossible to happen.
51              waitingListForSignInBonus.add(0, pk);
52          }
53      }

        // This is how the genesis miner acts when receiving a block.
        // The genesis miner examines whether or not to update local blockchain
        // just as every miner does. If the local blockchain is updated, the balance
        // of the genesis miner is displayed (not necessary though). If the
        // incoming block is rejected, genesis miner needs to take actions
        // differently from what a normal miner does.
54      protected void receiveMessageBlockBroadcast(MessageBlockBroadcast mbb){
55          Block block = mbb.getMessageBody();
56          boolean b = myWallet().verifyGuestBlock(block, myWallet().getLocalLedger());
57          boolean c = false;
58          if(b){
```

```
59                    c = this.myWallet().updateLocalLedger(block);
60                }
61                if(b && c){
62                    System.out.println("new block is added to the local "
                              + "blockchain, blockchain size = "
                              + this.myWallet().getLocalLedger().size());
                      // Display the balance of the genesis miner in detail for
                      // verification purpose. This statement can be commented out.
63                    displayWallet_MinerBalance(myWallet());
64                }else{
65                    System.out.println("new block is rejected");
                      // Check if this block is a sign-in bonus block, if it is, then need to
                      // re-mine it. This is likely to happen when a number of miners join
                      // the network and there are a number blocks to mine.
66                    if(block.getCreator().equals(myWallet().getPublicKey())){
67                        System.out.println("genesis miner needs to re-mine "
                                  + "a sign-in bonus block");
68                        String id = UtilityMethods.getKeyString(
                                  block.getTransaction(0).getOuputUTXO(0).getReceiver());
69                        KeyNamePair pk = users.get(id);
70                        if(pk != null){
                              // Add at the beginning in the waiting list.
71                            waitingListForSignInBonus.add(0, pk);
72                        }else{
                              // This should never happen.
73                            System.out.println("ERROR: an existing user for "
                                      + "sign-in bonus is not found. Program error");
74                        }
75                    }
76                }
77        }

78        protected void receiveMessageTransactionBroadcast(MessageTransactionBroadcast mtb){
              // Ignore such messages.
79        }

          // The MessageAddressPrivate must be from the message service provider.
80        protected void receiveMessageAddressPrivate(MessageAddressPrivate mp){
81            ArrayList<KeyNamePair> all = mp.getMessageBody();
82            for(int z=0; z<all.size(); z++){
83                KeyNamePair pk = all.get(z);
84                String ID = UtilityMethods.getKeyString(pk.getKey());
85                if(!pk.getKey().equals(myWallet().getPublicKey())
                                      && !users.containsKey(ID)){
86                    users.put(ID, pk);
87                    if(users.size() <= SIGN_IN_BONUS_USERS_LIMIT){
88                        this.waitingListForSignInBonus.add(pk);
89                    }
90                }
91            }
92        }

93        protected void receivePrivateChatMessage(MessageTextPrivate m){
              // Do nothing for the genesis miner.
94        }

95        protected void receiveMessageTextBroadcast(MessageTextBroadcast mtb){
              // Do nothing for the genesis miner.
96        }
```

```
97        protected void askForLatestBlockChain(){
              // Do nothing for the genesis miner.
98        }

          // This method may not be necessary. Its purpose is to display the
          // balance of the genesis miner in detail for verification purpose only.
          // It is also kind of redundant.
99        public static final void displayWallet_MinerBalance(Wallet miner){
100           ArrayList<UTXO> all = new ArrayList<UTXO>();
101           ArrayList<UTXO> spent = new ArrayList<UTXO>();
102           ArrayList<UTXO> unspent = new ArrayList<UTXO>();
103           ArrayList<Transaction> ts = new ArrayList<Transaction>();
104           double b = miner.getLocalLedger().findRelatedUTXOs(
                      miner.getPublicKey(), all, spent, unspent, ts);
105           System.out.println("{");
106           System.out.println("\t" + miner.getName() + ": balance="+b
                      + ",   local blockchain size=" + miner.getLocalLedger().size());
107           double income = 0;
108           System.out.println("\tAll UTXOs:");
109           for(int i=0; i<all.size(); i++){
110               UTXO ux = all.get(i);
111               System.out.println("\t\t" + ux.getFundTransferred() + "|" + ux.getHashID()
                          + "|from=" + UtilityMethods.getKeyString(ux.getSender())
                          + "|to=" + UtilityMethods.getKeyString(ux.getReceiver()));
112               income += ux.getFundTransferred();
113           }
114           System.out.println("\t---- total income = " + income + " ----------");
115           System.out.println("\tSpent UTXOs:");
116           income = 0;
117           for(int i=0; i<spent.size(); i++){
118               UTXO ux = spent.get(i);
119               System.out.println("\t\t" + ux.getFundTransferred() + "|" + ux.getHashID()
                          + "|from=" + UtilityMethods.getKeyString(ux.getSender())
                          + "|to=" + UtilityMethods.getKeyString(ux.getReceiver()));
120               income += ux.getFundTransferred();
121           }
122           System.out.println("\t---- total spending = " + income+" ----------");
123           double tsFee = ts.size() * Transaction.TRANSACTION_FEE;
124           if(tsFee > 0){
125               System.out.println("\t\tTransaction Fee " + tsFee + " is automatically "
                          + "deducted. Please not include it in the calculation");
126           }
127           System.out.println("\tUnspent UTXOs:");
128           income = 0;
129           for(int i=0; i<unspent.size(); i++){
130               UTXO ux = unspent.get(i);
131               System.out.println("\t\t" + ux.getFundTransferred() + "|" + ux.getHashID()
                          + "|from=" + UtilityMethods.getKeyString(ux.getSender())
                          + "|to=" + UtilityMethods.getKeyString(ux.getReceiver()));
132               income += ux.getFundTransferred();
133           }
134           System.out.println("\t---- total unspent = " + income + " ----------");
135           System.out.println("}");
136       }
137   }
```

Code line 5 specifies the number of sign-in bonus blocks the genesis miner will mine. Additional sign-in bonus transactions are broadcast so that other miners can collect them. This parameter should be part of the system configuration, i.e. it is better to be controlled by the Configuration class.

Code lines 16-27 present the whatToDo() method. In the WalletMessageTaskManager, this method does nothing. A genesis miner, however, makes use of this method to collect the addresses of new, incoming wallets and send out sign-in bonus to these users.

Code lines 28-53 include the codes for the method sendSignInBonus(). Each sign-in bonus is prepared as a transaction. Initially, the genesis miner constructs a block with only one transaction and mines the block. Once the genesis miner has mined a certain number of blocks, it broadcasts the transaction to let other miners take care of it.

Code lines 54-77 explain how the genesis miner reacts to an incoming block broadcast. Similar to a wallet or miner, the genesis miner needs to determine if the incoming block should be accepted. If accepted, the genesis miner would follow its usual protocols. If not, the genesis miner must examine whether the rejected block is for a sign-in bonus. A sign-in bonus block can only be rejected by a genesis miner after the genesis miner has updated its local blockchain with a block mined by other miners. When this happens, other wallets and miners may have rejected this sign-in block as well, indicating that the transactions inside this block are now in the public pool for every miner to collect. Thus, the genesis miner should try to re-mine the block as soon as possible. Note that this action is slightly revised in the chapter 9 programs.

The message routing services are provided in the program BlockchainMessageServiceProvider. The services provided include:
- accepting network connection requests;
- relaying messages to proper receivers;
- keeping a list of wallets (both name and public key);
- rendering each new, incoming wallet a genesis blockchain;
- providing a name discovery service.

Please notice that this program has three classes inside: the BlockchainMessageServiceProvider, the ConnectionChannelTaskManager, and the MessageCheckingTaskManager. The latter two classes are presented as inner classes as they are part of the server.
- Class BlockchainMessageServiceProvider provides the network server. Upon accepting an incoming connection, it creates a ConnectionChannelTaskManager thread to specifically manage the connection between the server and the client (where a client is a participating wallet). In addition, this class provides several storage and lookup services. There is only one instance of BlockchainMessageServiceProvider on the server side.
- Class ConnectionChannelTaskManager manages a connection channel and the messages received and sent through this connection channel. Upon receiving a message, it places the message into the designated queue. Every network connection has a dedicated instance of ConnectionChannelTaskManager, so there are multiple instances of it on the server side.
- Class MessageCheckingTaskManager constantly scrutinizes the message queue to process

messages based on their origins, destinations, and types. There is only one instance of MessageCheckingTaskManager on the server side.

The codes of the class BlockchainMessageServiceProvider are listed below. Comments are added to explain certain details and logics.

```
1    import java.security.PublicKey;
2    import java.io.ObjectOutputStream;
3    import java.io.ObjectInputStream;
4    import java.util.ArrayList;
5    import java.util.Hashtable;
6    import java.util.Iterator;
7    import java.util.concurrent.ConcurrentLinkedQueue;
8    import java.net.Socket;
9    import java.net.ServerSocket;
10   import java.security.KeyPair;

11   public class BlockchainMessageServiceProvider{
12       private ServerSocket serverSocket = null;
13       private boolean forever = true;
         // To store all network connections based on wallet public keys.
14       private Hashtable<String, ConnectionChannelTaskManager> connections = null;
         // All incoming messages are stored in this queue for processing.
15       private ConcurrentLinkedQueue<Message> messageQueue = null;
         // To store all names/addresses so that name discovery service can
         // be provided.
16       private Hashtable<String, KeyNamePair> allAddresses = null;
         // Genesis blockchain is a public asset in this system.
17       private static Blockchain genesisBlockchain = null;

         // The constructor.
18       public BlockchainMessageServiceProvider(){
19           System.out.println("BlockchainMessageServiceProvider is starting");
20           connections = new Hashtable<String, ConnectionChannelTaskManager>();
21           this.messageQueue = new ConcurrentLinkedQueue<Message>();
22           this.allAddresses = new Hashtable<String, KeyNamePair>();
23           try{
24               serverSocket = new ServerSocket(Configuration.networkPort());
25           }catch(Exception e){
26               System.out.println("BlockchainMessageServiceProvider failed to "
                         + "create server socket. Failed");
                 // If something goes wrong, the system should not start at all.
27               System.exit(1);
28           }
29       }

30       protected void startWorking(){
31           System.out.println("BlockchainMessageServiceProvider is ready");
             // The server needs a pair of public/private keys to represent the server.
32           KeyPair keypair = UtilityMethods.generateKeyPair();
             // Start the message checking thread.
34           MessageCheckingTaskManager checkingAgent =
                     new MessageCheckingTaskManager(this, messageQueue, keypair);
35           Thread agent = new Thread(checkingAgent);
36           agent.start();
37           System.out.println("BlockchainMessageServiceProvider generated "
                     + "MessageCheckingTaskManager, thread working");
```

```
                // The network server is supposed to run forever.
38              while(forever){
39                  try{
40                      Socket socket = serverSocket.accept();
41                      System.out.println("BlockchainMessageServiceProvider "
                                + "accepts one connection");
                        // Allocate a connection channel task manager for a connection.
42                      ConnectionChannelTaskManager st =
                                new ConnectionChannelTaskManager(this, socket, keypair);
43                      Thread tt = new Thread(st);
44                      tt.start();
45                  }catch(Exception e){
46                      System.out.println("BlockchainMessageServiceProvider runs into "
                                + "a problem: " + e.getMessage() + " --> exit now");
47                      System.exit(2);
48                  }
49              }
50          }

            // Discover the corresponding public key based on a hashID.
51          protected PublicKey findAddress(String ID){
52              KeyNamePair kp = this.allAddresses.get(ID);
53              if(kp != null){
54                  return kp.getKey();
55              }else{
56                  return null;
57              }
58          }

            // When a connection is closed, remove this connection from storage.
59          protected synchronized KeyNamePair removeAddress(String ID){
60              return this.allAddresses.remove(ID);
61          }

            // Obtain all addresses.
62          protected synchronized ArrayList<KeyNamePair> getAllAddresses(){
63              ArrayList<KeyNamePair> A = new ArrayList<KeyNamePair>();
64              Iterator<KeyNamePair> it = this.allAddresses.values().iterator();
65              while(it.hasNext()){
66                  A.add(it.next());
67              }
68              return A;
69          }

            // Find a connection channel task manager based on a connectionID.
70          protected synchronized ConnectionChannelTaskManager
                            findConnectionChannelTaskManager(String connectionID){
71              return this.connections.get(connectionID);
72          }

            // Retrieve all connection channel task managers, i.e. all connections.
73          protected synchronized ArrayList<ConnectionChannelTaskManager>
                            getAllConnectionChannelTaskManager(){
74              ArrayList<ConnectionChannelTaskManager> A =
                                new ArrayList<ConnectionChannelTaskManager>();
75              Iterator<ConnectionChannelTaskManager> V =
                                this.connections.values().iterator();
76              while(V.hasNext()){
77                  A.add(V.next());
```

```
78              }
79              return A;
80          }

            // Add one address into the address collection.
81          protected synchronized void addPublicKeyAddress(KeyNamePair knp){
82              this.allAddresses.put(UtilityMethods.getKeyString(knp.getKey()), knp);
83          }

            // Add one connection channel task manager.
84          protected synchronized void addConnectionChannel(ConnectionChannelTaskManager channel){
85              this.connections.put(channel.getConnectionChannelID(), channel);
86          }

            // Remove a connection channel task manager and the related address.
87          protected synchronized KeyNamePair removeConnectionChannel(String channelID){
88              this.connections.remove(channelID);
89              KeyNamePair kp = this.removeAddress(channelID);
90              return kp;
91          }

            // Add one message into the queue.
92          protected void addMessageIntoQueue(Message m){
93              this.messageQueue.add(m);
94          }

            // A static method that updates the genesis block. This method
            // is called only once.
95          protected static void updateGenesisBlock(Blockchain genesisBlock){
96              if(BlockchainMessageServiceProvider.genesisBlockchain == null){
97                  BlockchainMessageServiceProvider.genesisBlockchain = genesisBlock;
98              }
99          }

100         public static Blockchain getGenesisBlockchain(){
101             return BlockchainMessageServiceProvider.genesisBlockchain;
102         }
103     }

    // Inner class 1.
104 class ConnectionChannelTaskManager implements Runnable{
105         private Socket socket;
106         private ObjectOutputStream out = null;
107         private ObjectInputStream in = null;
108         boolean forever = true;
            // The connection clientID indicates which connection this thread is working for.
109         private String ConnectionID = null;
110         private BlockchainMessageServiceProvider server;
            // The private and public key pair of the server.
111         private KeyPair keypair;
            // The public key of the client (wallet).
112         private PublicKey delegatePublicKey;
            // The name of the client (wallet).
113         private String name = null;

            // The constructor.
114         protected ConnectionChannelTaskManager(BlockchainMessageServiceProvider
                                server, Socket s, KeyPair keypair){
115             this.server = server;
```

```java
116                this.socket = s;
117                this.keypair = keypair;
118                try{
119                    out = new ObjectOutputStream(socket.getOutputStream());
120                    in = new ObjectInputStream(socket.getInputStream());
121                    // The server sends the client its public key.
122                    MessageID toClient = new MessageID(this.keypair.getPrivate(),
                                   this.keypair.getPublic(), "ServiceProvider");
123                    out.writeObject(toClient);
124                    out.flush();
                       // The server will then wait for the client to send in a MessageForID.
125                    MessageID mid = (MessageID)in.readObject();
126                    // Examine if the communication is securely constructed.
127                    if(!mid.isValid()){
128                        throw new Exception("messageID is invalid. Something wrong.");
129                    }
                       // Store this connection and its ID.
130                    this.delegatePublicKey = mid.getPublicKey();
131                    this.ConnectionID = UtilityMethods.getKeyString(mid.getPublicKey());
132                    this.name = mid.getName();
133                    System.out.println("connection successfully established for "
                                   + this.getDelegateName() + "|" + this.ConnectionID);
134                    this.server.addConnectionChannel(this);
135                    this.server.addPublicKeyAddress(mid.getKeyNamePair());
136                    System.out.println("adding address for "
                                   + mid.getKeyNamePair().getName() + ", now send the genesis blockchain");
137                    // Let the new coming user get the genesis blockchain.
138                    MessageBlockchainPrivate mchain = new MessageBlockchainPrivate(
                                   BlockchainMessageServiceProvider.getGenesisBlockchain(),
                           BlockchainMessageServiceProvider.getGenesisBlockchain().getGenesisMiner(),
                                   this.delegatePublicKey);
139                    out.writeObject(mchain);
140                }catch(Exception e){
141                    System.out.println("ConnectionChannelTaskManager exception: "
                                   + e.getMessage());
142                    System.out.println("This ConnectionChannelTaskManager connection failed");
143                    System.out.println("aborting this connection now");
144                    this.activeClose();
145                }
146        }

           // Return the name of the client (wallet).
147        public String getDelegateName(){
148            return this.name;
149        }

           // Return the address (public key) of the client (wallet).
150        public PublicKey getDelegateAddress(){
151            return this.delegatePublicKey;
152        }

           // This method is synchronized so that messages are sent one at a time.
153        protected synchronized boolean sendMessage(Message m){
154            try{
155                out.writeObject(m);
156                out.flush();
157                return true;
158            }catch(Exception ee){
159                return false;
```

```
160                }
161            }

            // Implement the method run() as this class implements Runnable interface.
162        public void run(){
163            int count = 0;
164            while(forever){
165                try{
166                    Message m = (Message)in.readObject();
167                    this.server.addMessageIntoQueue(m);
168                }catch(Exception ie){
169                    count++;
                    // If the exception happened too many times,
                    // it would be wise to close this thread
170                    if(count >= 3){
171                        this.activeClose();
172                    }
173                }
174            }
175        }

            // Note that connectionID is the readable string of the client's public key.
176        protected String getConnectionChannelID(){
177            return this.ConnectionID;
178        }

            // This close action is initiated by the server side.
179        private void activeClose(){
180            this.forever = false;
181            try{
182                this.server.removeConnectionChannel(this.getConnectionChannelID());
183                System.out.println("ConnectionChannelTaskManager: preparing to "
                        + "close connection: " + this.getDelegateName()
                        + "|" + this.getConnectionChannelID());
                // Also ask the client side to close the connection.
184                MessageTextPrivate mc = new MessageTextPrivate(Message.TEXT_CLOSE,
                        this.keypair.getPrivate(), this.keypair.getPublic(),
                        this.getDelegateName(), this.delegatePublicKey);
185                this.sendMessage(mc);
                // Sleep enough time so that the above message can be processed.
186                Thread.sleep(1000);
187                System.out.println("ConnectionChannelTaskManager "
                        + this.getDelegateName() + " closed actively ("
                        + this.getConnectionChannelID() + ")");
188                in.close();
189                out.close();
190                socket.close();
191            }catch(Exception e){
192                e.printStackTrace();
193            }
194        }

            // This close action is initiated by the client side.
195        protected void passiveClose(){
196            this.forever = false;
197            try{
198                this.server.removeConnectionChannel(this.getConnectionChannelID());
199                in.close();
200                out.close();
```

```
201                     socket.close();
202                     System.out.println("ConnectionChannelTaskManager closed passively ("
                                    + this.getConnectionChannelID() + ")");
203             }catch(Exception e){
204                 e.printStackTrace();
205             }
206         }
207 }

        // Inner class 2.
208 class MessageCheckingTaskManager implements Runnable{
209         private boolean forever = true;
210         private long sleepTime = 100;
211         private BlockchainMessageServiceProvider server;
212         private ConcurrentLinkedQueue<Message> messageQueue;
            // The public and private key pair of the server.
213         private KeyPair keypair;

        // The constructor.
214         protected MessageCheckingTaskManager(BlockchainMessageServiceProvider server,
                        ConcurrentLinkedQueue<Message> messageQueue, KeyPair keypair){
215             this.server = server;
216             this.messageQueue = messageQueue;
217             this.keypair = keypair;
218         }

        // Implements the run() method of the Runnable interface.
219     public void run(){
220         while(forever){
221             try{
                    // Checking if there is any message in the queue.
222                 if(this.messageQueue.isEmpty()){
223                     Thread.sleep(this.sleepTime);
224                 }else{
                        // Process all available messages.
225                     while(!this.messageQueue.isEmpty()){
226                         Message m = this.messageQueue.poll();
227                         processMessage(m);
228                     }
229                 }
230             }catch(Exception e){
231                 e.printStackTrace();
232             }
233         }
234     }

        // This method processes messages depending on their types,
        // senders, and receivers.
235     private void processMessage(Message m) throws Exception{
236         if(m == null){
237             return;
238         }
            // All broadcast messages would be forwarded to all wallets.
239         if(m.isForBroadcast()){
240             ArrayList<ConnectionChannelTaskManager> all =
                        this.server.getAllConnectionChannelTaskManager();
241             for(int i=0; i<all.size(); i++){
242                 all.get(i).sendMessage(m);
243             }
```

```
244             }else if(m.getMessageType()==Message.TEXT_PRIVATE){
245                 MessageTextPrivate mt = (MessageTextPrivate)m;
246                 if(!mt.isValid()){
247                     return;
248                 }
249                 String text = null;
                    // Examine the receiver and check if it is the service provider first.
250                 if(mt.getReceiver().equals(this.keypair.getPublic())){
251                     text = mt.getMessageBody();
                        // There are only two types of private text messages for the message
                        // service provider. One is to inform the service provider that a
                        // connection should be closed, another one is to ask the service
                        // provider for the addresses of participating wallets.
252                     if(text.equals(Message.TEXT_CLOSE)){
                            // The client wants to close the connection.
                            // Find the corresponding connection to close it.
253                         System.out.println(mt.getSenderName() + " left the system.");
254                         ConnectionChannelTaskManager thread =
                                this.server.findConnectionChannelTaskManager(
                                    UtilityMethods.getKeyString(mt.getSenderKey()));
255                         if(thread != null){
256                             thread.passiveClose();
257                         }
258                     }else if(text.equals(Message.TEXT_ASK_ADDRESSES)){
                            // Display who is asking for the list of addresses. But do not
                            // display the requester's information if it is the genesis miner.
259                         if(!mt.getSenderKey().equals(
                            BlockchainMessageServiceProvider.getGenesisBlockchain().getGenesisMiner())){
260                             System.out.println(mt.getSenderName()
                                    + " is asking for a list of users.");
261                         }
262                         ArrayList<KeyNamePair> addresses = this.server.getAllAddresses();
                            // If there is no address, or only one address the same
                            // as the requester, ignore it.
263                         if(addresses.size() == 0){
264                             return;
265                         }
266                         if(addresses.size() == 1){
267                             KeyNamePair kp = addresses.get(0);
268                             if(kp.getKey().equals(mt.getSenderKey())){
269                                 return;
270                             }
271                         }
272                         ConnectionChannelTaskManager thread =
                                this.server.findConnectionChannelTaskManager(
                                    UtilityMethods.getKeyString(mt.getSenderKey()));
273                         if(thread != null){
274                             MessageAddressPrivate mp = new MessageAddressPrivate(addresses);
275                             thread.sendMessage(mp);
276                         }
277                     }else{
                            // Anything else to this message service provider will be ignored.
278                         System.out.println("Garbage message for service provider "
                                + " found: "+ text);
279                     }
280                 }else{
                        // It must be a message for a wallet. Forward the message.
281                     ConnectionChannelTaskManager thread =
                            this.server.findConnectionChannelTaskManager(
```

```
                                UtilityMethods.getKeyString(mt.getReceiver()));
                        // If thread is null, the user must have logged out.
282                     if(thread != null){
283                         thread.sendMessage(mt);
284                     }
285                 }
286             }else if(m.getMessageType() == Message.BLOCKCHAIN_PRIVATE){
                    // Try to forward this message to the proper receiver.
287                 System.out.println("forwarding a blockchain private message.");
288                 MessageBlockchainPrivate mcp = (MessageBlockchainPrivate)m;
289                 ConnectionChannelTaskManager thread =
                        this.server.findConnectionChannelTaskManager(
                            UtilityMethods.getKeyString(mcp.getReceiver()));
290                 if(thread != null){
291                     thread.sendMessage(mcp);
292                 }
293             }else{
294                 System.out.println("message type not supported currently, type="
                        + m.getMessageType() + ", object=" + m.getMessageBody());
295             }
296         }
297         public void close(){
298             forever = false;
299         }
300 }
```

Finally, it is time to develop the BlockchainPlatform class which jumpstarts the message service provider and the genesis miner. The genesis miner is created at the start of the blockchain system, which explains why the MinerGenesisSimulator class is included inside the BlockchainPlatform class as an inner class. (Recall that the genesis miner must first generate the genesis blockchain before any network connection is possible.) The message service provider is created right after the genesis miner but must be ready and on stand-by before the genesis miner can attempt network connection. Once the system is up and running, the genesis miner should be the first participant.

```
1   import java.util.Scanner;
2   import java.util.ArrayList;
3   public class BlockchainPlatform {
4       protected static Scanner keyboard = null;
5       public static void main(String[] args) {
5           keyboard = new Scanner(System.in);
            // Start the genesis miner first.
6           MinerGenesisSimulator genesisSimulator = new MinerGenesisSimulator();
7           Thread simulator = new Thread(genesisSimulator);
8           simulator.start();
9           System.out.println("Genesis simulator is up");
10          System.out.println("Starting the blockchain message service provider ...");
11          BlockchainMessageServiceProvider server =
                        new BlockchainMessageServiceProvider();
            // Obtain the genesis blockchain from the genesis miner.
            // If the genesis blockchain is not ready, the program execution
            // is blocked right here until the genesis blockchain is ready.
12          Blockchain ledger = genesisSimulator.getGenesisLedger();
            // Set up the genesis blockchain as a permanent asset.
13          BlockchainMessageServiceProvider.updateGenesisBlock(ledger);
            // Make sure that the genesisMiner's blockChain and the ledger here
            // are the same (this examination is not necessary in fact).
```

```
14              Blockchain ledger2 = genesisSimulator.getGenesisMiner().getLocalLedger();
15              if(ledger.size() != ledger2.size()){
16                  System.out.println("ERROR!!! the two genesis blockchains are "
                            + "different in size!, " + ledger.size() + "|" + ledger2.size());
17                  System.exit(1);
18              }
19              if(!ledger.getLastBlock().getHashID().equals(
                                    ledger2.getLastBlock().getHashID())){
20                  System.out.println("Error!!! the two genesis blockchains have "
                            + "different hashcodes!");
21                  System.out.println(ledger.getLastBlock().getPreviousBlockHashID()
                            + "\n" + ledger2.getLastBlock().getPreviousBlockHashID());
22                  System.exit(2);
23              }
24              System.out.println("**********************************************");
25              System.out.println("Blockchain message service provider is "
                            + "now ready to work");
26              System.out.println("**********************************************");
                // Start the server to run "forever".
27              server.startWorking();
                // If the program reaches here, that means the server is down.
28              System.out.println("=========Blockchain platform shuts down=========");
29          }
30  }

    // Inner class. Simulates a genesis miner.
31  final class MinerGenesisSimulator implements Runnable{
32      private Blockchain genesisLedger = null;
33      private Miner genesisMiner;
        // It is critical to make the method synchronized so that if the genesis
        // blockchain is not ready, the calling statement must wait. This is an
        // example of Java's power on concurrency handling.
34      protected synchronized Blockchain getGenesisLedger(){
35          if(genesisLedger == null){
36              System.out.println("Blockchain platform starts ...");
37              System.out.println("creating genesis miner, genesis transaction "
                        + "and genesis block");
                // Create a genesis miner to start a blockchain.
38              genesisMiner = getGenesisMiner();
                // Create the genesis block.
40              Block genesisBlock =
                        new Block("0", Configuration.blockMiningDifficultyLevel(),
                            genesisMiner.getPublicKey());
41              UTXO u1 = new UTXO("0", genesisMiner.getPublicKey(),
                            genesisMiner.getPublicKey(), 1000001.0);
42              UTXO u2 = new UTXO("0", genesisMiner.getPublicKey(),
                            genesisMiner.getPublicKey(), 1000000.0);
43              ArrayList<UTXO> inputs = new ArrayList<UTXO>();
44              inputs.add(u1);
45              inputs.add(u2);
46              Transaction gt = new Transaction(genesisMiner.getPublicKey(),
                            genesisMiner.getPublicKey(), 1000000.0, inputs);
47              boolean b = gt.prepareOutputUTXOs();
48              if(!b){
49                  System.out.println("genesis transaction failed.");
50                  System.exit(1);
51              }
52              gt.signTheTransaction(genesisMiner.getPrivateKey());
53              b = genesisBlock.addTransaction(gt, genesisMiner.getPublicKey());
```

```java
54              if(!b){
55                  System.out.println("failed to add the genesis transaction to "
                            + "the  genesis block. System quit");
56                  System.exit(2);
57              }
58              // Genesis miner mines the genesis block.
59              System.out.println("genesis miner is mining the genesis block");
60              b = genesisMiner.mineBlock(genesisBlock);
61              if(b){
62                  System.out.println("genesis block is successfully mined.");
63                  System.out.println(genesisBlock.getHashID());
64              }else{
65                  System.out.println("failed to mine genesis block. System exit");
66                  System.exit(3);
67              }
68              Blockchain ledger = new Blockchain(genesisBlock);
69              System.out.println("block chain genesis successful");
                // The genesis miner copies the blockchain to be its local ledger.
70              genesisMiner.setLocalLedger(ledger);
                // Set up the genesis blockchain.
71              this.genesisLedger = ledger.copy_NotDeepCopy();
72              System.out.println("genesis miner balance: "
                        + genesisMiner.getCurrentBalance(genesisMiner.getLocalLedger()));
73          }
74          return this.genesisLedger;
75      }
 
        // It is critical to make this method synchronized so that if the genesis miner
        // is in the process of construction, the calling statement must wait for
        // the construction to complete.
75      protected synchronized Miner getGenesisMiner(){
76          if(genesisMiner == null){
77              genesisMiner = new Miner("genesis", "genesis");
78          }
79          return genesisMiner;
80      }

        // Implement this run() method as this class implements Runnable.
81      public void run(){
82          System.out.println("Important!  You are the genesis miner, you must "
                    + "start before any other miners or wallet!");
83          System.out.println("With great ability comes the great responsibility ...");
84          System.out.println("");
85          Miner miner = getGenesisMiner();
86          getGenesisLedger();
87          System.out.println("Your name=" + miner.getName());
88          System.out.println("===== Important!  Has the "
                        + "ServiceRelayProvider started?===== (1=yes, 0= no)");
89          int yesno = UtilityMethods.guaranteeIntegerInputByScanner(
                        BlockchainPlatform.keyboard, 0, 1);
90          while(yesno == 0){
91              System.out.println("===== Important!  Has the "
                        + "ServiceRelayProvider started?===== (1=yes, 0= no)");
92              yesno = UtilityMethods.guaranteeIntegerInputByScanner(
                        BlockchainPlatform.keyboard, 0, 1);
93          }
94          double balance = miner.getCurrentBalance(miner.getLocalLedger());
95          System.out.println("checking genesis miner balance: " + balance);
96          System.out.println("To join the blockchain network, please enter "
```

```
                        + "the service provider IP address:");
97          System.out.println("If this simulator is on the same computer as "
                        + "the Service Provider, please enter 127.0.0.1 or hit Enter");
98          String ipAddress = BlockchainPlatform.keyboard.nextLine();
99          if(ipAddress== null || ipAddress.length()<5){
100             ipAddress = "localhost";
101         }
            // Start the connection agent for the genesis miner.
102         WalletConnectionAgent agent = new WalletConnectionAgent(
                        ipAddress, Configuration.networkPort(), miner);
103         Thread athread = new Thread(agent);
104         athread.start();
            // Start the message task manager for the genesis miner.
105         MinerGenesisMessageTaskManager taskManager =
                    new MinerGenesisMessageTaskManager(agent, miner, agent.getMessageQueue());
106         Thread tThread = new Thread(taskManager);
107         tThread.start();
108     }
109 }
```

With all the programs ready, it is time for the big unveiling, so let's begin by starting up the distributed blockchain system. The steps are listed below:

1. Compile the Java programs. The programs presented in the book are in a default Java package. If you are using the downloaded Java programs (the recommended choice), please be aware that they are in the Java package: mdsky.applications.blockchain. Please download the programs of this chapter at: https://github.com/hhohho/Learning-Blockchain-in-Java-Edition-2.

2. Assuming that you are executing the downloaded Java programs, start up the message service provider by the command:

    *java mdsky.applications.blockchain.BlockchainPlatform*

    Figure 12 shows the initial output when the platform launches. The genesis miner starts with an initial balance of 2000000.

3. Once you see the message "Blockchain message service provider is now ready to work", enter "1" as shown in Figure 12. Otherwise, wait until the message service provider is ready. After entering "1", you will be prompted for the IP address of the server. Since the genesis miner is on the same computer as the blockchain platform, you don't have to enter anything, i.e. hitting "Enter" is fine. The log messages will show that the message service provider has accepted a connection. This is shown in Figure 13.

4. Figure 14 illustrates the following scenario. After a wallet named client1 has joined the system, the message service provider will display log messages to indicate that 1) client1 is in; 2) the sign-in bonus for client 1 has been issued; and 3) the genesis miner has mined the sign-in bonus block.

5. Start a wallet or miner with the command:

    *java mdsky.applications.blockchain.WalletSimulator*

    You can achieve this on the same computer but in a different terminal window, or in a terminal window of a different computer. You will be asked for a name and then a password as shown in Figure 15.

    ```
    Genesis simulator is up
    Starting the blockchain message service provider ...
    Important! You are the genesis miner, you must start before any other miners or wallet!
    With great ability comes the great responsibility ...

    BlockchainMessageServiceProvider is starting
    A wallet exists with the same name and password. Loaded the existing wallet
    Blockchain platform starts ...
    creating genesis miner, genesis transaction and genesis block
    genesis miner is mining the genesis block
    genesis block is successfully mined. HashID:
    000000000000000000000100100001011110011011001110110101001001011011111111110010011
    110111010111111110010010001110110011010100001011111001000010101011101110010011
    001000110110011011011001101001001101100000110001111000111010100001011100001011
    0101110110011001
    block chain genesis successful
    genesis miner balance: 2000000.0
    Your name=genesis
    ===== Important! Has the ServiceRelayProvider started?===== (1=yes, 0= no)
    ********************************************************
    Genesis blockchain is set for service provider
    Blockchain message service provider is now ready to work
    ********************************************************
    BlockchainMessageServiceProvider is ready
    BlockchainMessageServiceProvider generated MessageCheckingTaskManager, thread working
    1
    ```

    **Figure 12** The initial output when BlockchainPlatform starts. Genesis miner starts first. After the genesis block is ready, the message service provider fetches it directly from the genesis miner. Entering 1 if the message service provider is now ready to work.

6. When asked if you would like to show public keys as the addresses, please enter "No" or

simply hit the "Enter" key. The last step is to enter the IP address of the server, and you will need to know the IP address of the computer running the message service provider. If everything works fine, a GUI window should pop up, as well as some log messages in a terminal window (shown in Figure 15).

7. Create at least another wallet or miner, either on the same or a different computer, so that you can try chatting and sending transactions to each other. Make sure that at least one of the users is a miner. To simulate a mining competition, at least two miners are necessary. The first time you initiate a private chat or start a transaction, you may find that there are no wallets available. If so, have everyone type a message into the public chat so that the local wallet can obtain the name and public key of every wallet except for the genesis miner. If you want to acquire the name and public key of every wallet including the genesis miner, click "Ask For", and then select "update users". After that, when you click "To Send" to send a private message, all available wallets are displayed for selection.

```
===== Important! Has the ServiceRelayProvider started?===== (1=yes, 0= no)
BlockchainMessageServiceProvider is ready
BlockchainMessageServiceProvider generated MessageCheckingTaskManager, thread working
1
checking genesis miner balance: 2000000.0
To join the blockchain network, please enter the service provider IP address:
If this simulator is on the same computer as the Service Provider, please enter 127.0.0.1

Begin to create agent for network communication
BlockchainMessageServiceProvider accepts one connection
obtained server address and stored it, now sending wallet public key to server
name=genesis
connection successfully established for
genesis|MIIBIjANBgkqhkiG9w0BAQEFAAOCAQ8AMIIBCgKCAQEAlCAylW4EZOYtR
aqKylbAdmDK+cnkxBQS9rje4YqhfB/cipOs2kutBjL0Kr2k1+mUkZksWbtRF6tTP0/Bwjq
hvqIKyVPQ3vK/lh/6tRRbz0r+qNncI3H3HSmRa3l4D17PVUJr1cn545jzF7xB8wRzy1XaN
1T/p7hb1Q+aojXlNjQ0P19YNOcp2AnV2a/jBRKy0TyKfR6AWki3eQu/8Oud9ame/Dgyr
L0UEsyGGudHhdZ5NuFlenBqlV5x2tNIKGTrpSe2DqKAflaWC7WYcuz2XWZ3TgWsMp
Tq0/YvCZGx7L/o7B7+rgkh3r7UOLrXvIYgVmh/ypdXehADy5OlhLhP7wIDAQAB
adding address for genesis, now send the genesis blockchain
genesis] Warning: the incoming blockchain is no longer than current local one, local size=1, incoming size=1
The genesis block chain set, everything ready ...
sent a message for latest blockchain
```

**Figure 13** Illustrating the acceptance of the genesis miner's connection after displaying its

**balance.**

8. You can click "Ask For" to display a wallet's balance. Figure 16 shows the balance of a miner named client1.

9. You can also show the content of a local blockchain. Figure 17 shows part of a blockchain.

10. It is important to examine if all wallets have the same blockchain content. To update a local blockchain, click "Ask For" → "update blockchain".

```
BlockchainMessageServiceProvider accepts one connection
connection successfully established for
client1 | MIIBIjANBgkqhkiG9w0BAQEFAAOCAQ8AMIIBCgKCAQEAg+AQQcDodIj56q/
L5OT1gVoVYJvAkEo6IASo1KGThnY8VXDmzEs7CM/2VkJWrbTKVcs9ZDFXuXBabV83
qEElvZYdRD7IBJ64ZWeauANTBLs1WEBp/ARkovDgQBvJBZvtNIKZLg41ywh5y6e+lQnl
6Hk+MRUpkamVwtDiy8RU6nvieAeIWHH7IV4YcrAFJqrEyPCWMIoJ2upbMALiQErKfroR
P8CECOf/hD9DgUi7+KjpcfmQ+lpgtyWvtf47VWWKVR6SnmPfF2AjYS4Sbb1B+/aCF7cJo
0iUMCSbbBAgbLbDJG5bXEm5YDdlTO4p/8l1qAKs31nMQj1FuYDsFdG+9wIDAQAB
adding address for client1, now send the genesis blockchain
genesis: sent local blockchain to the requester, chain size=1 | 1
forwarding a blockchain private message.
genesis is sending client1 sign-in bonus of 1000
genesis is mining the sign-in bonus block for client1 by himself
Miner genesis begins to mine a block. Competition starts.
genesis mined and signed the block, hashID is:
000000000000000000011110011110110100010111111100111111110101010000011101010111
100000001111011001010000001100111000000011010010011110011100111001000000010000011
010101001111010000101111000101111100001000011111011110111000101100001101110000100
0010010011111011000
it is a block broadcast message, check if it is necessary to update it
new block is added to the local blockchain, blockchain size = 2
{
genesis: balance=1999100.0,  local blockchain size=2
```

**Figure 14** The message service provider accepts a wallet named client1.

11. Warning! If you start and stop the blockchain message service provider through Eclipse, there might still be a Java thread running (e.g. the server socket is still listening at the given port).

This will prevent you from restarting the message service provider because the port is already "taken". If this happens, terminate the running Java thread. On Windows, you can do so by using the Windows Task Manager. On a Linux computer, you can search for this process and stop it based on its process ID.

```
please provide a name: client1
Please provide your password: client1
When showing balance, by default the public key is not shown as the address.
This is for simplicity. Do you like to show the public key as address (Yes/No)?? N
To join the blockchain network, please present the service provider IP address: 127.0.0.1
===== Congratulation, you are a miner, i.e. a full-power user who can mine blocks =====
A wallet exists with the same name and password. Loaded the existing wallet
Welcome client1, blockchain miner created for you.
Begin to create agent for network communication
obtained server address and stored it, now sending wallet public key to server
name=client1
The genesis block chain set, everything ready ...
miner connection agent started
miner task manager started
sent a message for latest blockchain
It is a blockchain private message, check if it is for me and if necessary to update the blockchain
client1] Warning: the incoming blockchain is no longer than current local one, local size=1, incoming size=1
rejected the new blockchain
it is a block broadcast message, check if it is necessary to update it
new block is added to the local blockchain
```

**Figure 15** A wallet (miner) is joining the blockchain system. Please observe that after the connection agent and task manager have started, the first thing a wallet does is to ask for the latest blockchain. In addition, the sign-in bonus for this wallet is presented as a new block mined by the genesis miner.

And that's a wrap! You've done it, you've made your own functional distributed blockchain system! It may be preliminary, but the purpose of this book is to help you understand the basics of blockchain through Java programming. As aforementioned, security, network and concurrency (multi-threading) are the top three priorities in a blockchain system. Hopefully this book did a decent job introducing you to these concepts, and giving you step-by-step hands-on experience to enrich your learning.

If you are interested in learning more about blockchain development, there are two more things you can challenge yourself to try. The first is to encrypt all transported messages in the system. The second is to discard the network star model and adopt the peer-to-peer network where every node is simultaneously a client and a server.

The blockchain system can be developed in many different languages. There are quite some voices advocating for JavaScript, Solidity and Python. It is surprised to notice that Java is not highly recommended for blockchain implementation, though Solidity has some similarities with Java. After some hands-on experience in Java, the emphasis on security, network and concurrency in blockchain operations should make a lot of sense. Java is very capable of both security and concurrency by default. Java has embedded concurrency management through its JVM. JMS would also work rather well as a platform for network communication in a blockchain setting. However, JMS is only available in the Java Enterprise Edition (JEE).

```
client1{
    All UTXOs:
        fund: 1000.0, receiver: client1, sender: genesis
        fund: 899.0, receiver: client1, sender: client1
        fund: 102.0, receiver: client1, sender: client1
    Spent UTXOs:
        fund: 1000.0, receiver: client1, sender: genesis
    Unspent UTXOs:
        fund: 899.0, receiver: client1, sender: client1
        fund: 102.0, receiver: client1, sender: client1
    Mining Rewards:
        fund: 102.0, receiver: client1, sender: client1
    Paid UTXOs:
        fund: 100.0, receiver: client3, sender: client1
    Paid Transaction Fee:
        1.0
    Balance=1001.0
}
```

**Figure 16** The balance of miner client 1 who has received a sign-in bonus from the genesis miner, made a payment of 100.0 to client 3, and mined a block of two transactions.

```
Blockchain{ number of blocks: 4
    Block{
        ID: 0000000000000000000001001111010000110101001011110101100111010000100011010001100000
        Transaction{
            ID: I6MqSaB+rmDl3xIq6LWGvyeSA1JIjIm7kDsngNI++NE=
            sender: MIIBIjANBgkqhkiG9w0BAQEFAAOCAQ8AMIIBCgKCAQEAljNyTqHXbDmdLe6F7q7M/PctZKGl
            fundToBeTransferred total: 1000000.0
            Input:
                fund: 1000001.0, receiver: MIIBIjANBgkqhkiG9w0BAQEFAAOCAQ8AMIIBCgKCAQEAljNyTq
                fund: 1000000.0, receiver: MIIBIjANBgkqhkiG9w0BAQEFAAOCAQ8AMIIBCgKCAQEAljNyTq
            Output:
                fund: 1000000.0, receiver: MIIBIjANBgkqhkiG9w0BAQEFAAOCAQ8AMIIBCgKCAQEAljNyTq
                change: 1000000.0
            transaction fee: 1.0
            signature verification: true
        }
    }
    Block{
        ID: 0000000000000000000000001111011000101010101111000011010010100000010010110011001000
        Transaction{
            ID: 8w/928CXPNgdK5yuFaVDFpISNKkD7XsF0zJnYqy04to=
```

Figure 17 Display partial content of a local blockchain which has four blocks. Some data are truncated.

# 9 PEER-TO-PEER BLOCKCHAIN SYSTEM

This will be a long chapter, too. We will start with programs from chapter 8, but I do not recommend you to import the source codes from Chapter 8. Instead, I recommend you to download the chapter 9 codes from https://github.com/hhohho/Learning-Blockchain-in-Java-Edition-2 and place them into a directory (folder) for chapter 9. If you are using Eclipse or other IDE tools, please create a Java project named chapter9 and import the chapter 9 source codes.

A blockchain system is not a "true" blockchain if its network environment is not peer-to-peer (P2P). Note that "peer" is an exchangeable word with "node". In fact, in this chapter "peer" is also exchangeable with "wallet". When nodes have equal roles in a network, they are called peers. There are two major categories of P2P networks: centralized and decentralized. In a centralized P2P network, there are servers that users can always connect to. Such a P2P realm has its advantage: peers can quickly get back into the network and find others. The disvantage is obvious also: if the servers are down, some peers can quickly become isolated, i.e. the network degenerates. In a decentralized P2P environment, there are no central servers. Such a decentralized P2P faces many challenges to make all peers connected directly or indirectly. When the number of peers increase, more and more peers connect with each other indirectly through other peers. However, peers are on and off, thus there is a possibility that at some moments some peers may be left isolated. A common solution is for all peers to exchange background messages time to time such that 1) new users can be found; 2) dynamic connections can be established among peers based on the ever-changing peer status. However, such a solution tremendously increases the network traffic.

When implementing a P2P network based on the TCP protocol, there are multiple different approaches we can adopt. Every TCP connection has a server and a client, each with an input stream and an output stream. In approach 1, a TCP connection between two peers is bidirectional, i.e. both the input and output streams are utilitized, and there is only one TCP connection between any two directly connected peers. This is illustrated in Figure 18. As shown in Figure 18, there is only one TCP connection between Peer 1 and Peer 2. One of them must act like the server and the other the client. The output stream of peer 1 and the input stream of peer 2 are inside the same pipe, i.e. they are connected. The same applies to the input stream of peer 1 and the output stream of peer 2. Thus, one TCP connection between two peers provides a bidirectional communication channel. However, peer1 is the server and peer2 is the client between these two peers.

Figure 18. There is a bidirectional TCP connections between two peers.

Figure 19. There are two bidirectional TCP connections between two peers.

Approach 2 is very similar to approach 1 except that there are two TCP connections between any two directly connected peers, as shown in Figure 19. In this approach, Peer 1 and Peer 2 are both a server and a client at the same time to each other. Certainly, approach 2 cost more network resources and can incur more network traffic.

Approach 3 is more complicated as it treats each TCP connection unidirectional. Though a TCP connection has two pipes, but only one pipe is used. Thus in approach 3, it is possible that between peer 1 and peer 2, the network traffic can only go from peer 2 to peer 1, or vice versa. Let's assume the connections a peer's server accepts are the incoming connections, and the client connections of the peer to other peers' servers are the outgoing connections, Figure 20 shows that a peer sends messages out only from its client/outgoing connections and receives messages only from its server/incoming connections. In Figure 20, between Peer 1 and Peer 2, the network traffic can only move from Peer 2 to Peer 1.

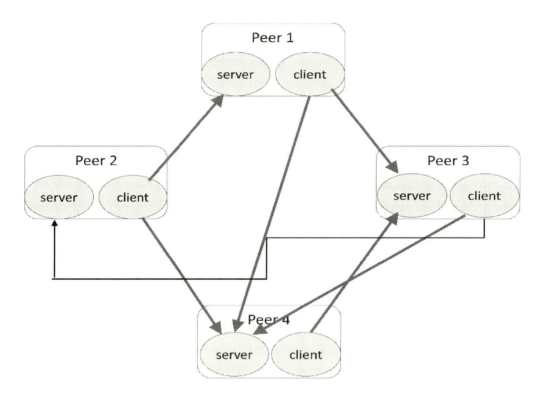

Figure 20. Connections between two peers are unidirectional in approach 3.

In this book, I will show you a simple implementation of approach 1 and approach 3. Note that a network implementing approach 2 can be easily obtained by slightly modifying approach 1 (this is explained in this chapter, too). As shown in Figure 20, both Peer 1 and Peer 4 can only accept messages from Peer 2. Messages to Peer 2 from either Peer 1 or Peer 4 must be routed through Peer 3. This is an disadvantage of approach 3 compared to approaches 1 and 2. Figure 21 illustrates a network adopting approach 1. Note that as there is only one TCP connection between any two peers, it is possible that a peer in approach 1 may only be in the server role such as Peer 3. In my opinion, approach 2 is the most reliable but most expensive, approach 1 is the most practical. Both approaches 2 and 3 are more decentralized than approach 1 as each peer is both a server and a client between two directly connected peers in approaches 2 and 3. However, approach 3 should be the last model to adopt when considering both network efficiency and reachability. This chapter will present you a simple TCP intranet implementation of approach 1, and the next chapter will present another simple TCP intranet implementation of approach 3.

This chapter's programs are derived from those of chapter 8. There are a few new programs which are introduced below. Before I introduce the new programs to you, let's review the modifications inside the Configuration class. The new codes are marked gray.

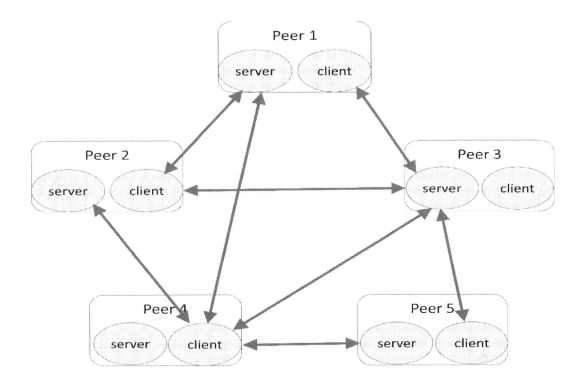

Figure 21. A P2P network adopting approach 1.

```
1    public final class Configuration {
2        private static String KEY_LOCATION = "keys";
3        public static final String keyLocation(){
4            return Configuration.KEY_LOCATION;
5        }

6        private static String HASH_ALGORITHM = "SHA-256";
7        public static final String hashAlgorithm(){
8        return Configuration.HASH_ALGORITHM;
9        }

10       private static final String SIGNATURE_ALGORITHM = "SHA256withRSA";
11       public static final String signatureAlgorithm(){
12           return Configuration.SIGNATURE_ALGORITHM;
13       }
```

```java
14        private static final String KEYPAIR_ALGORITHM = "RSA";
15        public static final String keyPairAlgorithm(){
16             return Configuration.KEYPAIR_ALGORITHM;
17        }

18        private static final int PORT = 1117;
19        public static final int networkPort(){
20             return Configuration.PORT;
21        }

22        private static final int BLOCK_MINING_DIFFICULTY_LEVEL = 20;
23        public static final int blockMiningDifficultyLevel(){
24             return Configuration.BLOCK_MINING_DIFFICULTY_LEVEL;
25        }

          // Control how many sign-in bonuses the genesis miner can issue.
26        private static int SIGN_IN_BONUS_USERS_LIMIT = 4;
27        public static final int genesisMiner_signInBonusUsersLimit(){
28             return Configuration.SIGN_IN_BONUS_USERS_LIMIT;
29        }

          // Specify how many sign-in bonus blocks the genesis miner can mine. Additional
          // sign-in blocks are mined by other miners.
30        private static int SELF_BLOCKS_TO_MINE_LIMIT = 2;
31        public static final int genesisMiner_selfBlocksToMineLimit(){
32             return Configuration.SELF_BLOCKS_TO_MINE_LIMIT;
33        }

          // The maximum number of transactions a block can have.
34        private static int BLOCK_TRANSACTION_UPPER_LIMIT = 100;
35        public static final int blockTransactionNumberUpperLimit(){
36             return Configuration.BLOCK_TRANSACTION_UPPER_LIMIT;
37        }

          // The minimum number of transactions a block must have. Note this does not apply
          // to the sign-in bonus block.
38        private static int BLOCK_TRANSACTION_LOWER_LIMIT = 2;
39        public static final int blockTransactionNumberLowerLimit(){
40             return Configuration.BLOCK_TRANSACTION_LOWER_LIMIT;
41        }

42        private static double MINING_REWARD = 100.0;
43             public static final double blockMiningReward(){
44                  return Configuration.MINING_REWARD;
45        }

          // A message that has been buried over this time limit won't be processed any more.
46        private static long MESSAGE_BURIED_TIME_LIMIT = 10 * 24 * 60 * 60 * 1000;
47        public static final long messageBuriedTimeLimit(){
48             return Configuration.MESSAGE_BURIED_TIME_LIMIT;
49        }

          // Specify a short time period a thread can sleep.
50        private static int THREAD_SLEEP_TIME_SHORT = 100;
51        public static final int threadSleepTimeShort(){
52             return Configuration.THREAD_SLEEP_TIME_SHORT;
53        }
```

```
54          // Specify a medium-sized time period a thread can sleep.
            private static int THREAD_SLEEP_TIME_MEDIUM = 250;
55          public static final int threadSleepTimeMedium(){
56              return THREAD_SLEEP_TIME_MEDIUM;
57          }

            // Specify a long time period a thread can sleep.
58          private static int THREAD_SLEEP_TIME_LONG = 1000;
59          public static final int threadSleepTimeLong(){
60              return THREAD_SLEEP_TIME_LONG;
61          }

            // Specify the bar for log messages. Log messages can be displayed on
            // standard output only if the log level is not less than the log bar.
62          private static int LOG_BAR = 0;
63          public static final int logBar(){
64              return LOG_BAR;
65          }

66          private static int LOG_MAX = 10;
67          public static final int logMax(){
68              return LOG_MAX;
69          }

70          public static final int logMin(){
71              return 0;
72          }

            // Specify the number of outgoing connections a peer can have.
73          private static int OUTGOING_CONNECTIONS_LIMIT = 6;
74          public static final int outGoingConnectionsLimit(){
75              return OUTGOING_CONNECTIONS_LIMIT;
76          }

            // Specify the number of incoming connections a peer can have.
77          private static int INCOMING_CONNECTIONS_LIMIT = 20;
78          public static final int incomingConnectionsLimit(){
79              return INCOMING_CONNECTIONS_LIMIT;
80          }

81          public static final int logMedium(){
82              return 5;
83          }
84      }
```

The first new class is LogManager. Java has its own LogManager class, but we would like to use our simple version which is demonstrated below.

```
1   public class LogManager{
2       public static void log(int logLevel, String message){
3           if(logLevel >= Configuration.logBar()){
4               System.out.println(message);
5           }
6       }
7   }
```

As shown by the IF statement in code lines 3-5, a log message can only be displayed if the input argument *LogLevel* is not less than the the *LOG_BAR* defined in the Configuration class. By default, *LOG_BAR* is set 0 so that all log messages can be displayed.

Message class is modified in this chapter. The following code section shows its content.

```
1     import java.security.PublicKey;
2     public abstract class Message implements java.io.Serializable{
3         private static final long serialVersionUID = 1L;
4         public static final int ID = 0;
5         public static final int TEXT_BROADCAST = 1;
6         public static final int TEXT_PRIVATE = 2;
          // A type of message specifically for closing connection.
7         public static final int TEXT_PRIVATE_CLOSE_CONNECTION = 3;
8         public static final int TRANSACTION_BROADCAST = 10;
9         public static final int BLOCK_BROADCAST = 20;
10        public static final int BLOCK_PRIVATE = 21;
11        public static final int BLOCK_ASK_PRIVATE = 22;
12        public static final int BLOCK_ASK_BROADCAST = 23;
13        public static final int BLOCKCHAIN_BROADCAST = 3;
14        public static final int BLOCKCHAIN_PRIVATE = 31;
15        public static final int BLOCKCHAIN_ASK_BROADCAST = 33;
          // A type of message requesting a blockchain between two peers.
16        public static final int BLOCKCHAIN_ASK_PRIVATE = 34;
          // A type of message requesting the receiving peer to initiate a connection.
17        public static final int ADDRESS_BROADCAST_MAKING_FRIEND = 40;
18        public static final int ADDRESS_PRIVATE = 41;
19        public static final int ADDRESS_ASK_BROADCAST = 42;
          // A message used to testify if the message transportation is tampered
20        public static final String JCOIN_MESSAGE = "This package is from mdsky.";
21        public abstract int getMessageType();
22        public static final String TEXT_CLOSE = "CLOSE_me";
23        public static final String TEXT_ASK_ADDRESSES = "TEXT_QUERY_ADDRESSES";
24        public abstract Object getMessageBody();
25        public abstract boolean isForBroadcast();
          // A unique ID of this message
26        public abstract String getMessageHashID();
          // Time stamp of a message: records when the message is created.
27        public abstract long getTimeStamp();
          // The sender of every message must be recorded.
28        public abstract PublicKey getSenderKey();
          // By default, a message sent by the peer won't be processed again by the same peer.
          // However, if this method returns true, then such a message will be processed
          // again by the same peer.
29        protected boolean selfMessageAllowed(){
30            return false;
31        }
32    }
```

Code line 7 specifies a new type of message that is dedicated to signal connection closing.

Code line 17 specifies a new type of message that is issued time to time by every peer. The receiving peers are requested to initiate a direct outgoing connection to the message-issuing peer.

Code lines 26-28 request that all messages must have a unique ID, a timestamp showing the creation time of the message, and a sender. In our P2P implementation, a peer finds other peers through its directly-connected neighbor(s). A peer sends out messages time to time to search for other peers in the network. The receiving peers are required to forward such messages to their directly-connected peers. Clearly, messages will be sent and received repeatedly. For example, assume Peer A has direct connection with Peers B, C, and D, while Peer X has direct connection with Peers A, C, and Y, and C has direct connection to A, X, and Y. When X sends a message to A, A will forward it to B, C, D and X. Now C will forward the same message to A, X, and Y, and Y would forward it to X and C. Clearly, the same message are repeatedly sent and received, and this becomes a serious and unnecessary overhead. There must be a mechanism to minimize this overhead. The solution we have in this chapter is to give every message a unique ID, timestamp, and a sender. Upon receiving, messages too old will be discarded, messages have been processed by a peer will be discarded by this peer, and by default, the sender of a message will discard the same message forwarded back to him.

Code lines 29-31 specify the default case that the sender of a message won't accept the same message forwarded back to him. However, there are two types of messages that a miner must accept for at least once: transaction broadcast and block broadcast messages sent by this miner. The reason is that, a miner can collect and mine its own transactions and blocks only after receiving them through network, i.e. a miner must broadcast its own transactions and blocks before collecting them.

Due to the modifications to Message class, all subclasses that extend Message are required to contain several methods. For example, considering the MessageID class, it is updated as the following:

```
1    import java.security.PrivateKey;
2    import java.security.PublicKey;
3    public final class MessageID extends MessageSigned{
4        private static final long serialVersionUID = 1L;
5        private String info = null;
6        private byte[] signature = null;
7        private PublicKey sender = null;
8        private String name = null;
9        private String uniqueHashID;
10       private long timeStamp = 0;
11       public MessageID(PrivateKey pk, PublicKey sender, String name){
12           this.info = Message.JCOIN_MESSAGE;
13           signature = UtilityMethods.generateSignature(pk, this.info);
14           this.sender = sender;
15           this.name = name;
16           this.timeStamp = UtilityMethods.getTimeStamp();
17           String v = UtilityMethods.getKeyString(sender) + name
                    + UtilityMethods.getUniqueNumber() + this.timeStamp;
18           this.uniqueHashID = UtilityMethods.messageDigestSHA256_toString(v);
19       }

20       public String getMessageBody(){
21           return this.info;
22       }

23       public boolean isValid(){
24           return UtilityMethods.verifySignature(this.getSenderKey(), signature, this.info);
25       }

26       public int getMessageType(){
27           return Message.ID;
```

```
28          }
29          public PublicKey getSenderKey(){
30              return this.sender;
31          }

32          public boolean isForBroadcast(){
33              return false;
34          }

35          public String getName(){
36              return this.name;
37          }

38          public KeyNamePair getKeyNamePair(){
39              KeyNamePair kp = new KeyNamePair(this.getSenderKey(), this.getName());
40              return kp;
41          }

42          public String getMessageHashID(){
43              return this.uniqueHashID;
44          }

45          public long getTimeStamp(){
46              return this.timeStamp;
47          }
48      }
```

Code lines 9-10 declare two new variables *uniqueHashID* and *timeStamp*. These two variables are initialized in the constructor by code lines 16-18.

Code line 42-44 implements the required method getMessageHashID().

Code lines 45-47 implements the required method getTimeStamp().

All other existing message classes follow the similar way to include the above two variables *uniqueHashID* and *timeStamp*, and implement the above two methods getMessageHashID() and getTimeStamp(). However, both MessageBlockBroadcast and MessageTransactionBroadcast classes override the method selfMessageAllowed() as shown below:

```
protected boolean selfMessageAllowed(){
    return true;
}
```

A new class added in this chapter is MessageTextCloseConnectionPrivate which is a subclass of MessageTextPrivate. The purpose of this class is to make the connection closing message more specific.

```
1   import java.security.PrivateKey;
2   import java.security.PublicKey;
3   public class MessageTextCloseConnectionPrivate extends MessageTextPrivate{
4       private static final long serialVersionUID = 1L;
5       public MessageTextCloseConnectionPrivate(PrivateKey prikey,
```

```
                            PublicKey senderKey, String senderName, PublicKey receiver){
6           super(Message.TEXT_CLOSE, prikey, senderKey, senderName, receiver);
7       }
8       public int getMessageType(){
9           return Message.TEXT_PRIVATE_CLOSE_CONNECTION;
10      }
11  }
```

MessageAskForBlockchainPrivate is also a new class. In chapter 8, the central server holds the genesis block and delivers it to every user when the user joins the blockchain network. As there is no central server in our P2P network, when a peer without any local ledger joins the blockchain network, this peer needs to obtain its initial local blockchain from the first neighbor it connects. This peers sends a MessageAskForBlockchainPrivate object to its neighbor to ask for a blockchain copy.

```
1   import java.security.PrivateKey;
2   import java.security.PublicKey;
3   class MessageAskForBlockchainPrivate extends MessageTextPrivate{
4       private static final long serialVersionUID = 1L;
5       private String uniqueHashID;
6       private long timeStamp;
7       private boolean must = false;
8       public MessageAskForBlockchainPrivate(String text, PrivateKey prikey,
                        PublicKey sender, String name, PublicKey receiver, boolean must){
9           super(text, prikey, sender, name, receiver);
10          this.timeStamp = UtilityMethods.getTimeStamp();
11          String v = UtilityMethods.getKeyString(sender) + name
                        + this.timeStamp+UtilityMethods.getUniqueNumber();
12          this.uniqueHashID = UtilityMethods.messageDigestSHA256_toString(v);
13          this.must = must;
14      }

15      public int getMessageType(){
16          return Message.BLOCKCHAIN_ASK_PRIVATE;
17      }

18      public String getMessageHashID(){
19          return this.uniqueHashID;
20      }

21      public long getTimeStamp(){
22          return this.timeStamp;
23      }

        // When this method returns true, it tells that the message owner does not
        // have a local ledger and must request a copy.
24      public boolean isMust(){
25          return this.must;
26      }
27  }
```

Code lines 24-26 present the only unique part of the MessageAskForBlockchainPrivate class. We will explain more about this method isMust() later.

The following code section introduces another new class MessageBroadcastMakingFriend.

```java
1     import java.security.PrivateKey;
2     import java.security.PublicKey;
3     public final class MessageBroadcastMakingFriend extends MessageSigned{
4         private static final long serialVersionUID = 1L;
5         private String info = null;
6         private byte[] signature = null;
7         private PublicKey sender = null;
8         private String name = null;
9         private String uniqueHashID;
10        private long timeStamp = 0;
11        private String IP;
12        public MessageBroadcastMakingFriend(PrivateKey pk, PublicKey sender,
                                               String name, String IP) {
13            this.info = Message.JCOIN_MESSAGE;
14            signature = UtilityMethods.generateSignature(pk, this.info);
15            this.sender = sender;
16            this.name = name;
17            this.timeStamp = UtilityMethods.getTimeStamp();
18            String v = UtilityMethods.getKeyString(sender) + name
                        + UtilityMethods.getUniqueNumber() + this.timeStamp;
19            this.uniqueHashID = UtilityMethods.messageDigestSHA256_toString(v);
20            this.IP = IP;
21        }

22        public String getMessageBody(){
23            return this.info;
24        }

25        public boolean isValid(){
26            return UtilityMethods.verifySignature(this.getSenderKey(), signature, this.info);
27        }

28        public int getMessageType(){
29            return Message.ADDRESS_BROADCAST_MAKING_FRIEND;
30        }

31        public PublicKey getSenderKey(){
32            return this.sender;
33        }

34        public boolean isForBroadcast(){
35            return true;
36        }

37        public String getName(){
38            return this.name;
39        }

40        public KeyNamePair getKeyNamePair(){
41            KeyNamePair kp = new KeyNamePair(this.getSenderKey(), this.getName());
42            return kp;
43        }

44        public String getMessageHashID(){
45            return this.uniqueHashID;
46        }

47        public long getTimeStamp(){
48            return this.timeStamp;
```

```
49          }
50          public String getIP(){
51              return this.IP;
52          }
53    }
```

Code lines 12-21 list the constructor of this class. Note that the constructor requires the IP address of the sending peer. The IP address is fetched by the program automatically when constructing an object of `MessageBroadcastMakingFriend`. The receiving peer needs the IP address to initiate a connection request.

Code lines 50-52 list the method that returns the IP address stored inside this message.

The UtilityMethods class is slightly modified in this chapter by adding the following method which determines if a message is too old to be accepted:

```
public static boolean isMessageTooOld(long timeStamp){
    long currentTime = getTimeStamp();
    return (currentTime - timeStamp) >= Configuration.messageBuriedTimeLimit();
}
```

Compared to chapter 8 programs, the most significant modification in this chapter is the removal of the central server. This means that there is no more BlockchainMessageServiceProvider class. Instead, there is the PeerServer class. The second most significant modification in this chapter is the addition of PeerIncomingConnection class and PeerOutgoingConnection class. The third most significant modification in this chapter is the removal of WalletConnectionAgent class. A similar class named PeerConnectionManager is created instead. PeerConnectionManager serves a similar role as WalletConnectionAgent but with a different name. The reasons for the name change are 1) the new class is no longer representing one connection, it manages all the network connections for a peer; 2) all the network connections it manages are peer connections. WalletMessageTaskManager and its two subclasses MinerMessageTaskManager and MinerGenesisMessageTaskManager are slightly modified, too. At the last, the BlockchainPlatform and WalletSimulator classes are modified accordingly.

```
1     import java.net.ServerSocket;
2     import java.net.Socket;
3     import java.net.InetAddress;
4     public class PeerServer implements Runnable{
5         private Wallet wallet;
6         private ServerSocket server;
7         private static String IP = null;
8         private boolean forever = true;
9         private PeerConnectionManager connectionManager;
10        private WalletMessageTaskManager messageManager;
11        PeerServer(Wallet wallet, WalletMessageTaskManager messageManager,
                        PeerConnectionManager connectionManager) throws Exception{
12            this.wallet = wallet;
13            this.connectionManager = connectionManager;
14            this.messageManager = messageManager;
15            server = new ServerSocket(Configuration.networkPort());
16            PeerServer.IP = server.getInetAddress().getLocalHost().getHostAddress();
```

```
17          }
18          public static String getServerIP(){
19                  return PeerServer.IP;
20          }




21          public void run(){
22                  LogManager.log(Configuration.logMax(), "peer server of "
                                    + this.wallet.getName()+" is listening now");
23              while(forever){
24                try{
25                    if(this.connectionManager.numberOfExistingIncomingConnections()
                                        >= Configuration.incomingConnectionsLimit()){
26                          Thread.sleep(Configuration.threadSleepTimeLong() * 100);
27                    }else{
28                          Socket socket = this.server.accept();
29                          InetAddress clientAddress = socket.getInetAddress();
30                          LogManager.log(Configuration.logMax(), "Got an incoming connection "
                                        + "request from " + clientAddress.getHostAddress());
31                          PeerIncomingConnection peer = new PeerIncomingConnection(wallet,
                                        socket, messageManager, connectionManager);
32                          Thread t = new Thread(peer);
33                          t.start();
34                          LogManager.log(Configuration.logMax(), "PeerIncomingConnection with "
                                        + peer.getConnectionIP() + " established");
35                          this.connectionManager.addIncomingConnection(peer);
36                    }
37                }catch(Exception ioe){
38                    LogManager.log(Configuration.logMax(), "Exception in PeerServer.run()["
                                    + ioe.getMessage());
39                    forever = false;
40                }
41            }
42            System.exit(0);
43          }
44   }
```

The above code sections present the PeerServer class.

Code line 4 defines that PeerServer class can be executed as an independent thread because it implements the interface Runnable. It is extremely important to execute the server as another thread so that it won't block the execution of the program.

Code line 5 specifies the wallet which this peer server is working on behalf of.

Code line 6 records the ServerSocket the server will create. Note that every TCP server must have a ServerSocket to accept incoming connection requests.

Code line 7 defines a static variable to hold the IP address of this PeerServer. Making this variable static is to render easy access to the IP address that a peer server is bound to. As one IP/port can bind one ServerSocket only, and in a single JVM there should be only one PeerServer instance, it is safe to make this variable static.

Code line 9 defines a PeerConnectionManager variable "connectionManager" which we will discuss later in detail. By now, please just be aware of it. The same applies to the WalletMessageTaskManager variable "messageManager" defined in code line 10.

Code lines 11-17 list the constructor. Note that to construct a PeerServer instance, the following objects must be given: Wallet, PeerConnectionManager, and WalletMessageTaskManager.

Code line 15 creats a ServerSocket based on the port number defined in Configuration class.

Code line 16 fetches the local IP address of the computer where the peer server is running. Note that some computers may have multiple IP addresses due to multiple network connections. If so, when testing this package, please make sure that the right IP address is used.

Code lines 21-43 list the method run(). Inside this method, the while loop (lines 23-41) keeps the server running forever until it is forced to shut down.

The IF statement in code lines 25-27 describes such a scenario: if the peer has already enough incoming connections, the peer server won't accept any connection request. Removing this IF statement will allow the peer server to accept as many incoming connections as possible.

Code line 28 creates a Socket instance upon a connection request. Note that this statement blocks the execution of PeerServer till a connection request arrives.

Code line 31 creates a PeerIncomingConnection based on the Socket instance, the Wallet instance, the PeerConnectionManager instance, and the WalletMessageTaskManager instance. Note that this PeerIncomingConnection object is started as a thread later in code lines 32-33.

Code line 34 adds this PeerIncomingConnection instance into PeerConnectionManager's pool.

Code line 42 is also important: when the peer server is interrupted or stoped, shuts down the JVM.

A PeerIncomingConnection is a TCP socket connection in which this incoming connection is on the server side. The PeerIncomingConnection class is explained by comments in the following code section:

```
1    import java.net.Socket;
2    import java.io.ObjectInputStream;
3    import java.io.ObjectOutputStream;
4    import java.io.IOException;
5    import java.security.PublicKey;
     // Define PeerIncomingConnection will be executed as a thread.
     // Refer to code lines 31-33 of PeerServer class.
6    public class PeerIncomingConnection implements Runnable{
         // The wallet which this connection works on behalf.
7        private Wallet wallet;
```

```
8              // The socket dedicated to this connection / channel.
               private Socket socket;
               // The input stream in the form of ObjectInputStream.
9              private ObjectInputStream in;
               // The output stream in the form of ObjectOutputStream.
10             private ObjectOutputStream out;
               // The public key of the peer that this incoming connection is connected to.
11             private PublicKey connectionPeerPubkey;
               // The name of the peer that this incoming connection is connected to.
12             private String connectionPeerName;
               // The use of this variable allows the thread execution to be terminated.
13             private boolean forever = true;
               // The PeerConnectionManager that manages this connection.
14             private PeerConnectionManager connectionManager;
               // The WalletMessageTaskManager that process messages from this incoming connection.
15             private WalletMessageTaskManager messageManager;
               // The constructor. Pay attention to the input arguments.
16             public PeerIncomingConnection(Wallet wallet, Socket socket,
                           WalletMessageTaskManager messageManager,
                           PeerConnectionManager connectionManager) throws Exception{
17                 this.wallet = wallet;
18                 this.messageManager = messageManager;
19                 this.connectionManager = connectionManager;
20                 this.socket = socket;
                   // Note that this output stream must be created before the input stream.
21                 this.out = new ObjectOutputStream(this.socket.getOutputStream());
22                 this.in = new ObjectInputStream(this.socket.getInputStream());
                   // Prepare a MessageID object containing the wallet information.
23                 MessageID mid = new MessageID(this.wallet.getPrivateKey(),
                               this.wallet.getPublicKey(), this.wallet.getName());
                   // Send the peer at another end the MessageID object. Note the another end
                   // is the corresponding PeerOutgoingConnection.
24                 this.out.writeObject(mid);
                   // Expect a MessageID object from another end of the connection.
25                 MessageID md = (MessageID)this.in.readObject();
                   // Fetch the public key and name of the peer on another end.
26                 this.connectionPeerPubkey = md.getSenderKey();
27                 this.connectionPeerName = md.getName();
                   // It is guaranteed that the peer on another end will send in a
                   // MessageAskForBlockchainPrivate object.
28                 MessageAskForBlockchainPrivate mabcb
                               = (MessageAskForBlockchainPrivate)this.in.readObject();
                   // If the MessageAskForBlockchainPrivate object says "isMust", this peer / wallet
                   // must respond with a MessageBlockchainPrivate object.
29                 if(mabcb.isMust()){
30                     PublicKey receiver = mabcb.getSenderKey();
31                     Blockchain bc = this.wallet.getLocalLedger().copy_NotDeepCopy();
32                     MessageBlockchainPrivate message = new MessageBlockchainPrivate(bc,
                                   wallet.getPublicKey(), receiver);
33                     this.sendMessage(message);
34                 }
                   // Record the public key and name of the peer on another end of the connection.
35                 this.connectionManager.addAddress(md.getKeyNamePair());
36             }

               // Must implement this run() method.
37             public void run(){
                   // The while loop keeps the object alive till being terminated.
38                 while(forever){
```

```
39                    try{
                          // Release some CPU time so that other processes can work.
40                        Thread.sleep(Configuration.threadSleepTimeMedium());
41                    }catch(InterruptedException ie){
                          // Display the error message when an exception occurs.
42                        LogManager.log(Configuration.logMin(), "Exception in "
                              + "PeerIncomingConnection.run()-1[" + ie.getMessage());
                          // Request to terminate this thread actively since an exception occurs.
43                        activeClose();
44                    }
45                    try{
                          // Wait for an incoming message. This statement blocks the execution
                          // of this PeerIncomingConnection instance. That is why it must be
                          // executed inside a thread.
46                        Message m = (Message)this.in.readObject();
47                        LogManager.log(Configuration.logMin(),"got a message in "
                              + "IncomingConnection:" + m.getMessageType()
                              + "|" + m.getMessageBody());
                          // In case the received message is to requsting connection closure,
                          // immediate action must be taken to shut down this thread.
48                        if(m.getMessageType() == Message.TEXT_PRIVATE_CLOSE_CONNECTION){
                              // Make sure that it is from the correct sender.
49                            MessageTextCloseConnectionPrivate mp
                                  = (MessageTextCloseConnectionPrivate)m;
50                            if(mp.getSenderKey().equals(this.connectionPeerPubkey)
                                  && mp.getReceiver().equals(this.wallet.getPublicKey())){
51                                LogManager.log(Configuration.logMax(),"The incomingConnection "
                                      + "from "+ getConnectionIP() + "/" + this.connectionPeerName
                                      + " is requested to be terminated.");
                                  // Start the passive closing action.
52                                this.close();
53                            }
54                        }else{
                              // Pass all other messages to the WalletMessageTaskManager.
55                            this.messageManager.addMessageIntoQueue(m);
56                        }
57                    }catch(Exception ioe){
                          // The log message explains what is happening.
58                        LogManager.log(Configuration.logMin(), "Exception in "
                              + "PeerIncomingConnection.run()-2[" + ioe.getMessage());
59                        this.close();
60                    }
61                }
62            }

              // A method dedicated to sending out messages.
63            protected synchronized boolean sendMessage(Message m){
                  // Never send a null.
64                if(m == null){
65                    return false;
66                }
67                try{
                      // Send out the message and then return true.
68                    this.out.writeObject(m);
69                    return true;
70                }catch(IOException e){
71                    LogManager.log(Configuration.logMax(), "Exception in "
                          + "PeerIncomingConnection.sendMessage()["
                          + "type=" + m.getMessageType() + "]" + e.getMessage());
```

```
                // Need to close and remove this connection
72              this.close();
73          }
74          return false;
75      }

        // A close action initiated by the peer owning this connection, i.e, the close action
        // is initiated on this end of the connection. Such an action requires a
        // connection-close-message to be sent to another end of the connection.
        // Note that this method is synchronized.
76      protected synchronized void activeClose(){
77          MessageTextCloseConnectionPrivate mc
                    = new MessageTextCloseConnectionPrivate(this.wallet.getPrivateKey(),
                    this.wallet.getPublicKey(), this.wallet.getName(), this.connectionPeerPubkey);
78          try{
79              this.out.writeObject(mc);
80              Thread.sleep(Configuration.threadSleepTimeShort());
81          }catch(Exception ee){
82              LogManager.log(Configuration.logMin(), "Exception in "
                        + "PeerIncomingConnection.activeClose()["+ee.getMessage());
83          }
            // Now close this thread.
84          this.close();
85      }

        // By setting forever = false, this method offers an opportunity to exit from the
        // while loop inside the run() method. Note that this method is synchronized.
86      private synchronized void close(){
87          this.forever = false;
88          try{
89              this.in.close();
90              this.out.close();
91          }catch(Exception e){
92              LogManager.log(Configuration.logMin(), "Exception in "
                        + "PeerIncomingConnection.close()["+e.getMessage());
93          }
            // Also remove this connection from the pool.
94          connectionManager.removePeerConnection(this);
95          LogManager.log(Configuration.logMin(), "IncomingConnection from "
                    + this.getConnectionIP() + "/" + this.connectionPeerName + " is closed");
96      }

        // Return the IP address of the peer on another end of the connection.
97      public String getConnectionIP(){
98          return this.socket.getInetAddress().getHostAddress();
99      }

        // Return the public key of the wallet on another end of the connection.
100     public PublicKey getConnectionPeerPublicKey(){
101         return this.connectionPeerPubkey;
102     }

        // Return the name of the wallet on another end of the connection.
103     public String getConnectionPeerName(){
104         return this.connectionPeerName;
105     }

        // Obtain the KeyNamePair of the peer on another end of the connection
106     public KeyNamePair getConnectionPeerNamePair(){
```

```
107                return new KeyNamePair(this.connectionPeerPubkey, this.connectionPeerName);
108        }
109 }
```

A PeerOutgoingConnection is a TCP socket connection in which this connection is a client socket. This class is explained in the follow code section with comments.

```
1    import java.io.ObjectInputStream;
2    import java.io.ObjectOutputStream;
3    import java.net.Socket;
4    import java.security.PublicKey;
     // Define PeerOutgoingConnection will be executed as a thread.
5    public class PeerOutgoingConnection implements Runnable{
         // The wallet for which this connection is working.
6        private Wallet wallet;
         // The TCP socket on the client side.
7        private Socket socket;
         // The IP address of the server socket that this outgoing connection is connected to.
8        private String connectionIP;
9        private ObjectInputStream in;
10       private ObjectOutputStream out;
         // The public key of the peer that this outgoing connection is connected to.
11       private PublicKey connectionPeerPubkey;
         // The name of the peer that this outgoing connection is connected to.
12       private String connectionPeerName;
13       private boolean forever = true;
         // The PeerConnectionManager that manages this connection together with others.
14       private PeerConnectionManager connectionManager;
         //The WalletMessageTaskManager that process messages from this outgoing connection.
15       private WalletMessageTaskManager messageManager;
         // The constructor. Pay attention to the input arguments. It needs the IP address
         // of the peer server.
16       protected PeerOutgoingConnection(String serverIP, Wallet wallet,
                     WalletMessageTaskManager messageManager,
                     PeerConnectionManager connectionManager) throws Exception{
17           this.wallet = wallet;
18           this.messageManager = messageManager;
19           this.connectionManager = connectionManager;
20           LogManager.log(Configuration.logMax(), wallet.getName()
                  + " is creating a peer outgoing connection to " + serverIP);
             // Record the peer server IP address.
21           this.connectionIP = serverIP;
             // Create a socket on the client side.
22           socket = new Socket(serverIP, Configuration.networkPort());
             // It is important to create the output stream before input stream.
23           out = new ObjectOutputStream(socket.getOutputStream());
24           in = new ObjectInputStream(socket.getInputStream());
             // Expect MessageID from the peer server side.
25           MessageID fromPeerServer = (MessageID)in.readObject();
             // Make sure that the message is in good standing
26           if(fromPeerServer.isValid()){
                 // Record the public key and name of the peer server.
27               this.connectionPeerPubkey = fromPeerServer.getSenderKey();
28               this.connectionPeerName = fromPeerServer.getName();
29           }else{
30               throw new Exception("MessageID from peer server is invalid.");
31           }
32           LogManager.log(Configuration.logMax(), "obtained peer server address and "
```

```
                        + "stored it, now sending wallet public key to peer server");
33              LogManager.log(Configuration.logMax(), "name="+this.wallet.getName());
                // If everything works well by far, sends the peer server a responding MessageID
                // because the server's PeerIncomingConnection is waiting for a MessageID.
34              MessageID mid = new MessageID(this.wallet.getPrivateKey(),
                        this.wallet.getPublicKey(), this.wallet.getName());
35              out.writeObject(mid);
36              LogManager.log(Configuration.logMax(), "A peer client outgoingconnection to "
                        + this.connectionIP + " is established successfully.");
                // If this peer/wallet has no local blockchain set, i.e. this peer just
                // joins the network, it needs to obtain a blockchain immediately.
37              if(this.wallet.getLocalLedger() == null){
                    // Directly ask for a blockchain before doing anything else. Note that
                    // the last input argument is true.
38                  MessageAskForBlockchainPrivate m = new
                        MessageAskForBlockchainPrivate("update blockchain", wallet.getPrivateKey(),
                        wallet.getPublicKey(), wallet.getName(), this.connectionPeerPubkey, true);
                    // Send the request.
39                  out.writeObject(m);
                    // Wait for such a response.
40                  MessageBlockchainPrivate mbcb = (MessageBlockchainPrivate)in.readObject();
41                  LogManager.log(Configuration.logMin(), "In PeerOutgoingConnection.constructor["
                        + "It is a blockchain private message, check if it is for me and "
                        + "if necessary to update the blockchain");
                    // The wallet sets its blockchain.
42                  boolean b = this.wallet.setLocalLedger(mbcb.getMessageBody());
43                  if(b){
44                      LogManager.log(Configuration.logMax(), "blockchain updated successfully");
45                  }else{
46                      LogManager.log(Configuration.logMax(), "In PeerOutgoingConnection. "
                            + "constructor[blockchain update failed for "
                            + this.wallet.getName() + " from " + this.getConnectionIP());
47                      throw new RuntimeException("In In PeerOutgoingConnection.constructor["
                            + "blockchain update failed for " + this.wallet.getName()
                            + " from " + this.getConnectionIP());
48                  }
49              }else{
                    // If the peer/wallet has a local blockchain, still send such a message but
                    // the last input argument is false (then no responding object is expected).
50                  MessageAskForBlockchainPrivate m = new
                        MessageAskForBlockchainPrivate("update blockchain", wallet.getPrivateKey(),
                        wallet.getPublicKey(), wallet.getName(), this.connectionPeerPubkey, false);
51                  out.writeObject(m);
52              }
                // Add the information of the connected peer into the pool.
53              this.connectionManager.addAddress(fromPeerServer.getKeyNamePair());
54          }

            // A method dedicated to sending messages.
55          public synchronized boolean sendMessage(Message m){
                // Double ensure that no null message is sent.
56              if(m == null){
57                  LogManager.log(Configuration.logMin(), "message is null, cannot send");
58                  return false;
59              }
60              try{
                    // Send the message.
61                  this.out.writeObject(m);
62                  return true;
```

```
63              }catch(Exception e){
64                  LogManager.log(Configuration.logMax(), "Exception in "
                        + "PeerOutgoingConnection.sendMessage()|" + this.getConnectionIP()
                        + "|failed to send message [" + e.getMessage());
                    // When an exception occurs here, the network will be terminated.
                    // Thus, we need to recreate this connection for at least one time.
65                  if(!this.connectionManager.recreatePeerOutgoingConnection(this)){
                        // The connection recovery effort failed, must close the connection.
66                      this.close();
67                  }
68                  return false;
69              }
70          }

            // Obtain the public key of the peer on another end of the connection.
71          public PublicKey getConnectionPeerPublicKey(){
72              return this.connectionPeerPubkey;
73          }

            // Obtain the name of the peer on another end of the connection.
74          public String getConnectionPeerName(){
75              return this.connectionPeerName;
76          }

            // Obtain the KeyNamePair of the peer on another end of the connection.
77          public KeyNamePair getConnectionPeerNamePair(){
78              return new KeyNamePair(this.connectionPeerPubkey, this.connectionPeerName);
79          }

            // Obtain the IP of the peer on another end of the connection,
            // i.e. the IP address of the peer server this connection connected to.
80          public String getConnectionIP(){
81              return this.connectionIP;
82          }

            // A close action initiated by the peer owning this connection, i.e, the close
            // action is initiated on this end of the connection. Such an action requires
            // a connection-close-message to be sent to another end of the connection.
83          protected void activeClose(){
                // Prepare the message to be sent.
84              MessageTextCloseConnectionPrivate mc = new
                    MessageTextCloseConnectionPrivate(this.wallet.getPrivateKey(),
                    this.wallet.getPublicKey(), this.wallet.getName(),
                    this.getConnectionPeerPublicKey());
                // Send the message.
85              this.sendMessage(mc);
                // Wait for a little bit.
86              try{
87                  Thread.sleep(Configuration.threadSleepTimeShort());
88              }catch(Exception ee){
89                  LogManager.log(Configuration.logMax(), "Exception in "
                        + "PeerOutgoingConnection.activeClose()|"
                        + this.getConnectionIP() + "[" + ee.getMessage());
90              }
                // Close this connection.
91              this.close();
92          }

            // Close the input and output stream of the connection.
```

```
                // In addition, remove this connection from the pool.
93      private void close(){
94          this.forever = false;
95          try{
96              this.in.close();
97              this.out.close();
98          }catch(Exception e){
                // Do nothing
99          }
100         this.connectionManager.removePeerConnection(this);
101         LogManager.log(Configuration.logMax(), "Peer outgoing connection to "
                    + this.connectionIP + "/" + this.getConnectionPeerName() + " is terminated.");
102     }

        // Must implement this method.
103     public void run(){
            // Use a while loop to keep this thread alive.
104         while(forever){
105             try{
106                 Thread.sleep(Configuration.threadSleepTimeMedium());
                    // Receive a message.
107                 Message m = (Message)in.readObject();
                    // Log message. Can be turned off.
108                 LogManager.log(Configuration.logMin(), "got a message in "
                            + "outgoingConnection:" + m.getMessageType() + "|from "
                            + this.connectionIP + "/" + this.connectionPeerName
                            + "|" + m.getMessageBody());
                    // If the received message is to close the connection.
109                 if(m.getMessageType() == Message.TEXT_PRIVATE_CLOSE_CONNECTION){
110                     MessageTextCloseConnectionPrivate mp
                            = (MessageTextCloseConnectionPrivate)m;
                        // Double check if such a message is for me.
111                     if(mp.getSenderKey().equals(this.getConnectionPeerPublicKey())
                                && mp.getReceiver().equals(this.wallet.getPublicKey())){
                            // Close the connection and release resources.
112                         this.close();
113                         LogManager.log(Configuration.logMax(), this.getConnectionIP()
                                + "/" + this.getConnectionPeerName() + " initiates "
                                + "connection close, the peer outgoing connection "
                                + "is closing now.");
114                     }
115                 }else{
                        // All other messages are passed to WalletMessageTaskManager.
116                     this.messageManager.addMessageIntoQueue(m);
117                 }
118             }catch(Exception e){
119                 LogManager.log(Configuration.logMax(), "Exception in "
                            + "PeerOutgoingConnection.run()|" + this.getConnectionIP() + "/"
                            + this.getConnectionPeerName() + "[ "+e.getMessage());
                    // If an exception occurs, close the connection.
120                 this.close();
121             }
122         }
123     }
124 }
```

The PeerConnectionManager class is a critical class as it manages all the network connections and peer information. Currently, we are implementing the P2P approach 1. However, if the approach 2 is desired, a minor modification inside the PeerConnectionManager class can turn the approach 1 implementaion into an approach 2 implementation. This class is explained by the following code section (pay attention to the comments):

```java
1    import java.security.PublicKey;
2    import java.util.ArrayList;
3    import java.util.Hashtable;
4    import java.util.Iterator;
5    import java.util.Enumeration;
     // The connection manager must be executed as a thread.
6    public class PeerConnectionManager implements Runnable{
         // The wallet that this manager is working for.
7        private Wallet wallet;
         // The pool to store the names and public keys of all wallets connected
         // directly or indirectly. The key is the string representation of the
         // public key.
8        private Hashtable<String, KeyNamePair> allAddresses
                 = new Hashtable<String, KeyNamePair>();
         // A boolean variable used to control the while loop inside the method run().
9        private boolean forever = true;
         // The message manager that this connection manager collaborates with.
10       private WalletMessageTaskManager messageManager;
         // The pool to store the peer's outgoing connections that this connection
         // manager is managing.
11       private Hashtable<String, PeerOutgoingConnection> outgoingConnections
                 = new Hashtable<String, PeerOutgoingConnection>();
         // The pool to store the peer's incoming connections that this connection
         // manager is managing.
12       private Hashtable<String, PeerIncomingConnection> incomingConnections
                 = new Hashtable<String, PeerIncomingConnection>();
         // The number of times that this connection manager has tried to find peers
         // to establish direct connections with. Note that in this package, except for
         // the genesis miner, when a peer starts, it must make a direct connection with
         // another peer so that it can join the network. It is important to find other
         // peers through this directly-connected peer, especially when it joins the
         // network. However, such attempts should be minimized to avoid traffic jam
         // once the network has been established. This is why we need to count how many
         // such attemps have been made.
13       private int autoMakingFriends = 0;
         // Another variable used to control how often the making-friend attempts should
         // be made.
14       private int idleTimes = 0;
         // The constructor.
15       public PeerConnectionManager(Wallet wallet, WalletMessageTaskManager messageManager){
16           this.wallet = wallet;
17           this.messageManager = messageManager;
18       }

19       protected void setWalletMessageTaskManager(WalletMessageTaskManager messageManager){
20           this.messageManager = messageManager;
21       }

         // Must implement this method that defines the actions of this connection manager.
22       public void run(){
             // Note the use of the boolean variable forever. If forever is switched to be
             // false, the while loop will be exited and then the life this connection
             // manager is soon finished.
23           while(forever){
```

```
24              try{
                    // In a non-busy network, the thread should sleep long.
                    // However, in a busy network, the thread should sleep short.
25                  Thread.sleep(Configuration.threadSleepTimeLong());
26              }catch(InterruptedException ie){
27                  LogManager.log(Configuration.logMin(), "Exception in "
                        + "PeerConnectionManager.run()-1[" + ie.getMessage());
28              }
                // Control when to attempt to make friends. The idea is to attempt three
                // times when the peer starts. Actually, attempting once is good enough.
                // It is hard-coded three times here, though it should be better to control
                // this number in the Configuration class.
29              if((idleTimes+2) %10 == 0 && autoMakingFriends < 3){
30                  makingFriends();
31                  autoMakingFriends++;
32              }
33              try{
34                  Thread.sleep(Configuration.threadSleepTimeLong());
35                  idleTimes++;
36              }catch(InterruptedException ie){
37                  LogManager.log(Configuration.logMin(), "Exception in "
                        + "PeerConnectionManager.run()-2[" + ie.getMessage());
38              }
39              if(idleTimes % 100 == 0){
40                  idleTimes = 0;
41              }
42          }
43      }

        // The method "makingFriends". In this method, a MessageBroadcastMakingFriend message
        // is sent to all available peers in the network. All peers receiving such a message
        // will attempt to make an outgoing connection to this peer, including those whom
        // this peer has already directly connected. Certainly, this can incur quite some
        // unnecessary network traffic.
44      protected void makingFriends(){
45          if(PeerServer.getServerIP() != null && this.numberOfExistingIncomingConnections()
                    < Configuration.incomingConnectionsLimit()){
46              MessageBroadcastMakingFriend mf =
                new MessageBroadcastMakingFriend(this.wallet.getPrivateKey(),
                    this.wallet.getPublicKey(), this.wallet.getName(), PeerServer.getServerIP());
47              this.sendMessageByAll(mf);
48          }
49      }

        // This  method creates an outgoing connection to the given IP address.
        // The creation takes place only if 1) this peers does not have enough outgoing
        // connections; 2) there is no existing incoming connection to the same IP address;
        // 3) there is no existing outgoing connection to the same IP address.
50      protected synchronized boolean createOutgoingConnection(String peerServerIP){
            // Examine if there are enough outgoing connections. If yes, quit.
51          if(this.outgoingConnections.size() >= Configuration.outGoingConnectionsLimit()){
52              LogManager.log(Configuration.logMax(), "cannot create the outgoing "
                    + "connection to " + peerServerIP + " because the current size of "
                    + this.outgoingConnections.size() +" has already reached the limit of "
                    + Configuration.outGoingConnectionsLimit());
53              return false;
54          }
            // Examine if there is an incoming connection from the same IP address.
            // If yes, quit.
```

```java
                PeerIncomingConnection pi = this.incomingConnections.get(peerServerIP);
                if(pi != null){
                    LogManager.log(Configuration.logMin(), "cannot create the outgoing "
                            + "connection to " + peerServerIP +" because there is already "
                            + "an incoming connection from " + pi.getConnectionIP()
                            + "/" + pi.getConnectionPeerName());
                    return false;
                }
                try{
                    // Examine if there is an outgoing connection from the same IP address.
                    // If yes, do not proceed.
                    PeerOutgoingConnection client = outgoingConnections.get(peerServerIP);
                    if(client == null){
                        // Create an outgoing connection.
                        client = new PeerOutgoingConnection(peerServerIP,
                                    this.wallet, this.messageManager, this);
                        // Execute the outgoing connection as a thread.
                        Thread t = new Thread(client);
                        t.start();
                        // Add this outgoing connection into the pool.
                        outgoingConnections.put(UtilityMethods.getKeyString(
                                    client.getConnectionPeerPublicKey()), client);
                        outgoingConnections.put(peerServerIP, client);
                        // Store the name and public key information of the connected peer.
                        this.addAddress(client.getConnectionPeerNamePair());
                        LogManager.log(Configuration.logMax(),
                            "created an outgoing connection to " + peerServerIP);
                        return true;
                    }
                }catch(Exception e){
                    LogManager.log(Configuration.logMax(), "Exception in "
                        + "PeerConnectionManager.createOutgoingConnection|"
                        + peerServerIP + "[" + e.getMessage());
                    return false;
                }
                return false;
            }
            
            // An effort to re-create a PeerOutgoingConnection based a retired
            // outgoing connection.
            protected boolean recreatePeerOutgoingConnection(PeerOutgoingConnection con){
                this.removePeerConnection(con);
                return createOutgoingConnection(con.getConnectionIP());
            }
            
            // Add an incoming connection into its pool.
            protected void addIncomingConnection(PeerIncomingConnection con){
                this.incomingConnections.put(UtilityMethods.getKeyString(
                                con.getConnectionPeerPublicKey()), con);
                this.incomingConnections.put(con.getConnectionIP(), con);
            }
            
            // An overloaded method to remove an outgoing connection.
            protected synchronized void removePeerConnection(PeerOutgoingConnection con){
                outgoingConnections.remove(con.getConnectionIP());
                outgoingConnections.remove(UtilityMethods.getKeyString(
                                    con.getConnectionPeerPublicKey()));
            }
```

```
            // An overloaded method to remove an outgoing connection.
 90         protected synchronized void removePeerConnection(PeerIncomingConnection con){
 91             incomingConnections.remove(con.getConnectionIP());
 92             incomingConnections.remove(UtilityMethods.getKeyString(
                        con.getConnectionPeerPublicKey()));
 93         }

            // Send the given message by all connections, both incoming and outgoing.
 94         protected synchronized void sendMessageByAll(Message m){
 95             Enumeration<PeerOutgoingConnection> E = outgoingConnections.elements();
 96             while(E.hasMoreElements()){
 97                 PeerOutgoingConnection p = E.nextElement();
 98                 p.sendMessage(m);
 99             }
100             Enumeration<PeerIncomingConnection> E2 = incomingConnections.elements();
101             while(E2.hasMoreElements()){
102                 PeerIncomingConnection p = E2.nextElement();
103                 p.sendMessage(m);
104             }
105         }

            // Send the given message based on the given public key. This method tries
            // to find a connection based on the given public key, either incoming
            // or outgoing. Upon finding such a connection, send the message through it
            // and return true; otherwise return false.
106         protected synchronized boolean sendMessageByKey(PublicKey key, Message m){
107             String v = UtilityMethods.getKeyString(key);
108             PeerOutgoingConnection p = outgoingConnections.get(v);
109             if(p != null){
110                 p.sendMessage(m);
111                 return true;
112             }
                //find the connection inside the incomingConnections
113             PeerIncomingConnection pi = incomingConnections.get(v);
114             if(pi != null){
115                 pi.sendMessage(m);
116                 return true;
117             }
118             return false;
119         }

            // Return all public key/name pairs stored by this connection manager.
            // The pairs are returned inside a newly constructed ArrayList.
120         public ArrayList<KeyNamePair> getAllStoredAddresses(){
121             Iterator<KeyNamePair> E = this.allAddresses.values().iterator();
122             ArrayList<KeyNamePair> A = new ArrayList<KeyNamePair>();
123             while(E.hasNext()){
124                 A.add(E.next());
125             }
126             return A;
127         }

            // Add a KeyNamePair into the pool. If the same KeyNamePair has been
            // added before, it won't matter. A better implementation of this method
            // should be checking the existence of the KeyNamePair first.
128         public void addAddress(KeyNamePair address){
129             this.allAddresses.put(UtilityMethods.getKeyString(address.getKey()), address);
130         }
```

```java
        // This method tells if the public key exists in the name-key pool.
        // Note that this method does not examine if a connection to the given public key exists.
        // Generally speaking, if a connection to the given public key exists, then this
        // public key must also exist inside the name-key pool. The vice versa is not true,
        // however.
131     public boolean isExistingUserByPK(PublicKey pk){
132         return this.allAddresses.containsKey(UtilityMethods.getKeyString(pk));
133     }

        // Find the name matching the public key from the KeyNamePair pool.
        // If not found, return the string representation of the public key.
134     public String getNameFromAddress(PublicKey key){
            //if the key is self, then return the wallet's name
135         if(key.equals(this.wallet.getPublicKey())){
136             return this.wallet.getName();
137         }
138         String address = UtilityMethods.getKeyString(key);
139         KeyNamePair kp = this.allAddresses.get(address);
140         if(kp != null){
141             return kp.getName();
142         }else{
143             return address;
144         }
145     }

        // Find the KeyNamePair based on the given public key.
        // If not found, null is returned.
146     public KeyNamePair findKeyNamePair(PublicKey pk){
147         return this.allAddresses.get(UtilityMethods.getKeyString(pk));
148     }

        // This method initiates the closing of all peer connections, both incoming
        // and outgoing.
149     protected synchronized void closeAllPeerConnectionsActively(){
150         Enumeration<PeerOutgoingConnection> Eo = outgoingConnections.elements();
151         while(Eo.hasMoreElements()){
152             PeerOutgoingConnection po = Eo.nextElement();
153             po.activeClose();
154             this.removePeerConnection(po);
155         }
156         Enumeration<PeerIncomingConnection> Ei = incomingConnections.elements();
157         while(Ei.hasMoreElements()){
158             PeerIncomingConnection pi = Ei.nextElement();
159             pi.activeClose();
160             this.removePeerConnection(pi);
161         }
162     }

        // This method closes all peer connections first, then terminate this
        // connection manager.
163     protected synchronized void shutdownAll(){
164         closeAllPeerConnectionsActively();
165         this.forever = false;
166     }

        // This method creates a Transaction for the wallet based on the given
        // public key (as the transcation recipient) and the transfer amount.
        // The Transaction is wrapped into a MessageTransactionBroadcast object
        // before it is sent through all connections, both incoming and outgoing.
```

```
                // If success, return true; otherwise return false.
167     protected boolean sendTransaction(PublicKey receiver, double fundToTransfer){
168         Transaction T = this.wallet.transferFund(receiver, fundToTransfer);
169         if(T != null && T.verifySignature()){
170             MessageTransactionBroadcast m = new MessageTransactionBroadcast(T);
171             this.sendMessageByAll(m);
172             return true;
173         }
174         return false;
175     }
        // This method sends a private message to the given public key. The content
        // of the message is the given text. It tries to send the message through
        // the direct connection to the given public key. However, if there is no such
        // a direct connection, it then sends the message through all direct connections.
        // Some network bandwidth is wasted when the message is sent through all direct
        // connections. So, this method can be improved.
176     protected boolean sendPrivateMessage(PublicKey receiver, String text){
177         MessageTextPrivate m = new MessageTextPrivate(text,
                    this.wallet.getPrivateKey(), this.wallet.getPublicKey(),
                    this.wallet.getName(), receiver);
178         if(!this.sendMessageByKey(receiver, m)){
179             this.sendMessageByAll(m);
180         }
181         return true;
182     }

        // This method sends out a message through all direct connections in request of
        // the latest blockchain. This method is called once inside WalletSimulator class
        // when a peer is first created. The purpose is to get the latest blockchain.
183     protected void broadcastRequestForBlockchainUpdate(){
184         MessageAskForBlockchainBroadcast m = new MessageAskForBlockchainBroadcast(
                    "update blockchain", wallet.getPrivateKey(),
                    wallet.getPublicKey(), wallet.getName());
185         LogManager.log(Configuration.logMin(), "sending message for "
                    + "updating local blockchain of " + this.wallet.getName());
186         this.sendMessageByAll(m);
187     }

        // This method examines if there is any direction connection between this peer and
        // the given public key (representing another peer or wallet). An integer is returned
        // by this method. 0 = no direct connection, 1 = has direct incoming connection,
        // 2 = has direct outgoing connection, and 3= has both direct incoming and
        // outgoing connections. This method is used once inside WalletSimulator GUI to show
        // users's status. See WalletSimulator.FramePrivateMessage.
188     protected int hasDirectConnection(PublicKey key){
189         int n = 0;
190         String v = UtilityMethods.getKeyString(key);
191         if(this.incomingConnections.get(v) != null
                        && this.outgoingConnections.get(v) != null){
192             n = 3;
193         }else if(this.outgoingConnections.get(v) != null){
194             n = 2;
195         }else if(this.incomingConnections.get(v) != null){
196             n = 1;
197         }
198         return n;
199     }

        // Return the number of existing outgoing connections inside this manager's pool.
```

```
200         protected int numberOfExistingOutgoingConnections(){
201             return this.outgoingConnections.size();
202         }

            // Return the number of existing incoming connections inside this manager's pool.
203         protected int numberOfExistingIncomingConnections(){
204             return this.incomingConnections.size();
205         }
206    }
```

Code line 6 specifies that a connection manager will be executed as a thread later. This is critical.

Code lines 44-49 (the makingFriends() method) and code lines 29-32 (inside the run() method) need further discussion. When peer A executes its PeerConnectionManager instance as a thread, the "makingFriends" method is executed for three times to broadcast making-friend requests. When peer B receives such a request, its response it to construct an outgoing connection to A unless B has enough outgoing connections already. Let's consider a scenario. Assume that a peer can have maximum 10 outgoing connections. Given a P2P network in which all existing peers have already had 10 outgoing connections, a new coming peer Z's request to make friend will be rejected by all existing peers. In this case, peer Z cannot have any incoming connections from any peers but can have only one outgoing connection to an existing peer. However, if the existing peer X that Z tries to connect at its instantiation has already had maximum incoming connections, then Z will fail to start. Of course Z can try other peers, but this won't be a pleasant experience for Z. So you see, ensuring full reachability in a P2P network requires detailed consideration.

Code lines 55-59 inside the `createOutgoingConnection()` method are of special importance. If they are removed, then a peer can have both an incoming and an outgoing connection at the same time to another peer. That means our current approach 1 implemention is switched to approach 2 implementation.

WalletMessageTaskManager is another critical player in this blockchain network. Its main goal is to sort received messages. Some messages will be rejected or ignored, some will be processed according to their types. WalletMessageTaskManager of this chapter is very similar to its peer in chapter 8, though there are significant modifications. This class is explained in the following code section by comments:

```
1      import java.util.ArrayList;
2      import java.util.concurrent.ConcurrentLinkedQueue;
3      import java.util.Hashtable;
4      import java.util.Enumeration;
5      public class WalletMessageTaskManager implements Runnable{
6          private boolean forever = true;
           // The Wallet this task manager is working for.
7          private Wallet wallet;
           // Store messages that have been processed. If a message has been processed,
           // then the arrival of the same message will be ignored.
8          private Hashtable<String, Message> existingMessages = new Hashtable<String, Message>();
           //The message queue that stores current message waiting to be processed.
9          private ConcurrentLinkedQueue<Message> messageQueue
                           = new ConcurrentLinkedQueue<Message>();
```

```java
10      private PeerConnectionManager connectionManager;
        // The WalletSimulator instance that this message manager cooperate with.
11      private WalletSimulator simulator = null;
        // A variable used in the run() method to help arrange thread sleep status.
12      private int idleTimes = 0;
        // The constructor.
13      public WalletMessageTaskManager(Wallet wallet, PeerConnectionManager connectionManager){
14          this.wallet = wallet;
15          this.connectionManager = connectionManager;
16      }

17      public void setSimulator(WalletSimulator simulator){
18          this.simulator = simulator;
19      }


        // This method adds a given message into the queue of messages waiting to be processed.
        // The following incoming messages will NOT be added into the queue by default:
        // 1) Messages originally sent by this wallet;
        // 2) Messages that have already been processed before;
        // 3) Messages that are too old.
20      public void addMessageIntoQueue(Message msg){
            // Check if msg is sent by this wallet. Generally speaking, if a message
            // is sent by this wallet, it won't be added into the queue except when its
            // selfMessageAllowed() method returns true.
21          if(msg.getSenderKey().equals(this.wallet.getPublicKey())
                                        && !msg.selfMessageAllowed()){
22              return;
23          }
            // Examine if the given message is too old.
24          if(UtilityMethods.isMessageTooOld(msg.getTimeStamp())){
25              return;
26          }
            // Check if this messsage has been processed before.
27          Message m = existingMessages.get(msg.getMessageHashID());
28          if(m != null){
29              return;
30          }
            // Mark that this message as being processed.
31          existingMessages.put(msg.getMessageHashID(), msg);
            // As this message is valid, add it into the queue to be processed in order.
32          this.messageQueue.add(msg);
33      }

        // A wallet does not need to do anything inside this method.
34      public void whatToDo(){ }

        // Must implement this method.
35      public void run(){
36          while(forever){
                try{
                    // Sleep a while to release CPU resource.
37                  Thread.sleep(Configuration.threadSleepTimeMedium());
38                  idleTimes ++;
                }catch(InterruptedException ee){
39
40                  LogManager.log(Configuration.logMin(), "Exception in "
                            + "WalletMessageTaskManager.run()["+ee.getMessage());
41              }
42              if(idleTimes >= 400000){
```

```
43                        //let's discard the messages that is too old inside processedMessages
                          idleTimes = 0;
44                        discardObseleteMessages();
45                    }
46                    if(this.messageQueue.isEmpty()){
                          // When there is no message to process, find something else to do.
47                        whatToDo();
48                        try{
49                            Thread.sleep(Configuration.threadSleepTimeLong());
50                        }catch(InterruptedException ie){
51                            LogManager.log(Configuration.logMin(), "Exception in "
                                  + "WalletMessageTaskManager.run()-2["+ie.getMessage());
52                        }
53                    }else{
                          // When there are messages to process, process them first.
54                        while(!(this.messageQueue.isEmpty())){
                              // Dequeue a message.
55                            Message m = this.messageQueue.poll();
                              // Process the message.
56                            processMessage(m);
57                        }
58                    }
59                }
60            }

          // This method goes through all processed messages (stored in
          // existingMessages) to find obsolete message(s) and delete them.
61        private synchronized void discardObseleteMessages(){
              // Fetch all the processed messages.
62            Enumeration<Message>  E = existingMessages.elements();
              // Use a loop to go over each message one by one.
63            while(E.hasMoreElements()){
64                Message m = E.nextElement();
                  // Examine if a message is too old
65                if(UtilityMethods.isMessageTooOld(m.getTimeStamp())){
                      // Yes, remove it.
66                    existingMessages.remove(m.getMessageHashID());
67                }
68            }
69        }

          // This is the major method of this class. Messages are processed based on their types.
          // Note that each message type has a specific method written for.
70        protected void processMessage(Message message) {
              // Avoid any null messages.
71            if(message == null){
72                return;
73            }
              // For non-broadcast message types.
74            if(!message.isForBroadcast()){
                  // If it is a private chat message
75                if(message.getMessageType() == Message.TEXT_PRIVATE){
76                    MessageTextPrivate m = (MessageTextPrivate)message;
                      // Ignore tampered messages.
77                    if(!m.isValid()){
78                        LogManager.log(Configuration.logMax(), "In WalletMessageTaskManager"
                              + ".processMessage()[text private message tampered");
79                        return;
80                    }
```

```
                    // Process a private chat message.
81                      receivePrivateChatMessage(m);
                    // If it is a message asking for information about available peers.
82                  }else if(message.getMessageType() == Message.ADDRESS_PRIVATE){
83                      MessageAddressPrivate mp = (MessageAddressPrivate)message;
84                      receiveMessageAddressPrivate(mp);
                    // If it is a private blockchain request message.
85                  }else if(message.getMessageType() == Message.BLOCKCHAIN_PRIVATE){
86                      MessageBlockchainPrivate mbcb = (MessageBlockchainPrivate)message;
87                      receiveMessagaeBlockchainPrivate(mbcb);
                    // Unknown private message type(s). This should never happen.
88                  }else{
89                      LogManager.log(Configuration.logMax(), "In WalletMessageTaskManager"
                                + ".processMessage()[....weird private message, not supported, "
                                + "please check ......");
90                  }
                // If it is a block broadcast message.
91              }else if(message.getMessageType() == Message.BLOCK_BROADCAST){
                    // Upon receiving a block message, a wallet validates the block before trying
                    // to update its local ledger with the block.
92                  LogManager.log(Configuration.logMin(), "In WalletMessageTaskManager"
                            + ".processMessage()[it is a block broadcast message, check "
                            + "if it is necessary to update it");
93                  MessageBlockBroadcast mbb = (MessageBlockBroadcast)message;
                                        this.receiveMessageBlockBroadcast(mbb);
                // If it is a blockchain broadcast message.
94              }else if(message.getMessageType() == Message.BLOCKCHAIN_BROADCAST){
95                  LogManager.log(Configuration.logMin(), "In WalletMessageTaskManager"
                            + ".processMessage()[It is a blockchain broadcast message, check "
                            + "if it is necessary to update the blockchain");
96                  MessageBlockchainBroadcast mbcb = (MessageBlockchainBroadcast)message;
                    //Modification in chapter 9 (compared to chapter 8).
97                  boolean b = receiveBlockchainBroadcast(mbcb);
98                  if(b){
99                      LogManager.log(Configuration.logMin(), "In WalletMessageTaskManager"
                                + ".processMessage()[blockchain is updated!");
100                 }else{
101                     LogManager.log(Configuration.logMin(), "In WalletMessageTaskManager"
                                + ".processMessage()[rejected the new blockchain");
102                 }
                // If it is a transaction broadcast message.
103             }else if(message.getMessageType() == Message.TRANSACTION_BROADCAST){
                    // As a wallet does not collect transaction a wallet will just pay
                    // attention to the transaction that has payment to herself/himself.
104                 LogManager.log(Configuration.logMin(), "In WalletMessageTaskManager"
                            + ".processMessage()[It is a transaction broadcast message");
105                 MessageTransactionBroadcast mtb = (MessageTransactionBroadcast)message;
106                 this.receiveMessageTransactionBroadcast(mtb);
                // If it is a message asking recipients to respond with their local ledgers.
107             }else if(message.getMessageType() == Message.BLOCKCHAIN_ASK_BROADCAST){
108                 MessageAskForBlockchainBroadcast mabcb
                            = (MessageAskForBlockchainBroadcast)message;
109                 if(mabcb.isValid()){
110                     receiveMessageForBlockchainBroadcast(mabcb);
111                 }
                // If it is an open chat text message.
112             }else if(message.getMessageType() == Message.TEXT_BROADCAST){
113                 MessageTextBroadcast mtb = (MessageTextBroadcast)message;
114                 receiveMessageTextBroadcast(mtb);
```

```
                // It is is a message requesting to make friend with.
115             }else if(message.getMessageType() == Message.ADDRESS_BROADCAST_MAKING_FRIEND){
116                 receiveMessageBroadcastMakingFriend((MessageBroadcastMakingFriend)message);
                // If it is a message requesting to respond with available peer information.
117             }else if(message.getMessageType() == Message.ADDRESS_ASK_BROADCAST){
118                 receiveMessageAddressBroadcastAsk((MessageAddressBroadcastAsk)message);
119             }
120         }

            // Process a MessageAddressBroadcastAsk message.
121         protected void receiveMessageAddressBroadcastAsk(MessageAddressBroadcastAsk m){
                // Forward it first. This is how a P2P network works.
122             this.connectionManager.sendMessageByAll(m);
                // Prepare a responding message and then send it. Note "address" means
                // public key.
123             KeyNamePair self = new KeyNamePair(this.wallet.getPublicKey(),
                                    this.wallet.getName());
124             ArrayList<KeyNamePair> pair = this.connectionManager.getAllStoredAddresses();
125             pair.add(self);
126             MessageAddressPrivate map = new MessageAddressPrivate(pair,
                                    this.wallet.getPublicKey(), m.getSenderKey());
                // Try to find a direction connection to the requester too send the message first.
                // If failed, then send it through all direct connections.
127             if(!this.connectionManager.sendMessageByKey(m.getSenderKey(), map)){
128                 this.connectionManager.sendMessageByAll(map);
129             }
130         }

            // Process a MessageBroadcastMakingFriend message.
131         protected void receiveMessageBroadcastMakingFriend(MessageBroadcastMakingFriend m){
                // Forward it first.
                this.connectionManager.sendMessageByAll(m);
                // Try to make a direct connection.
132             this.connectionManager.createOutgoingConnection(m.getIP());
133         }

            // Process a MessageTextBroadcast message.
134         protected void receiveMessageTextBroadcast(MessageTextBroadcast mtb) {
                // Forward it first.
135             this.connectionManager.sendMessageByAll(mtb);
                // Display the message on the message board.
136             String text = mtb.getMessageBody();
137             String name = mtb.getSenderName();
138             this.simulator.appendMessageLineOnBoard(name+"]: "+text);
                // Automatically store the user information (can be self).
139
140             this.connectionManager.addAddress(new KeyNamePair(mtb.getSenderKey(),
                                        mtb.getSenderName()));
141         }

            // Process a MessageAddressPrivate message.
142         protected void receiveMessageAddressPrivate(MessageAddressPrivate mp){
                // Make sure that this message is for this wallet.
143             if(mp.getReceiverKey().equals(this.wallet.getPublicKey())){
                    // Take out the addresses (peer information).
144                 ArrayList<KeyNamePair> all = mp.getMessageBody();
145                 LogManager.log(Configuration.logMin(), "In WalletMessageTaskManager"
                        + ".receiveMessageAddressPrivate()[There are these many addresses "
                        + " (users) available (in addition to yourself): ");
                    // Add them one by one into the pool.
```

```
146                     for(int z=0; z<all.size(); z++){
147                         KeyNamePair pk = all.get(z);
148                         if(!pk.getKey().equals(wallet.getPublicKey())){
149                             connectionManager.addAddress(pk);
150                             LogManager.log(Configuration.logMin(), "In WalletMessageTaskManager"
                                    + ".receiveMessageAddressPrivate()[" + pk.getName()
                                    + "| key=" + UtilityMethods.getKeyString(pk.getKey()));
151                         }
152                     }
153             }else{
                    // If not for this wallet, forward it.
154                 if(!this.connectionManager.sendMessageByKey(mp.getReceiverKey(),mp)){
155                     this.connectionManager.sendMessageByAll(mp);
156                 }
157             }
158         }

            // Process a MessageTextPrivate message.
159         protected void receivePrivateChatMessage(MessageTextPrivate m){
                // Check if this chat message is really for me. If not, need to relay it.
160             if(!(m.getReceiver().equals(this.wallet.getPublicKey()))){
161                 boolean done = this.connectionManager.sendMessageByKey(m.getReceiver(), m);
162                 if(!done){
                        // The message recipient is not directly connected. Got to relay.
163                     this.connectionManager.sendMessageByAll(m);
164                 }
165             }else{
                    // The message is for me. Display it on the message board.
166                 String text = m.getMessageBody();
167                 String name = m.getSenderName();
168                 this.simulator.appendMessageLineOnBoard("private<--"+name+"]: "+text);
                    // Automatically store the peer information.
169                 connectionManager.addAddress(new KeyNamePair(m.getSenderKey(),
                            m.getSenderName()));
170             }
171         }

            // A wallet does not respond to a blockchain request message in this implementation.
172         protected void receiveMessageForBlockchainBroadcast(
                            MessageAskForBlockchainBroadcast mabcb){
173             LogManager.log(Configuration.logMin(), "In WalletMessageTaskManager"
                        + ".receiveQueryForBlockchainBroadcast()[I am just a wallet, I can only "
                        + "forward the request for blockchain.");
174             this.connectionManager.sendMessageByAll(mabcb);
175         }

            // Process a MessageBlockchainBroadcast message.
176         protected boolean receiveBlockchainBroadcast(MessageBlockchainBroadcast mbcb){
                // In a P2P environment, we need to forward the message first.
177             this.connectionManager.sendMessageByAll(mbcb);
178             return this.wallet.setLocalLedger(mbcb.getMessageBody());
179         }

            // This is the version for Wallet only. The wallet can either ignore it or
            // send a THNAK YOU message to the transaction publisher.
180         protected void receiveMessageTransactionBroadcast(MessageTransactionBroadcast mtb){
                // Forward it first.
181             this.connectionManager.sendMessageByAll(mtb);
                // Examine if there is anything to this wallet.
```

```
182             Transaction ts = mtb.getMessageBody();
                // If the sender is self, quit.
183             if(ts.getSender().equals(this.wallet.getPublicKey())){
184                 return;
185             }
                // Go through every UTXO to count if there is any payment to me.
186             int n = ts.getNumberOfOutputUTXOs();
187             int total = 0;
188             for(int i=0; i<n; i++){
189                 UTXO ut = ts.getOuputUTXO(i);
190                 if(ut.getReceiver().equals(this.wallet.getPublicKey())){
191                     total += ut.getFundTransferred();
192                 }
193             }
194             if(total > 0){
195                 LogManager.log(Configuration.logMin(), "In WalletMessageTaskManager"
                        + ".receiveMessageTransactionBroadcast()[in the transaction, "
                        + "there is payment of " + total+" to me. Sending THANK YOU to the payer");
196                 MessageTextPrivate mtp = new MessageTextPrivate(
                        "Thank you for the fund of " + total + ", waiting for its publishing.",
                        this.wallet.getPrivateKey(), this.wallet.getPublicKey(),
                        this.wallet.getName(), ts.getSender());
197                 this.connectionManager.sendMessageByKey(mtb.getSenderKey(), mtp);
198             }
199         }

            // Process a MessageBlockBroadcas message. The same as that of chapter 8.
200         protected boolean receiveMessageBlockBroadcast(MessageBlockBroadcast mbb){
                // Different from the client-server model, in a P2P environment, we need
                // to forward the message first.
201             this.connectionManager.sendMessageByAll(mbb);
                // Now update local blockchain.
202             Block block = mbb.getMessageBody();
203             boolean b = this.wallet.updateLocalLedger(block);
204             if(b){
205                 LogManager.log(Configuration.logMin(), "In WalletMessageTaskManager"
                        + ".receiveMessageBlockBroadcast()"
                        + "[new block is added to the local blockchain");
206             }else{
207                 int size = block.getTotalNumberOfTransactions();
208                 int counter = 0;
209                 for(int i=0; i<size; i++){
210                     Transaction T = block.getTransaction(i);
211                     if(!this.wallet.getLocalLedger().isTransactionExist(T)){
212                         MessageTransactionBroadcast mt = new MessageTransactionBroadcast(T);
213                         this.connectionManager.sendMessageByAll(mt);
214                         counter++;
215                     }
216                 }
217                 LogManager.log(Configuration.logMin(), "In WalletMessageTaskManager"
                        + ".receiveMessageBlockBroadcast()[new block is rejected, "
                        + "released "+ counter+" unpublished transactions into the pool");
218             }
219             return b;
220         }

            // Process a MessageBlockchainPrivate message.
221         protected void receiveMessagaeBlockchainPrivate(MessageBlockchainPrivate mbcb){
222             LogManager.log(Configuration.logMin(), "In WalletMessageTaskManager"
```

```
                        + ".receiveMessagaeBlockchainPrivate()[It is a blockchain private "
                        + "message, check if it is for me and if necessary to update the blockchain");
                    // Check if this message is for me.
223                 if(mbcb.getReceiver().equals(this.wallet.getPublicKey())){
224                     boolean b = this.wallet.setLocalLedger(mbcb.getMessageBody());
225                     if(b){
226                         LogManager.log(Configuration.logMin(), "In WalletMessageTaskManager"
                                + ".receiveMessagaeBlockchainPrivate()[blockchain is updated!");
227                     }else{
228                         LogManager.log(Configuration.logMin(), "In WalletMessageTaskManager"
                                + ".receiveMessagaeBlockchainPrivate()[rejected the new blockchain");
229                     }
230                 }else{
                        // Since the message is not for me, forward it.
231                     if(!this.connectionManager.sendMessageByKey(mbcb.getReceiver(), mbcb)){
232                         this.connectionManager.sendMessageByAll(mbcb);
233                     }
234                 }
235         }

236         protected void close(){
237             forever = false;
238         }
239 }
```

The MinerMessageTaskManager in this chapter is slightly modified. There are two major modifications.

1) The original WalletConnectionAgent is replaced by PeerConnectionManager. This modification results in a few other necessary modifications.
2) The method `receiveMessageBlockBroadcast()` is added to override the same method inside WalletMessageTaskManager class.

Modifications are marked in the following code section for MinerMessageTaskManager class.

```
1   import java.security.PublicKey;
2   import java.util.ArrayList;
3   public class MinerMessageTaskManager extends WalletMessageTaskManager implements Runnable{
4       private boolean miningAction = true;
5       private ArrayList<Transaction> existingTransactions = new ArrayList<Transaction>();
6       private Miner miner;
        // Modification in chapter 9. There are other modifications derived from this modification.
7       private PeerConnectionManager connectionManager;
8       public MinerMessageTaskManager(Miner miner, PeerConnectionManager connectionManager){
9           super(miner, connectionManager);
10          this.miner = miner;
11          this.connectionManager = connectionManager;
12      }

13      protected synchronized void resetMiningAction(){
14          this.miningAction = true;
15      }

16      protected synchronized boolean getMiningAction(){
17          return this.miningAction;
18      }
```

```java
19      protected synchronized void raiseMiningAction(){
20          this.miningAction = false;
21      }

22      protected void receiveMessageForBlockchainBroadcast(
                        MessageAskForBlockchainBroadcast mabcb){
23          PublicKey receiver = mabcb.getSenderKey();
24          Blockchain bc = miner.getLocalLedger().copy_NotDeepCopy();
25          MessageBlockchainPrivate message = new MessageBlockchainPrivate(bc,
                        miner.getPublicKey(), receiver);

26          if(!this.connectionManager.sendMessageByKey(receiver, message)){
27              this.connectionManager.sendMessageByAll(message);
28          }
29      }

30      protected void receiveMessageTransactionBroadcast(MessageTransactionBroadcast mtb){
            // Modification in chapter 9. Forward the message first.
31          this.connectionManager.sendMessageByAll(mtb);
            // Process the message.
33          Transaction ts = mtb.getMessageBody();
            // First, make sure that this transaction does not exist in the current pool
34          for(int i=0; i<this.existingTransactions.size(); i++){
35              if(ts.equals(this.existingTransactions.get(i))){
36                  return;
37              }
38          }
            // Add this into the existing storage.
39          if(!miner.validateTransaction(ts)){
40              LogManager.log(Configuration.logMax(), "Miner " + miner.getName()
                        + " found an invalid transaction. Should broadcast it though");
41              return;
42          }
43          this.existingTransactions.add(ts);
            // Check if it meets the requirement to build a block.
44          if(Configuration.blockTransactionNumberLowerLimit() <=
                        this.existingTransactions.size() && this.getMiningAction() ){
45              this.raiseMiningAction();
46              LogManager.log(Configuration.logMax(),miner.getName()
                        +" has enough transactions to mine the block now, "
                        +"mining_action_block_size requirement meets. Start mining a new block");
                // Modification in Chapter 9:
                // Copy transactions into another arraylist for the worker to build a block.
                // Remove those transactions from the original pool once copied.
47              ArrayList<Transaction> tts = new ArrayList<Transaction>();
48              for(int i=0,j=0; i<this.existingTransactions.size() &&
                        j<Configuration.blockTransactionNumberUpperLimit(); i++,j++){
49                  tts.add(this.existingTransactions.get(i));
50                  this.existingTransactions.remove(i);
51                  i--;
52              }
53              MinerTheWorker worker = new MinerTheWorker(miner,
                        this, this.connectionManager, tts);
54              Thread miningThread = new Thread(worker);
55              miningThread.start();
                // Modification in chapter 9:
                //this.existingTransactions = new ArrayList<Transaction>();
56          }
57      }
```

```
    /**
     * Modification in chapter 9:
     * Overwrite this method so that when a block is accepted, the miner needs to
     * re-examine its transaction pool in case some existing transactions should be
     * invalidated by this newly accepted block.
     */
58  protected boolean receiveMessageBlockBroadcast(MessageBlockBroadcast mbb){
59      boolean b = super.receiveMessageBlockBroadcast(mbb);
60      if(b){
61          Block block = mbb.getMessageBody();
            // Examine if any transactions in the pool also exist inside this block.
            // If does, remove it from the pool.
62          for(int i=0; i<block.getTotalNumberOfTransactions(); i++){
63              Transaction t = block.getTransaction(i);
                // Test if t exists in the pool.
64              for(int j=0; j<this.existingTransactions.size(); j++){
65                  Transaction t2 = this.existingTransactions.get(j);
66                  if(t.equals(t2)){
67                      this.existingTransactions.remove(j);
68                      break;
69                  }
70              }
71          }
72      }
73      return b;
74  }
75  }
```

In Chapter 8, the genesis miner is very special. It is closely bound with the central server. In this chapter, however, the genesis miner is like any other miners except for 1) it must start first to prepare the genesis block; 2) it sends out sign-in bonus to new peers; 3) it only mines the sign-in bonus blocks. Thus, the MinerGenesisMessageTaskManager is also modified. It is explained in the following code section. Please pay attention to the comments.

```
1   import java.util.ArrayList;
2   import java.util.HashMap;
3   public final class MinerGenesisMessageTaskManager
                    extends MinerMessageTaskManager implements Runnable{
4       private int blocksMined = 0;
5       private HashMap<String, KeyNamePair> users = new HashMap<String, KeyNamePair>();
        // Modification in this chapter. This modification results a few other modifications.
6       private PeerConnectionManager connectionManager;
7       private final int signInBonus = 1000;
8       private ArrayList<KeyNamePair> waitingListForSignInBonus = new ArrayList<KeyNamePair>();
9       private ArrayList<Transaction> waitingTransactionForSignInBonus
                                = new ArrayList<Transaction>();
10      private Miner miner;
11      private int idleTimes = 0;
12      public MinerGenesisMessageTaskManager(Miner miner,
                        PeerConnectionManager connectionManager) {
13          super(miner, connectionManager);
14          this.connectionManager = connectionManager;
15          this.miner = miner;
16      }

        // Override this method so that the genesis miner can poll peer informations from other
```

```
                // peers time to time. This is for sending sign-in bonus.
17          public void whatToDo(){
18              try{
19                  Thread.sleep(Configuration.threadSleepTimeMedium());
20                  if(waitingListForSignInBonus.size() == 0 &&
                                users.size() < Configuration.genesisMiner_signInBonusUsersLimit()){
21                      this.idleTimes++;
                        // Send a message out to find new users
22                      if(this.idleTimes >= 100){
23                          this.idleTimes = 0;
24                          MessageAddressBroadcastAsk m = new
                                    MessageAddressBroadcastAsk(miner.getPublicKey(), miner.getName());
25                          this.connectionManager.sendMessageByAll(m);
26                      }
27                  }else if(users.size() < Configuration.genesisMiner_signInBonusUsersLimit()
                                && waitingListForSignInBonus.size()>0){
28                      sendSignInBonus();
29                  }
30              }catch(Exception e){}
31          }

32          private void sendSignInBonus(){
33              if(waitingTransactionForSignInBonus.size()<= 0
                                && waitingListForSignInBonus.size() <= 0){
34                  return;
35              }
36              Transaction T = null;
37              String recipient = null;
38              if(waitingTransactionForSignInBonus.size() > 0){
39                  T = waitingTransactionForSignInBonus.get(0);
40                  recipient = this.connectionManager.getNameFromAddress(
                                    T.getOuputUTXO(0).getReceiver());
41                  LogManager.log(Configuration.logMax(), "Re-mine a block for the "
                            + "bonus transaction to " + recipient);
42              }else if(waitingListForSignInBonus.size() > 0){
43                  KeyNamePair pk = waitingListForSignInBonus.remove(0);
44                  recipient = pk.getName();
45                  T = miner.transferFund(pk.getKey(), signInBonus);
46                  if(T != null && T.verifySignature()){
47                      LogManager.log(Configuration.logMax(), miner.getName()
                                +" is sending "+ recipient +" sign-in bonus of "+signInBonus);
48                  }else{
49                      waitingListForSignInBonus.add(0, pk);
50                      return;
51                  }
52              }
53              if(blocksMined < Configuration.genesisMiner_selfBlocksToMineLimit()
                                && this.getMiningAction()){
54                  blocksMined++;
55                  this.raiseMiningAction();
56                  LogManager.log(Configuration.logMin(), miner.getName()
                            + " is mining the sign-in bonus block for " + recipient + " by himself");
57                  ArrayList<Transaction> tss = new ArrayList<Transaction>();
58                  tss.add(T);
59                  MinerTheWorker worker = new MinerTheWorker(miner, this,
                                    this.connectionManager, tss);
60                  Thread miningThread = new Thread(worker);
61                  miningThread.start();
62              }else{
```

```
63                // Broadcast this transaction
                  LogManager.log(Configuration.logMin(), miner.getName()
                      + " is broadcasting the transaction of sign-in bonus for " + recipient);
64                MessageTransactionBroadcast mtb = new MessageTransactionBroadcast(T);
65                this.connectionManager.sendMessageByAll(mtb);
66            }
67        }

          // Modification in this chapter.
          // Override this method so that the genesis miner can send sign-in bonus
          // to new coming users.
68        protected void receiveMessageBroadcastMakingFriend(MessageBroadcastMakingFriend m){
              // Forward the message first.
69            this.connectionManager.sendMessageByAll(m);
70            this.connectionManager.createOutgoingConnection(m.getIP());
71            this.connectionManager.addAddress(m.getKeyNamePair());
72            String id = UtilityMethods.getKeyString(m.getSenderKey());
73            if(!(m.getSenderKey().equals(miner.getPublicKey())) && !users.containsKey(id)){
74                users.put(id, m.getKeyNamePair());
75                if(users.size() <= Configuration.genesisMiner_signInBonusUsersLimit()){
76                    this.waitingListForSignInBonus.add(m.getKeyNamePair());
77                }
78            }
79        }

          /**
           * Modification in this chapter.
           * To make the system simple, the genesis miner does not compete in mining.
           * It does not collect any published transaction.
           */
80        protected void receiveMessageTransactionBroadcast(MessageTransactionBroadcast mtb){
              // Just forward the message.
81            this.connectionManager.sendMessageByAll(mtb);
82        }

83        protected boolean receiveMessageBlockBroadcast(MessageBlockBroadcast mbb){
              // Forward the message first.
84            this.connectionManager.sendMessageByAll(mbb);
85            Block block = mbb.getMessageBody();
86            boolean b = miner.verifyGuestBlock(block, miner.getLocalLedger());
87            boolean c = false;
88            if(b){
89                c = this.miner.updateLocalLedger(block);
90            }
91            if(b && c){
92                LogManager.log(Configuration.logMin(), "new block is added "
                      + "to the local blockchain, blockchain size = "
                      + this.miner.getLocalLedger().size());
93            }else{
94                LogManager.log(Configuration.logMin(),"new block is rejected");
                  // Got to check if this block is a sign-in bonus block, if it is,
                  // then needs to re-mine it.
95                if(block.getCreator().equals(miner.getPublicKey())){
96                    LogManager.log(Configuration.logMin(),"genesis miner's block is "
                          + "rejected. It must be a sign-in bonus block. Check if "
                          + "this transaction has been published by others.");
                      // Got to redo. This is likely to happen if mining competition
                      // becomes tight.
97                    String id = UtilityMethods.getKeyString(
```

```
                                block.getTransaction(0).getOuputUTXO(0).getReceiver());
98                          KeyNamePair pk = users.get(id);
                            // Modification in chapter 9.
                            // Make sure that this user exists and this sign-in transaction
                            // does not exist in the local blockchain. Why should we examine if
                            // the sign-in transaction exists in the local blockchain? Well,
                            // if the sign-in transaction has been published by other miners,
                            // this sign-in block will always be rejected by the genesis miner.
                            // If we do not check the existence of this transaction, the genesis
                            // miner will run into a loop mining this block until this transaction
                            // is released to other miners after the genesis miner has mined
                            // enough blocks.
99                          Transaction T = block.getTransaction(0);
100                         if(pk != null && !(this.miner.getLocalLedger().isTransactionExist(T))){
                                // Insert the transation at the beginning, do not update miningAction.
101                             waitingTransactionForSignInBonus.add(0, T);
102                         }else if(pk == null){
103                             System.out.println("ERROR: an existing user for sign-in "
                                    + "bonus is not found. Program error");
104                         }
105                     }
106                 }
107             return b && c;
108         }

109         protected void receiveMessageAddressPrivate(MessageAddressPrivate mp){
110             ArrayList<KeyNamePair> all = mp.getMessageBody();
111             for(int z=0; z<all.size(); z++){
112                 KeyNamePair pk = all.get(z);
113                 this.connectionManager.addAddress(pk);
114                 String ID = UtilityMethods.getKeyString(pk.getKey());
115                 if(!pk.getKey().equals(miner.getPublicKey()) && !users.containsKey(ID)){
116                     users.put(ID, pk);
117                     if(users.size() <= Configuration.genesisMiner_signInBonusUsersLimit()){
118                         this.waitingListForSignInBonus.add(pk);
119                     }
120                 }
121             }
                // Forward the message.
122             if(!this.connectionManager.sendMessageByKey(mp.getReceiverKey(),mp)){
123                 this.connectionManager.sendMessageByAll(mp);
124             }
125         }
126     }
```

Code lines 95-105 deal with the scenario when the sign-in block is rejected by the genesis miner. You may wonder how this can happen. Yes, it can. Assume that the current last block is B, the sign-in bonus block C is built upon B's hash. However, when there are many transactions published and there are a number of miners, the genesis miner's local ledger is updated with block D which arrives before his own block C. When C arrives, C will be rejected by the genesis miner and all other wallets. Note that all other wallets/miners will publish the bonus transaction inside the sign-in bonus block C in an effort to keep alive unpublished transactions. Now the bonus transaction is in public pool and is collected by all other miners. The genesis miner itself, however, is still trying to re-mine the bonus block and he may lose again in the competition. When the genesis miner loses again, the specific bonus transaction is updated into the genesis miner's blockchain together with other transactions in another block. Thus, the genesis miner must examine his own blockchain to assess if the specific bonus transaction has already been inside his local ledger. If it does, then he should quit mining this bonus block B. That is why code line 100 examines the existence of the bonus transaction first before placing it into the waiting list again in code line 101.

The WalletSimulator is the driver class to start a wallet a miner. The GUI part is very similar to that in chapter 8, so I won't present you the GUI code section of this class in this chapter. The most significant modification in this class is the replacement of WalletConnectionAgent with PeerConnectionManager. The second modification is the inclusion of PeerServer in the main method of WalletSimulator. The follow code section lists the main method of WalletSimulator class.

```
1      public static void main(String[] args){
2          Random rand = new Random();
           // Let's make the chance to be a miner is 3 out 4, while the chance
           // to be a wallet is 1 out of 4
3          int chance = rand.nextInt(4);
4          Scanner in = new Scanner(System.in);
5          LogManager.log(Configuration.logMax(), "please provide a name:");
6          String wname = in.nextLine();
7          LogManager.log(Configuration.logMax(),"Please provide your password:");
8          String wpassword = in.nextLine();
9          LogManager.log(Configuration.logMax(), "When showing balance, "
                           + "by default the public key is not shown as the address.\n"
                           + "This is for simplicity. "
                           + "Do you like to show the public key as address (Yes/No)??");
10         String yesno = in.nextLine();
11         boolean show = false;
12         if(yesno.toUpperCase().startsWith("Y")){
13             show = true;
14         }
15         LogManager.log(Configuration.logMax(),"To join the blockchain network, "
                           + "please present the IP address of a peer.");
16         String ipAddress = in.nextLine();
17         try{
18             if(chance == 0){
19                 LogManager.log(Configuration.logMax(),
                       "===== Congratulation, you are a wallet, i.e. a general user =====");
20                 Wallet wallet = new Wallet(wname, wpassword);
21                 LogManager.log(Configuration.logMax(), "Welcome " + wname
                           + ", blockchain wallet created for you.");
22                 WalletMessageTaskManager manager = null;
                   // Modification in this chapter.
23                 PeerConnectionManager agent = new PeerConnectionManager(wallet, manager);
24                 manager = new WalletMessageTaskManager(wallet, agent);
25                 agent.setWalletMessageTaskManager(manager);
26                 if(!agent.createOutgoingConnection(ipAddress)){
27                     LogManager.log(Configuration.logMax(),
                           "connection to the " + ipAddress+" failed.");
28                     LogManager.log(Configuration.logMax(),
                           "The user has no local blockchain initiated.");
29                     System.exit(2);
30                 }
                   // Modification in this chapter.
31                 PeerServer peerServer = new PeerServer(wallet, manager, agent);
32                 Thread managerThread = new Thread(manager);
```

```
33                    Thread agentThread = new Thread(agent);
34                    Thread serverThread = new Thread(peerServer);
35                    WalletSimulator simulator = new WalletSimulator(wallet, agent, manager);
36                    manager.setSimulator(simulator);
37                    serverThread.start();
38                    LogManager.log(Configuration.logMax(),"peer server started");
39                    agentThread.start();
40                    LogManager.log(Configuration.logMax(),"peer clients manager started");
41                    managerThread.start();
42                    LogManager.log(Configuration.logMax(),"wallet task manager started");
43                    simulator.setBalanceShowPublicKey(show);
                      // Modification in this chapter.
44                    agent.broadcastRequestForBlockchainUpdate();
45                }else{
46                    LogManager.log(Configuration.logMax(),"===== Congratulation, you are a miner, "
                              + "i.e. a full-power user who can mine blocks =====");
47                    Miner miner = new Miner(wname, wpassword);
48                    LogManager.log(Configuration.logMax(),"Welcome " + wname
                              + ", blockchain miner created for you.");
49                    MinerMessageTaskManager manager = null;
                      // Modification in this chapter.
50                    PeerConnectionManager agent = new PeerConnectionManager(miner, manager);
51                    manager = new MinerMessageTaskManager(miner, agent);
52                    agent.setWalletMessageTaskManager(manager);
53                    if(!agent.createOutgoingConnection(ipAddress)){
54                        LogManager.log(Configuration.logMax(),
                                  "connection to the " + ipAddress+" failed.");
55                        LogManager.log(Configuration.logMax(),
                                  "The user has no local blockchain initiated.");
56                        System.exit(2);
57                    }
                      // Modification in this chapter.
58                    PeerServer peerServer = new PeerServer(miner, manager, agent);
59                    Thread managerThread = new Thread(manager);
60                    Thread agentThread = new Thread(agent);
61                    Thread serverThread = new Thread(peerServer);
62                    WalletSimulator simulator = new WalletSimulator(miner, agent, manager);
63                    manager.setSimulator(simulator);
64                    serverThread.start();
65                    LogManager.log(Configuration.logMax(),"peer server started");
66                    agentThread.start();
67                    LogManager.log(Configuration.logMax(),"peer clients manager started");
68                    managerThread.start();
69                    LogManager.log(Configuration.logMax(),"wallet task manager started");
70                    simulator.setBalanceShowPublicKey(show);
                      // Modification in this chapter.
71                    agent.broadcastRequestForBlockchainUpdate();
72                }
73            }catch(Exception e){
74                e.printStackTrace();
75                System.exit(1);
76            }
77    }
```

The last class we will learn is the BlockchainPlatform class. It used to be the driver of the central server. However, it becomes the unique class to start the genesis miner. The majority codes in this class look similar, but there are some modifications. Again, it is true that the genesis miner must be started first.

```
1     import java.util.ArrayList;
2     public class BlockchainPlatform {
3         public static void main(String[] args){
4             Miner genesisMiner = new Miner("genesis", "genesis");
              // Create the genesis block.
5             Block genesisBlock = new Block("0",
                  Configuration.blockMiningDifficultyLevel(), genesisMiner.getPublicKey());
              // Manually create some UTXO
6             UTXO u1 = new UTXO("0", genesisMiner.getPublicKey(),
                  genesisMiner.getPublicKey(), 1000001.0);
7             UTXO u2 = new UTXO("0", genesisMiner.getPublicKey(),
                  genesisMiner.getPublicKey(), 1000000.0);
              // Place the UTXOs into an array list.
8             ArrayList<UTXO> inputs = new ArrayList<UTXO>();
9             inputs.add(u1);
10            inputs.add(u2);
              // Manually create a Transaction object.
11            Transaction gt = new Transaction(genesisMiner.getPublicKey(),
                  genesisMiner.getPublicKey(), 1000000.0, inputs);
              // Prepare output.
12            boolean b = gt.prepareOutputUTXOs();
              // If the preparation of output is not successful, quit now.
13            if(!b){
14                System.out.println("genesis transaction failed.");
15                System.exit(1);
16            }
              // Sign the transaction.
17            gt.signTheTransaction(genesisMiner.getPrivateKey());
              // Add the transaction into the genesis block. If this action is not
              // successful, quit now.
18            b = genesisBlock.addTransaction(gt, genesisMiner.getPublicKey());
19            if(!b){
20                System.out.println("failed to add the genesis transaction to "
                      + "the genesis block. System quit");
21                System.exit(2);
22            }
              // The genesis miner mines the genesis block
23            System.out.println("genesis miner is mining the genesis block");
24            b = genesisMiner.mineBlock(genesisBlock);
25            if(b){
26                System.out.println("genesis block is successfully mined. HashID:");
27                System.out.println(genesisBlock.getHashID());
28            }else{
29                System.out.println("failed to mine genesis block. System exit");
30                System.exit(3);
31            }
              // Construct the genesis blockchain.
32            Blockchain ledger = new Blockchain(genesisBlock);
33            System.out.println("block chain genesis successful");
              // GenesisMiner copies the blockchain to his local ledger
34
35            genesisMiner.setLocalLedger(ledger);
36            System.out.println("genesis miner local copy of blockchain set.");
37            System.out.println("genesis miner balance: "
                      + genesisMiner.getCurrentBalance(genesisMiner.getLocalLedger()));
              // Start the WalletSimulator for the genesis miner.
38            try{
39                MinerMessageTaskManager manager = null;
40                PeerConnectionManager agent = new PeerConnectionManager(genesisMiner, manager);
```

```
41                manager = new MinerGenesisMessageTaskManager(genesisMiner, agent);
42                agent.setWalletMessageTaskManager(manager);
43                PeerServer peerServer = new PeerServer(genesisMiner, manager, agent);
44                Thread managerThread = new Thread(manager);
45                Thread agentThread = new Thread(agent);
46                Thread serverThread = new Thread(peerServer);
47                WalletSimulator simulator = new WalletSimulator(genesisMiner, agent, manager);
48                manager.setSimulator(simulator);
49                serverThread.start();
50                System.out.println("peer server started");
51                agentThread.start();
52                System.out.println("peer clients manager started");
53                managerThread.start();
54                System.out.println("wallet task manager started");
55                simulator.setBalanceShowPublicKey(false);
56                System.out.println("Genesis miner is up, blockchain platform ready. "
                      + "IP address=" + PeerServer.getServerIP());
57            }catch(Exception e){
58                e.printStackTrace();
59                System.exit(1);
60            }
61        }
62    }
```

Other classes in this chapter are very much the same as those in chapter 8. So we do not need to go over them again. With all the programs ready, it is time to experience our blockchain P2P network. Note that you need multiple computers inside the same intranet. The package does not support working through firewall or other network safeguard. So, it is a good idea to test the package inside an intranet. At least three computers are need to have a minimum experience, and the more the better. The steps are listed below:

1. Compile the Java programs. The programs presented in the book are in a default Java package. If you are using the downloaded Java programs (the recommended choice), please be aware that they are in the Java package: mdsky.applications.blockchain. Please download the programs of this chapter at: https://github.com/hhohho/Learning-Blockchain-in-Java-Edition-2.

2. Assuming that you are executing the downloaded Java programs, start up genesis miner on computer A by the command:

   *java mdsky.applications.blockchain.BlockchainPlatform*

   The IP address of computer A will be displayed after the genesis miner starts. Remember the IP address of computer A if you do not know how to find it.

3. On computer B, start a wallet or miner by the command:

   *java mdsky.applications.blockchain.WalletSimulator*

   When prompted for the IP address of a peer, please enter the IP address of computer A, i.e. this peer must connect to the genesis miner.

4.  Repeat step 3 on other computers. However, when prompted for the IP address of a peer, you can enter the IP address of computer A or computer B, or another computer as long as this computer is already in our blockchain network.

That's it! Once you have enough peers, you will find that all peers are automatically connected. However, it is important to make sure that there is at least one miner in addition to the genesis miner. The reason is that the genesis miner does not mine any blocks other than its own sign-in bonus blocks. If there is no other miners inside your P2P blockchain network, all transactions you made will be lost as there is no miner to collect them, construct blocks, mine the blocks, and publish the blocks. For example, if your network has three wallets and the genesis miner, then all transactions will be lost.

A robust blockchain system should examine if every message reaches its destination, especially those messages about Transactions. In our current implementation, if a transaction is lost, it is lost, and there is no way to retrieve it. A better implementation should require every peer to examine if any of its transactions have been processed when a new block is added to its local ledger. If not, this peer should re-broadcast its unprocessed transactions.

And that concludes yet another chapter. You can download the programs from chapter 9 at: https://github.com/hhohho/Learning-Blockchain-in-Java-Edition-2. In the next chapter we will learn how to implement a P2P blockchain network based on the aforementioned approach 3.

# 10 UNIDIRECTIONAL P2P BLOCKCHAIN SYSTEM

We will start with programs from chapter 9, so please copy all of the chapter 9 programs into a directory (folder) for chapter 10. If you are using Eclipse or other IDE tools, please create a Java project named chapter10 and import the chapter 9 source codes.

In last chapter we mentioned how to transition from approach 1 implementation to approach 2 implementation by modifying the PeerConnectionManager class. Approach 2 has its advantage compared to approach 1, though it has disadvantages, too. In this chapter, we will learn how to implement approach 3 in which every connection is unidirectional. That means, the incoming connections can only receive messages, while the outgoing connections only send messages. Please refer to Figure 20. In my opinion, there is little gain but only losses by switching from approach 1 to approach 3. The reason why we are learning the implementation of approach 3 is for education purpose only. So, you can skip this chapter if you want.

Transition from approach 1 implementation to unidirectional P2P implementation, the approach 3 implementation, is very straightforward, too. We only need to modify four classes: PeerServer, PeerIncomingConnection, PeerOutgoingConnection, and PeerConnectionManager. All other classes from chapter 9 remain unchanged. The following code section shows the modified PeerServer class. Note that the modified codes are underlined.

```
1    import java.net.ServerSocket;
2    import java.net.Socket;
3    import java.net.InetAddress;
4    public class PeerServer implements Runnable{
         // The wallet this peer server is working on behalf of
5        private Wallet wallet;
6        private ServerSocket server;
7        private static String IP = null;
8        private boolean forever = true;
9        private PeerConnectionManager connectionManager;
10       private WalletMessageTaskManager messageManager;
11       PeerServer(Wallet wallet, WalletMessageTaskManager messageManager,
```

```
12                  PeerConnectionManager connectionManager) throws Exception{
                this.wallet = wallet;

13              this.connectionManager = connectionManager;
14              this.messageManager = messageManager;
15              server = new ServerSocket(Configuration.networkPort());
16              PeerServer.IP = server.getInetAddress().getLocalHost().getHostAddress();
17          }

18          public static String getServerIP(){
19              return PeerServer.IP;
20          }

21          public void run(){
22              LogManager.log(Configuration.logMax(), "peer server of "
                            + this.wallet.getName()+" is listening now");
23              while(forever){
24                  try{
25                      if(this.connectionManager.numberOfExistingIncomingConnections()
                                    >= Configuration.incomingConnectionsLimit()){
26                          Thread.sleep(Configuration.threadSleepTimeLong() * 100);
27                      }else{
28                          Socket socket = this.server.accept();
29                          InetAddress clientAddress = socket.getInetAddress();
30                          LogManager.log(Configuration.logMax(),"Got an incoming "
                                    + "connection request from " + clientAddress.getHostAddress());
31                          PeerIncomingConnection peer = new PeerIncomingConnection(wallet,
                                            socket, messageManager, connectionManager);
32                          Thread t = new Thread(peer);
33                          t.start();
34                          LogManager.log(Configuration.logMax(), "PeerIncomingConnection with "
                                    + peer.getConnectionIP() + " established");
35                          this.connectionManager.addIncomingConnection(peer);
                            // Also try to create an outgoing connection at the same time.
36                          this.connectionManager.createOutgoingConnection(
                                            clientAddress.getHostAddress());
37                      }
38                  }catch(Exception ioe){
39                      LogManager.log(Configuration.logMax(),
                                "Exception in PeerServer.run()[" + ioe.getMessage());
40                      forever = false;
41                  }
42              }
43              System.exit(0);
44          }
45      }
```

The addition of code line 36 is the only difference between this PeerServer class and that of chapter 9. Code line 36 creates an outgoing connection from this peer to another peer that has just requested an incoming connection. However, the creation of the outgoing connection is contingent upon the number of this peer's existing outgoing connections.

The PeerIncomingConnection class in this chapter has only one additional statement compared to its peer in chapter 9, too. So, I will only present you the run() method which contains the additional statement. Again, the difference is underlined.

```
1      public void run(){
2          while(forever){
3              try{
4                  Thread.sleep(Configuration.threadSleepTimeMedium());
5              }catch(InterruptedException ie){
6                  LogManager.log(Configuration.logMin(), "Exception in "
                        + "PeerIncomingConnection.run()-1[" + ie.getMessage());
7                  activeClose();
8              }
9              try{
10                 Message m = (Message)this.in.readObject();
11                 LogManager.log(Configuration.logMin(),"got a message "
                        + "in IncomingConnection:" + m.getMessageType()
                        + "|" + m.getMessageBody());
12                 if(m.getMessageType() == Message.TEXT_PRIVATE_CLOSE_CONNECTION){
13                     MessageTextCloseConnectionPrivate mp
                            = (MessageTextCloseConnectionPrivate)m;
14                     if(mp.getSenderKey().equals(this.connectionPeerPubkey)
                            && mp.getReceiver().equals(this.wallet.getPublicKey())){
15                         LogManager.log(Configuration.logMax(), "The incomingConnection "
                            + "from " + getConnectionIP() + "/" + this.connectionPeerName
                            + " is requested to be terminated.");
16                         this.close();
                           // Also shutdown the outgoing connection to this peer if possible.
17                         this.connectionManager.removeOutgoingConnection(
                                            mp.getSenderKey());
18                     }
19                 }else{
20                     this.messageManager.addMessageIntoQueue(m);
21                 }
22             }catch(Exception ioe){
23                 LogManager.log(Configuration.logMin(), "Exception in "
                        + "PeerIncomingConnection.run()-2[" + ioe.getMessage());
24                 this.close();
25             }
26         }
27     }
```

The PeerOutgoingConnection class has two modifications that are underlined. The first notable modification is that it no longer implements Runnable, which is why this class does not implement the method run(). The second modification is at its constructor method heading at which it does not require a WalletMessageTaskManager object as an argument. Please examine the following code section:

```
1     import java.io.ObjectInputStream;
2     import java.io.ObjectOutputStream;
3     import java.net.Socket;
4     import java.security.PublicKey;
5     public class PeerOutgoingConnection{
6         private Wallet wallet;
7         private Socket socket;
          // The IP address of the server socket that this outgoing connection is connected to
8         private String connectionIP;
9         private ObjectInputStream in;
10        private ObjectOutputStream out;
          // The public key of the peer that this outgoing connection is connected to
```

```
11      private PublicKey connectionPeerPubkey;
        // The name of the peer that this outgoing connection is connected to
12      private String connectionPeerName;
13      private PeerConnectionManager connectionManager;
        // The second modification in this chapter is that the constructor does not
        // require a WalletMessageTaskManager object as an argument.
        // This is because the PeerOutgoingConnection only sends messages out,
        // it does not need to queue any messages. Everything else is pretty much the same
        // as the PeerOutgoingConnection in last chapter.
14      protected PeerOutgoingConnection(String serverIP, Wallet wallet,
                    PeerConnectionManager connectionManager) throws Exception{
15          this.wallet = wallet;
16          this.connectionManager = connectionManager;
17          LogManager.log(Configuration.logMax(), wallet.getName()
                    + " is creating a peer outgoing connection to " + serverIP);
18          this.connectionIP = serverIP;
19          socket = new Socket(serverIP, Configuration.networkPort());
20          out = new ObjectOutputStream(socket.getOutputStream());
21          in = new ObjectInputStream(socket.getInputStream());
            // The peer client will get a MessageForID from the peer server
22          MessageID fromPeerServer = (MessageID)in.readObject();
            // Make sure that the message is in good standing
23          if(fromPeerServer.isValid()){
24              this.connectionPeerPubkey = fromPeerServer.getSenderKey();
25              this.connectionPeerName = fromPeerServer.getName();
26          }else{
27              throw new Exception("MessageID from peer server is invalid.");
28          }
            // If everything works well, the agent sends the server a responding MessageForID
            // because the server is waiting for the client to send in a MessageForID.
29          LogManager.log(Configuration.logMax(), "obtained peer server address "
                    + "and stored it, now sending wallet public key to peer server");
30          LogManager.log(Configuration.logMax(), "name="+this.wallet.getName());
31          MessageID mid = new MessageID(this.wallet.getPrivateKey(),
                    this.wallet.getPublicKey(), this.wallet.getName());
32          out.writeObject(mid);
33          LogManager.log(Configuration.logMax(), "A peer client outgoingconnection to "
                    + this.connectionIP + " is established successfully.");
34          if(this.wallet.getLocalLedger() == null){
                // Directly ask for a blockchain before doing anything.
35              MessageAskForBlockchainPrivate m =
                        new MessageAskForBlockchainPrivate("update blockchain",
                        wallet.getPrivateKey(), wallet.getPublicKey(),
                        wallet.getName(), this.connectionPeerPubkey, true);
36              out.writeObject(m);
                // Wait for such a response.
37              MessageBlockchainPrivate mbcb = (MessageBlockchainPrivate)in.readObject();
38              LogManager.log(Configuration.logMin(), "In PeerOutgoingConnection.constructor["
                        + "It is a blockchain private message, check if it is for me and if "
                        + "necessary to update the blockchain");
39              boolean b = this.wallet.setLocalLedger(mbcb.getMessageBody());
40              if(b){
41                  LogManager.log(Configuration.logMax(), "blockchain updated successfully");
42              }else{
43                  LogManager.log(Configuration.logMax(),
                            "In PeerOutgoingConnection.constructor["
                            + "blockchain update failed for " + this.wallet.getName()
                            + " from " + this.getConnectionIP());
44                  throw new RuntimeException("In In PeerOutgoingConnection.constructor["
```

```
                              + "blockchain update failed for " + this.wallet.getName()
                              + " from " + this.getConnectionIP());
45                    }
46              }else{
47                    MessageAskForBlockchainPrivate m =
                              new MessageAskForBlockchainPrivate("update blockchain",
                                      wallet.getPrivateKey(), wallet.getPublicKey(),
                                      wallet.getName(), this.connectionPeerPubkey, false);
48                    out.writeObject(m);
49              }
50              this.connectionManager.addAddress(fromPeerServer.getKeyNamePair());
51        }
          // Other codes are omitted because they are the same, except that this class does not
          // implement the method run() compared to its peer in the last chapter.
52  }
```

The only difference between PeerConnectionManager in this chapter and that in the last chapter lies in the method createOutgoingConnection. This is because the PeerOutgoingConnection in this chapter does not need to implement Runnable. The following code section presents the createOutgoingConnection method:

```
1    protected synchronized boolean createOutgoingConnection(String peerServerIP){
2        if(this.outgoingConnections.size() >= Configuration.outGoingConnectionsLimit()){
3            LogManager.log(Configuration.logMax(), "cannot create the outgoing connection to "
                    + peerServerIP + " because the current size of "
                    + this.outgoingConnections.size() + " has already reached the limit of "
                    + Configuration.outGoingConnectionsLimit());
4            return false;
5        }
6        try{
7            PeerOutgoingConnection client = outgoingConnections.get(peerServerIP);
8            if(client == null){
9                client = new PeerOutgoingConnection(peerServerIP, this.wallet, this);
                 // Add this peer client into the outgoingConnections.
10               outgoingConnections.put(UtilityMethods.getKeyString(
                         client.getConnectionPeerPublicKey()), client);
11               outgoingConnections.put(peerServerIP, client);
12               this.addAddress(client.getConnectionPeerNamePair());
13               LogManager.log(Configuration.logMax(), "created an outgoing connection to "
                         + peerServerIP);
14               return true;
15           }
16       }catch(Exception e){
17           LogManager.log(Configuration.logMax(),
                      "Exception in PeerConnectionManager.createOutgoingConnection|"
                      +peerServerIP+"["+e.getMessage());
18           return false;
19       }
20       return false;
21   }
```

Pay close attention to code lines 8-10. If you compare them with the corresponding codes in the last chapter, you will notice the difference.

By now you should have observed that once we have the approach 1 implemented, implementing approaches 2 and 3 are fairly straightforward, requiring one a few modifications. You can download the programs from chapter 10 at: https://github.com/hhohho/Learning-Blockchain-in-Java-Edition-2.

# 11 SECURE CODING

Blockchain technology has gained popularity in recent years, but it is far from being mainstream. It is still not ubiquitous enough that we can use it to pay the bills or buy groceries. Where this technology ends up is still unknown. Internet is by default a distributed environment with a dominant presence in our lives. It is a powerful environment that distributes many services, especially information, and allows everyone to participate. However, the Internet is a heterogeneous environment that is short of trust. Blockchain technology can complement this shortage by distributing trust among participants. The trust would not be placed on a single server or entity. As long as the majority of participants stays honest, blockchain will remain trustworthy. Blockchain's accessibility is also one of its selling points. It is very possible that in the near future, anyone with network access and computational power (equal to that of a common PC) would be able to provide certain blockchain services. The possibilities are endless.

Cloud computing makes use of a network of server farms to offer computational services anytime and anywhere. From this perspective, cloud computing is distributed because its computational power is distributed. However, cloud services are provided by large companies with a network of powerful servers distributed throughout the Internet. The services are owned by these companies and are provided through servers. In this sense, it is centralized. We could argue that cloud computing makes use of distributed technology to achieve centralized services. Blockchain technology, however, walks one giant step further on the way of decentralization. Take bitcoin for example: any network node can join the bitcoin network and become an equal node in the system, so long as it complies with bitcoin protocols. Certainly, blockchain is more open than cloud computing. Cloud computing had significantly impact on the IT industry in the past decade, so what will blockchain's effect look like?

The largest challenge blockchain faces is that most of its applications are in cryptocurrency, serving as a transaction platform. Even in the cryptocurrency world, blockchain is confronting many challenges. Throughout this book, we have been talking about secure coding practices and security risks.

Blockchain is an open environment, making it susceptible to malicious threats that have been meticulously planned before being carried out. Therefore, secure cryptography alone is not enough to protect blockchain applications. We need to be more proactive and write secure codes.

In July 2017, Parity Ethereum was attacked and lost $30,000,000 dollars worth of Ethereum coins (Ether). The attack was based on a minor piece of unsecure coding: two library methods that should have been internal (similar to being private in Java) but were not. To understand this attack, we first need to go over Ethereum, Smart Contract, and Solidity.

Bitcoin was the work of genius, opening a Pandora's Box of possibilities. Bitcoin was intended for digital currency only, but its blockchain paradigm led to the birth of Ethereum. The goal of Ethereum was to broaden the usage of blockchain, providing a "world computer" or global platform on which different applications can be deployed. To achieve this, Ethereum blockchain adopts Smart Contract and has developed Ethereum protocol and Ethereum Virtual Machine (EVM). Smart contracts are like digital vending machines with strictly specified rules and triggers. When you insert money into a vending machine, you get your drink. Smart contracts work in the same way. You provide the necessary digital payment and in return, you get what you paid for. Applications are deployed as smart contracts. In this sense, you can think of Ethereum as a distributed iOS platform upon which different applications can be developed. Ethereum blockchain has the potential to become the evolved platform of the Internet, and it is one of the reasons why blockchain technology is so alluring.

To understand the Ethereum malicious attack aforementioned, let us learn the following vocab:
1) Smart contracts are programs. Solidity is a high level programming language dedicated for smart contract programming.
2) Parity Ethereum blockchain has a type of wallet called multi-signature wallet which is supposed to be very secure. The initialization logic of a multi-signature wallet is contained in a shared external library as well. A library method can be called through an EVM instruction *delegatecall*. Whichever method issues a *delegatecall*, the *delegatecall* finds a method in the library with the same method name to execute. The execution is, however, with the contract's current state.
3) When a certain type of method is unknown, Parity Ethereum falls back to the method payable(). As shown in the Solidity codes below, _walletLibrary.delegatecall(msg.data) will be executed under a certain condition:

```
function() payable{
    if(msg.value > 0)
        Deposit(msg.sender, msg.value);
    else if (msg.data.length > 0)
        _walletLibrary.delegatecall(msg.data);
}
```

4) The attacker called the method initWallet() which does not exist inside the multi-signature wallet but is defined in the shared external library. Thus, payable() is called which in turn calls the initWallet() method in the library with the contract's current state. The library method initWallet() is presented below. This method re-initializes the wallet based on the input

arguments, meaning the existing wallet would switch its ownership to the addresses provided by the attacker, allowing the attacker to transfer tokens out of the wallet.

```
function initWallet(address[] _owners, uint _required, uint _daylimit){
    initDaylimit(_daylimit);
    initMultiowned(_owners, _required);
}
```

In Solidity, functions are public by default. So now you can tell, had the functions initWallet() and initMultiowned() been internal, this attack could have been avoided. That being said, it is a very good example of secure coding. In Java, methods are specified as either public, private or protected. It is important to think twice about who could possibly call a specific method, and it is simply a bad practice to define all methods as public. Methods only used inside the class they are made in should be specified as private.

Another lesson we can learn from this attack is that the use of implicit action should be minimized. When an unexpected scenario occurs, we may be tempted to design a default action as the response. This can solve a lot of troubles, but it can also leave an open ground for unknown attacks. Secure coding requires that there are no implicit actions in programs. Whatever the program does under a certain condition should be explicitly stated. This may seem obvious, but in more complicated cases, things can get tricking. The creation of the Decentralized Autonomous Organization (The DAO) was announced on April 30, 2016 by a few members of the Ethereum community. It was built upon the Ethereum blockchain via Smart Contract and Solidity. It was initially very successful until June 2016 when an attacker exploited the DAO by taking advantage of a loophole in the coding which included an implicit recursive call. The loophole was actually a combination of several unsecure codes. The states of related variables were not updated under a certain condition during the recursive call, causing the recursive call non-stop. What the attacker did was to create such a condition so that a wallet's fund was sent to the attacker's account multiple times (recursively) until the attacked account was drained. The technical details of this attack will take pages to explain – so we won't go into the depth. But one lesson learned from this attack is to explicitly address all possible states in programming.

The selfish mining attack presents a different scenario. When a powerful miner does not broadcast a freshly mined block and successfully wins the competition for next block, this miner creates a blockchain branch longer than everyone else's local blockchain. By the commonly accepted rule of mining, this longer blockchain invalidates every other blockchain copy. As this longer blockchain has one block different from every other local blockchain, some transactions published and accepted by every other wallet can be invalidated when this longer blockchain is announced. In May 2018, digital cryptocurrency Monacoin in Japan suffered a selfish mining attack. This raises a question about how selfish mining attacks can be avoided. A similar scenario could involve a group of nodes making a large number of transactions internally and mining the corresponding blocks selfishly for advantages. For example, our Wallet class has the following method:

```
1    public Transaction transferFund(PublicKey[] receivers, double[] fundToTransfer){
2        ArrayList<UTXO> unspent = new ArrayList<UTXO>();
3        double available = this.getLocalLedger().findUnspentUTXOs(
                    this.getPublicKey(), unspent);
```

```
4          double totalNeeded = Transaction.TRANSACTION_FEE;
5          for(int i=0; i<fundToTransfer.length; i++){
6              totalNeeded += fundToTransfer[i];
7          }
8          if(available < totalNeeded){
9              System.out.println(this.walletName+" balance="+available
                   +", not enough to make the transfer of "+totalNeeded);
10             return null;
11         }
12         ArrayList<UTXO> inputs = new ArrayList<UTXO>();
13         available = 0;
14         for(int i=0; i<unspent.size() && available < totalNeeded; i++){
15             UTXO uxo = unspent.get(i);
16             available += uxo.getFundTransferred();
17             inputs.add(uxo);
18         }
19         Transaction T = new Transaction(this.getPublicKey(), receivers, fundToTransfer, inputs);
20         boolean b = T.prepareOutputUTXOs();
21         if(b){
22             T.signTheTransaction(this.getPrivateKey());
23             return T;
24         }else{
25             return null;
26         }
27     }
```

This method has a serious loophole. Java allows an array to be size zero. Thus, the two input arguments (code line 1) can both be empty arrays. As long as the sender's available fund can cover the transaction fee, the sender can initiate a valid transaction without any receiver. If the sender is also a malicious miner, he can make a large number of such transactions and collect them for mining rewards. Therefore, it is necessary to require that the length of the two arguments in this method must be greater than zero. For the same reason, the method prepareOutputUTXOs() of the class Transaction must be revised as well.

In April 2018, a digital cryptocurrency in China, Beauty Chain (BEC), suffered an attack because of unsecure coding. This attack almost completely cleared out the value of BEC as the attacker created more than $10^{58}$ additional BEC tokens. Let's take a look at the attacked Solidity codes below.

```
1      function batchTransfer(address[] _receivers, uint256 _value)
                         public whenNotPaused returns (bool) {
2          uint cnt = _receivers.length;
3          uint256 amount = uint256(cnt) * _value;
4          require(cnt > 0 && cnt <= 20);
5          require(_value > 0 && balances[msg.sender] >= amount);
6          balances[msg.sender] = balances[msg.sender].sub(amount);
7          for (uint i = 0; i < cnt; i++) {
8              balances[_receivers[i]] = balances[_receivers[i]].add(_value);
9              Transfer(msg.sender, _receivers[i], _value);
10         }
11         return true;
12     }
```

The maximum integer of uint256 is $2^{256}$ – a giant number, but it can still overflow. When the input _value (code line 1) is large enough, multiplying it with the length of _receivers (it was 2 in this case), an overflow can happen and set *amount* to be 0 (code line 3). Thus, all the assessments in the function (specifically the second require statement at code line 5) are useless while each receiver address can obtain *_value* tokens (lines 6-10).

Java has number overflow, too. In Java, both *int* and *Long* data types can have overflow. When an overflow happens, the resulting value is unpredictable. In most cases, it is a negative number. Please examine the following codes. However, both double and float do not have overflow. When a number exceeds Double.MAX_VALUE, it becomes infinity.

```java
public class Overflow {
    public static void main(String[] args) {
        long x = Long.MAX_VALUE;
        System.out.println(x);
        x = x * 10;
        System.out.println(x);
        double d = Double.MAX_VALUE;
        System.out.println(d);
        d = d * 10.0;
        System.out.println(d);
    }
}
```

As you can imagine, our blockchain system is not fortified either. For example, in the aforementioned method *transferFund()* in the class Wallet, double is used. In Java, the maximum value of double is as large as $2^{1023}$, large enough for any tasks we may have. It is true that Java's double would not have the overflow risk because once a double number is over the limit, it becomes infinity. However, double, like any other floating point numbers, is an approximated value when it becomes large. For example, a double number as large as $2^{37}$ cannot differentiate itself from another double number that is 0.00001 larger. One as large as $2^{60}$ cannot tell the difference as large as 100. Will an intelligent attacker be able to abuse this difference to accumulate a significant loss on others?

The `mineTheBlock()` method in the Block class can result in an overflow and should be revised. The variable nonce was originally declared as "int", which may not have enough variations for a valid hash to be generated if the difficulty level is set too high. Even if it is declared as long, it may still fail. Recall that the class MinerTheWorker is dedicated to block mining. If the mining fails because no qualified hash ID can be found, the transactions inside the block should be re-examined to determine if they should be re-broadcast – a scenario that our program does not take into consideration in the MinerTheWorker class.

Secure coding also requires that as many scenarios as possible are considered. This is a necessary but difficult task because human mind is not error proof. In our blockchain system, a miner collects a number of valid transactions to construct a block. Some transactions might have been invalidated after a new block is accepted (i.e. these transactions exist inside the blockchain by now) when they are still waiting in the pool. This requires that when a new block is accepted, the transaction pool should be re-examined. Otherwise, a miner may end up mining a block containing invalid transactions. Again, this is a scenario that our program should deal with. There are a few additional revisions that our programs should undertake to make them more robust. They are not discussed here, however.

Blockchain still faces many unexpected challenges and attacks as a new technology involved in momentary transactions. This is why the blockchain community needs people like you who are interested in blockchain and are willing to make it more robust and secure, and most importantly, improve and extend upon possible applications. Hopefully this book has been helpful to you and your blockchain endeavors.

# INDEX

Address, 22, 59, 82, 84, 86, 90, 91, 104, 116, 117, 120, 122, 126, 135, 148, 149, 150, 151, 152, 155, 159, 160, 219, 220, 221
AES, 17, 18, 36, 37, 38, 40, 43, 109
AND, 5, 13, 31, 36, 46, 82
Asset, 149, 156
Asymmetric, 15
Attack, 38, 69, 218, 219, 220
   attacker, 2, 218, 219, 220, 221
BEC, 220
Bitcoin, 2, 13, 91, 107, 108, 218
   Satoshi Nakamoto, 1, 3, 108
BlockchainPlatform, 54, 74, 79, 80, 81, 156, 158, 159, 160, 209
C++, 2, 3
Cipher, 17, 18, 19, 20, 36, 37, 38, 40
Class Loader, 10, 23
Collision, 6
Concurrency, 3, 157, 163, 164
Consensus, 1, 100
CPU, 11, 99, 100, 124, 141
Cryptography, 2, 3, 5, 6, 10, 15, 17, 37, 38, 41, 218
DAO, 219
Datagram
   DatagramPacket, 82, 83, 84, 85
   DatagramSocket, 82, 83, 84, 85, 86
Decentralized, 3
Decrypt, 15, 16, 17, 18, 19, 35, 36, 38, 39, 43, 44
Deserialization, 10, 23, 89, 109
Distributed, 1, 2, 3, 13, 53, 54, 55, 82, 91, 107, 159, 163, 166, 211, 217, 218
DSA, 19
Eclipse, 5, 7, 13, 31, 46, 59, 61, 82, 107, 162, 166, 211
Encrypt, 15, 16, 18, 19, 35, 36, 41, 43, 109, 163
Ethereum, 2, 3, 218, 219
   Ether, 218
   EVM, 3, 218
   Parity Ethereum, 218
FIBRE, 91
   Fast Internet Bitcoin Relay Engine, 91
Genesis, 4, 50, 51, 55, 56, 68, 69, 70, 71, 73, 74, 75, 76, 79, 108, 116, 120, 144, 145, 146, 147, 148, 151, 152, 155, 156, 157, 158, 159, 160, 161, 163, 164
   genesis block, 50, 51, 55, 68, 69, 70, 74, 75, 108, 120, 148, 151, 152, 156, 157, 158, 160
   genesis miner, 55, 56, 68, 70, 71, 73, 74, 75, 76, 108, 116, 144, 145, 146, 147, 148, 155, 156, 157, 158, 159, 160, 161, 163, 164
GUI, 101, 102, 104, 108, 117, 123, 126, 128, 129, 130, 134, 161
Hacker, 16, 219
Hash, 5, 6, 7, 8, 10, 11, 16, 21, 22, 23, 24, 27, 35, 47, 51, 52, 58, 59, 60, 62, 64, 68, 69, 72, 221
   hashing, 5, 6, 27, 68
   HashMap, 5, 49, 52, 65, 66, 97, 123, 144
   Hashtable, 5, 97, 99, 100, 120, 149
   MessageDigest, 6, 7, 8, 10, 17
IP, 82, 84, 86, 90, 91, 104, 135, 159, 161
   127.0.0.1, 86, 91, 159
Java
   Java Message Service, 3, 164
   JCA, 6, 17
   JCE, 6, 38
   JDK, 3, 6, 18, 19, 164
JavaScript, 163
LedgerList, 48, 49, 51, 59, 65, 69

Localhost, 86, 91, 104, 135, 159
Memory, iii, 3, 23, 59, 60
Merkle Tree, 59, 60, 62, 64
MessageDigest, 6, 7, 8, 10, 17
Mining, 3, 5, 7, 8, 9, 11, 12, 14, 24, 44, 51, 54, 55, 58, 68, 69, 72, 75, 76, 77, 79, 80, 108, 140, 141, 142, 143, 144, 145, 158, 161, 219, 220, 225
   consensus, 1, 100
   reward, 24, 51, 58, 59, 61, 62, 63, 64, 66, 69, 75, 76, 78, 79, 118
Monacoin, 219
multi-signature wallet, 218
Nodes, 3, 14, 44, 59, 60, 107, 109, 113, 144, 217, 219
Nonce, 8, 9, 10, 46, 47, 60, 62, 63, 69, 221
ObjectInputStream, 41, 43, 44, 88, 89, 97, 98, 99, 101, 102, 105, 120, 149, 151, 152
ObjectOutputStream, 41, 42, 43, 88, 89, 97, 98, 101, 102, 119, 120, 149, 151, 152
OR, 35, 43
Overflow, 220, 221
Peer-to-Peer, 2, 91, 107, 163
PrintStream, 32, 33, 61, 117
Proof of Work, 2, 5, 7, 72
Python, 3, 163
Reward, 24, 51, 58, 59, 61, 62, 63, 64, 66, 69, 75, 76, 78, 79, 118
RSA, 15, 18, 19, 20, 21, 119
Runnable, 97, 98, 99, 100, 101, 104, 120, 123, 140, 142, 144, 151, 153, 154, 157, 158
RuntimeException, 6, 7, 21, 37, 40, 42, 83, 85, 100, 104, 130, 131
Safe coding, 27, 48, 62, 217, 218, 219, 220
Salt, 36, 37, 38, 39, 40
Satoshi Nakamoto, 1, 3, 108
Secret Key, 15, 16, 18, 36, 38, 40, 109

Selfish mining attack
   Monacoin, 219
Selfish Mining Attack, 69
Serializable, 9, 10, 22, 23, 24, 43, 46, 48, 49, 61, 65, 89, 96, 109, 110, 111, 114
   serialVersionUID, 9, 10, 22, 23, 24, 46, 48, 49, 61, 65, 70, 96, 110, 111, 112, 113, 114, 115, 116
SHA, 5, 6, 7, 20, 119
   SHA-1, 5, 6, 20
   SHA-2, 5, 6, 7, 20, 119
Signature, 15, 16, 19, 20, 21, 24, 25, 26, 27, 33, 62, 64, 68, 72, 73, 111, 112, 113, 118, 218
Smart Contract, 218, 219
Socket, 85, 87, 88, 89, 90, 91, 97, 98, 101, 102, 120, 149, 150, 151
   ServerSocket, 87, 88, 97, 149
Solidity, 3, 163, 218, 219, 220
StringBuilder, 8, 9, 25, 47, 62, 117, 118, 134, 135
Symmetric, 15, 18
Synchronized, 49, 51, 53, 69, 70, 71, 97, 98, 121, 142, 150, 151, 152, 157, 158
TCP, 82, 87, 88, 89, 91, 95, 100, 105, 107
Third Party, 3, 14, 19
Thread, 88, 89, 90, 91, 97, 98, 99, 100, 101, 102, 104, 105, 121, 124, 136, 140, 141, 142, 143, 144, 145, 148, 149, 150, 151, 153, 154, 155, 156, 159, 162
TIOBE, 3
Transaction fee, 14, 26, 28, 33, 51, 53, 54, 58, 63, 69, 117, 220
Trust, 1, 2, 14, 217
UDP, 82, 83, 84, 85, 86, 87, 89, 91
Unspent, 13, 49, 50, 51, 52, 53, 54, 66, 67, 79, 134, 147, 219, 220
XOR, 35, 36, 37, 43

## ABOUT THE AUTHOR

Hong Zhou is currently a professor of computer science and mathematics at University of Saint Joseph, Connecticut, USA. Dr. Zhou has 20 years of Java programming experience. Before going back to school for his doctoral degree in Scientific Computing, Hong was working as a Java developer at Silicon Valley. Since obtaining his doctoral degree in 2004, Dr. Zhou has been teaching various courses in computer science, mathematics and data science at University of Saint Joseph. His major research interests include bioinformatics, software agents, data mining, and recently blockchain.

Made in the USA
Middletown, DE
05 November 2019